W9-ATI-793

Bloom's Modern Critical Interpretations

Bloom's Modern Critical Interpretations

Bloom's Modern Critical Interpretations

George Orwell's
1984
Updated Edition

Edited and with an introduction by
Harold Bloom
Sterling Professor of the Humanities
Yale University

CHELSEA HOUSE
P U B L I S H E R S
An imprint of Infobase Publis

Bloom's Modern Critical Interpretations: 1984, Updated Edition

Copyright ©2007 by Infobase Publishing

Introduction ©2007 by Harold Bloom

Chelsea House
An imprint of Infobase Publishing
132 West 31st Street
New York NY 10001

Library of Congress Cataloging-in-Publication Data
George Orwell's 1984 / Harold Bloom, editor. — Updated ed.
    p. cm. — (Bloom's modern critical interpretations)
  Includes bibliographical references and index.
  ISBN 0-7910-9300-X
 1. Orwell, George, 1903-1950. Nineteen eighty-four. 2. Science
fiction, English—History and criticism. 3. Dystopias in literature.
I. Bloom, Harold. II. Title: George Orwell's Nineteen eighty-four.
III. Series.

  PR6029.R8N4944 2006
  823'.912—dc22   2006025343

Contributing Editor: Pamela Loos
Cover designed by Ben Peterson
Cover illustration by Ben Peterson

Printed in the United States of America
Bang EJB 10 9 8 7 6 5 4 3 2 1

This book is printed on acid-free paper.

Contents

Editor's Note

My introduction, written twenty years ago, in the presidency of Ronald Reagan, seems even more apt to me in 2006, during the reign of George W. Bush. I discount *1984* as aesthetic achievement, but celebrate Orwell's excellence as a pamphleteer in the tradition of Defoe, Carlyle, and Ruskin.

The British Marxist critic Raymond Williams, writing in 1984, still admired the book, but found it somewhat obsolete in the era of the Cold War.

Sue Lonoff rather dangerously compares *1984* to Dickens, while Erika Gottlieb praises the supposed imagistic power of demonic Oceania.

A certain reservation as to the plausibility of *1984* is sensibly ventured by Laurence Lerner, after which Robert Plank ponders Orwell's musings upon the social effect of a general loss of belief in immortality.

Roger Fowler shows Orwell's limitations as the inventor of Newspeak, while Malcolm Pittock argues that the hell of *1984* is more pervasive than even Orwell intended.

In a shrewd essay, Steven Carter opposes to the dystopias of Orwell and of Aldous Huxley our contemporary do-it-yourself style of dystopia.

Anthony Stewart is able to detect more optimism in Orwell's vision than Orwell could, while Homi K. Bhabha praises the "fragile and compelling freedom" that Orwell's rather limited fiction-making power seems to offer.

HAROLD BLOOM

Introduction

I

There is an equivocal irony to reading, and writing, about George Orwell in 1986. I have just reread *1984*, *Animal Farm*, and many of the essays for the first time in some years, and I find myself lost in an interplay of many contending reactions, moral and aesthetic. Orwell, aesthetically considered, is a far better essayist than a novelist. Lionel Trilling, reviewing *1984*, in 1949, praised the book, with a singular moral authority:

> The whole effort of the culture of the last hundred years has been directed toward teaching us to understand the economic motive as the irrational road to death, and to seek salvation in the rational and the planned. Orwell marks a turn in thought; he asks us to consider whether the triumph of certain forces of the mind, in their naked pride and excess, may not produce a state of things far worse than any we have ever known. He is not the first to raise the question, but he is the first to raise it on truly liberal or radical grounds, with no intention of abating the demand for a just society, and with an overwhelming intensity and passion. This priority makes his book a momentous one.

The book remains momentous; perhaps it always will be so. But there is nothing intrinsic to the book that will determine its future importance. Its very genre will be established by political, social, economic events. Is it satire or science fiction or dystopia or countermanifesto? Last week I read newspaper accounts of two recent speeches, perorations delivered by president Reagan and by Norman Podhoretz, each favorably citing Orwell. The President, awarding medals to Senator Barry Goldwater and Helen Hayes, among others, saw them as exemplars of Orwell's belief in freedom and individual dignity, while the sage Podhoretz allowed himself to observe that Orwell would have become a neoconservative had he but survived until this moment. Perhaps irony, however equivocal, is inadequate to represent so curious a posthumous fate as has come to the author of *Homage to Catalonia*, a man who went to Barcelona to fight for the Party of Marxist Unity and the Anarcho-Syndicalists.

V. S. Pritchett and others were correct in describing Orwell as the best of modern pamphleteers. A pamphlet certainly can achieve aesthetic eminence; "tracts and pamphlets" is a major genre, particularly in Great Britain, where its masters include Milton, Defoe, Swift, Dr. Johnson, Burke, Blake, Shelley, Carlyle, Ruskin, and Newman. Despite his celebrated mastery of the plain style, it is rather uncertain that Orwell has joined himself to that company. I suspect that he is closer to the category that he once described as "good bad books," giving Harriet Beecher Stowe's *Uncle Tom's Cabin* as a supreme instance. Aesthetically considered, *1984* is very much the *Uncle Tom's Cabin* of our time, with poor Winston Smith as Uncle Tom, the unhappy Julia as little Eva, and the more-than-sadistic O'Brien as Simon Legree. I do not find O'Brien to be as memorable as Simon Legree, but then that is part of Orwell's point. We have moved into a world in which our torturers also have suffered a significant loss of personality.

II

Orwell's success as a prophet is necessarily a mixed one, since his relative crudity as a creator of character obliges us to read *1984* rather literally. What works best in the novel is its contextualization of all the phrases it has bequeathed to our contemporary language, though whether to *the* language is not yet certain. Newspeak and doublethink, "War Is Peace," "Freedom Is Slavery," "Ignorance Is Strength," "Big Brother Is Watching You," the Thought Police, the Two Minutes Hate, the Ministry of Truth, and all the other Orwellian inventions that are now wearisome clichés, are restored to some force, though little freshness, when we encounter them where they first arose.

Unfortunately, in itself that does not suffice. Even a prophetic pamphlet requires eloquence if we are to return to it and find ourselves affected at least as much as we were before. *1984* can hurt you a single time, and most likely when you are young. After that, defensive laughter becomes the aesthetic problem. Rereading *1984* can be too much like watching a really persuasive horror movie; humor acquires the validity of health. Contemporary reviewers, even Trilling, were too overwhelmed by the book's relevance to apprehend its plain badness as narrative or Orwell's total inability to represent even a curtailed human personality or moral character. Mark Schorer's response in the *New York Times Book Review* may have seemed appropriate on June 12, 1949, but its hyperboles now provoke polite puzzlement:

> No real reader can neglect this experience with impunity. He will be moved by Smith's wistful attempts to remember a different kind of life from his. He will make a whole new discovery of the beauty of love between man and woman, and of the strange beauty of landscape in a totally mechanized world. He will be asked to read through pages of sustained physical and psychological pain that have seldom been equaled and never in such quiet, sober prose. And he will return to his own life from Smith's escape into living death with a resolution to resist power wherever it means to deny him his individuality, and to resist for himself the poisonous lures of power.

Would it make a difference now if Orwell had given his book the title "1994"? Our edge of foreboding has vanished when we contemplate the book, if indeed we ought to regard it as a failed apocalypse. Yet all apocalypses, in the literary sense, are failed apocalypses, so that if they fade, the phenomenon of literary survival or demise clearly takes precedence over whatever status social prophecy affords. The limits of Orwell's achievement are clarified if we juxtapose it directly to the authentic American apocalypses of our time: Faulkner's *As I Lay Dying*, Nathanael West's *Miss Lonelyhearts*, Thomas Pynchon's *Gravity's Rainbow*. Why do they go on wounding us, reading after reading, while *1984* threatens to become a period piece, however nightmarish? It would be absurdly unfair to look at *1984* side by side with Kafka and Beckett; Orwell was in no way an aspirant after the sublime, however demonic or diminished. But he was a satirist, and in *1984* a kind of phantasmagoric realist. If his O'Brien is not of the stature of the unamiable Simon Legree, he is altogether nonexistent as a Satanic rhetorician if we attempt to bring him into the company of West's Shrike.

Can a novel survive praise that endlessly centers upon its author's humane disposition, his indubitable idealism, his personal honesty, his political courage, his moral nature? Orwell may well have been the exemplary and representative Socialist intellectual of our time (though Raymond Williams, the crucial Marxist literary critic in Great Britain, definitely does not think so). But very bad men and women have written superb novels, and great moralists have written unreadable ones. *1984* is neither superb nor unreadable. If it resembles the work of a precursor figure, that figure is surely H. G. Wells, as Wyndham Lewis shrewdly realized. Wells surpasses Orwell in storytelling vigor, in pungency of characterization, and in imaginative invention, yet Wells now seems remote and Orwell remains very close. We are driven back to what makes *1984* a good bad book: relevance. The book substitutes for a real and universal fear: that in the political and economic area, the dreadful is still about to happen. Yet the book again lacks a defense against its own blunderings into the ridiculous. As social prophecy, it is closer to Sinclair Lewis's now forgotten *It Can't Happen Here* than to Nathanael West's still hilarious *A Cool Million*, where Big Brother, under the name of Shagpoke Whipple, speaks uncannily in the accents shared by Calvin Coolidge and Ronald Reagan. Why could not Orwell have rescued his book by some last touch of irony or by a valid invocation of the satiric Muse?

III

What Max Horkheimer and T. W. Adorno grimly called the Culture Industry has absorbed Orwell, and his *1984* in particular. Is this because Orwell retains such sentimentalities or soft idealisms as the poignance of true love? After all, Winston and Julia are terrorized out of love by brute pain and unendurable fear; no one could regard them as having been culpable in their forced abandonment of one another. This is akin to Orwell's fantastic and wholly unconvincing hope that the proles might yet offer salvation, a hope presumably founded upon the odd notion that Oceania lets eighty-five percent of its population go back to nature in the slums of London and other cities. Love and the working class are therefore pretty much undamaged in Orwell's vision. Contrast Pynchon's imaginative "paranoia" in *Gravity's Rainbow*, where all of us, of whatever social class, live in the Zone which is dominated by the truly paranoid System, and where authentic love can be represented only as sado-masochism. There is a Counterforce in *Gravity's Rainbow* that fights the System, but it is ineffectual, farcical, and can be animated only by the peculiar ideology that Pynchon calls sado-anarchism, an ideology that the Culture Industry cannot absorb, and that I suspect Adorno gladly would have embraced.

I don't intend this introduction as a drubbing or trashing of Orwell and *1984*, and *Gravity's Rainbow*, being an encyclopedic prose epic, is hardly a fair agonist against which *1984* should be matched. But the aesthetic badness of *1984* is palpable enough, and I am a good enough disciple of the divine Oscar Wilde to wonder if an aesthetic inadequacy really can be a moral splendor? Simon Legree beats poor old Uncle Tom to death, and O'Brien pretty well wrecks Winston Smith's body and then reduces him to supposed ruin by threatening him with some particularly nasty and hungry rats. Is Uncle Tom's Cabin actually a moral achievement, even if Harriet Beecher Stowe hastened both the Civil War and the Emancipation Proclamation? Is *1984* a moral triumph, even if it hastens a multiplication of neoconservatives?

The defense of a literary period piece cannot differ much from a defense of period pieces in clothes, household objects, popular music, movies, and the lower reaches of the visual arts. A period piece that is a political and social polemic, like *Uncle Tom's Cabin* and *1984*, acquires a curious charm of its own. What partly saves *1984* from Orwell's overliteralness and failures in irony is the strange archaism of its psychology and rhetoric:

> He paused for a few moments, as though to allow what he had been saying to sink in.
>
> "Do you remember," he went on, "writing in your diary, 'Freedom is the freedom to say that two plus two make four'?"
>
> "Yes," said Winston.
>
> O'Brien held up his left hand, its back toward Winston, with the thumb hidden and the four fingers extended.
>
> "How many fingers am I holding up, Winston?"
>
> "Four."
>
> "And if the Party says that it is not four but five—then how many?"
>
> "Four."
>
> The word ended in a gasp of pain. The needle of the dial had shot up to fifty-five. The sweat had sprung out all over Winston's body. The air tore into his lungs and issued again in deep groans which even by clenching his teeth he could not stop. O'Brien watched him, the four fingers still extended. He drew back the lever. This time the pain was only slightly eased.
>
> "How many fingers, Winston?"
>
> "Four."
>
> The needle went up to sixty.
>
> "How many fingers, Winston?"

"Four! Four! What else can I say? Four!"

The needle must have risen again, but he did not look at it. The heavy, stern face and the four fingers filled his vision. The fingers stood up before his eyes like pillars, enormous, blurry, and seeming to vibrate, but unmistakably four.

"How many fingers, Winston?"

"Four! Stop it, stop it! How can you go on? Four! Four!"

"How many fingers, Winston?"

"Five! Five! Five!"

"No, Winston, that is no use. You are lying. You still think there are four. How many fingers, please?"

"Four! Five! Four! Anything you like. Only stop it, stop the pain!"

Abruptly he was sitting up with O'Brien's arm round his shoulders. He had perhaps lost consciousness for a few seconds. The bonds that had held his body down were loosened. He felt very cold, he was shaking uncontrollably. His teeth were chattering, the tears were rolling down his cheeks. For a moment he clung to O'Brien like a baby, curiously comforted by the heavy arm round his shoulders. He had the feeling that O'Brien was his protector, that the pain was something that came from outside, from some other source, and that it was O'Brien who would save him from it.

"You are a slow learner, Winston," said O'Brien gently.

"How can I help it?" he blubbered. "How can I help seeing what is in front of my eyes? Two and two are four."

"Sometimes. Winston. Sometimes they are five. Sometimes they are three. Sometimes they are all of them at once. You must try harder. It is not easy to become sane."

He laid Winston down on the bed. The grip on his limbs tightened again, but the pain had ebbed away and the trembling had stopped, leaving him merely weak and cold. O'Brien motioned with his head to the man in the white coat, who had stood immobile throughout the proceedings. The man in the white coat bent down and looked closely into Winston's eyes, felt his pulse, laid an ear against his chest, tapped here and there; then he nodded to O'Brien.

"Again," said O'Brien.

The pain flowed into Winston's body. The needle must be at seventy, seventy-five. He had shut his eyes this time. He knew that the fingers were still there, and still four. All that mattered was somehow to stay alive until the spasm was over. He had ceased to notice whether he was crying out or not. The pain lessened again. He opened his eyes. O'Brien had drawn back the lever.

"How many fingers, Winston?"

"Four. I suppose there are four. I would see five if I could. I am trying to see five."

"Which do you wish: to persuade me that you see five, or really to see them?"

"Really to see them."

"Again," said O'Brien.

If we took this with high seriousness, then its offense against any persuasive mode of representation would make us uneasy. But it *is* a grand period piece, parodying not only Stalin's famous trials, but many theologically inspired ordeals before the advent of the belated Christian heresy that Russian Marxism actually constitutes. Orwell was a passionate moralist, and an accomplished essayist. The age drove him to the composition of political romance, though he lacked nearly all of the gifts necessary for the writer of narrative fiction. *1984* is an honorable aesthetic failure, and perhaps time will render its crudities into so many odd period graces, remnants of a vanished era. Yet the imagination, as Wallace Stevens once wrote, is always at the end of an era. Lionel Trilling thought that O'Brien's torture of Winston Smith was "a hideous parody on psychotherapy and the Platonic dialogues." Thirty-seven years after Trilling's review, the scene I have quoted above seems more like self-parody, as though Orwell's narrative desperately sought its own reduction, its own outrageous descent into the fallacy of believing that only the worst truth about us can be the truth.

Orwell was a dying man as he wrote the book, suffering the wasting away of his body in consumption. D. H. Lawrence, dying the same way, remained a heroic vitalist, as his last poems and stories demonstrate. But Lawrence belonged to literary culture, to the old, high line of transcendental seers. What wanes and dies in *1984* is not the best of George Orwell, not the pamphleteer of *The Lion and the Unicorn* nor the autobiographer of *Homage to Catalonia* nor the essayist of *Shooting an Elephant*. That Orwell lived and died an independent Socialist, hardly Marxist but really a Spanish Anarchist, or an English dissenter and rebel of the line of Cromwell and of Cromwell's celebrators, Milton and Carlyle. *1984* has the singular power, not aesthetic but social, of being the product of an age, and not just of the man who set it down.

RAYMOND WILLIAMS

Afterword:
Nineteen Eighty-Four *in 1984*

I

It was never at all likely that any actual society, in 1984, would much resemble the hellhole of Orwell's novel. He was in any case not making that kind of prediction:

> I do not believe that the kind of society I describe necessarily *will* arrive, but I believe (allowing of course for the fact that the book is a satire) that something resembling it *could* arrive. (CEJL, IV, 502)

The qualification is important. He had written earlier:

> This is a novel about the future—that is, it is in a sense a fantasy, but in the form of a naturalistic novel. That is what makes it a difficult job—of course as a book of anticipations it would be comparatively simple to write. (CEJL, IV, 329–30)

This difficulty of the form needs emphasis, as we try in his arbitrarily dated year to reassess his vision. The form is in fact more complex than the combination, in his terms, of 'fantasy' and 'naturalistic novel'. For there is a

From *Orwell*. © 1991 by Raymond Williams.

third element, most clearly represented by the extracts from the notorious Book and by the appendix on 'The Principles of Newspeak'. In the case of the Book, especially, the method of the writing is that of argument: the historical and political essay. There are then in effect three layers in the novel.

First, an infrastructure, immediately recognisable from Orwell's other fiction, in which the hero-victim moves through a squalid world in a series of misunderstandings and disappointments, trying and failing to hold on to the possibility—as much a memory as a vision—of a sweeter kind of life. Second, a structure of argument, indeed of anticipations, in the extracts from the Book and in some of the more general descriptions of the actual society. Third, a superstructure, including many of the most memorable elements, in which, by a method ranging from fantasy to satire and parody, the cruelty and repression of the society are made to appear at once ludicrous and savagely absurd.

The three levels are of course interconnected, though, as he recognised, imperfectly. The figure of the hero-victim is connected because at the centre of his memory or vision is an idea of truth, which the social order is determined to destroy. The everyday squalor is more generally connected, in the argument that the state of perpetual war has been instituted to keep people poor, but also as a bitter reversal of the normal condition of the authoritarian Utopia, in which material plenty is commonplace. Similarly, the most bizarre elements of the superstructure— the spy telescreen, Newspeak, the memory hole, the Two Minutes Hate, the Anti-Sex League—are satirical projections of the state of mind of the central social order:

> I believe ... that totalitarian ideas have taken root in the minds of intellectuals everywhere, and I have tried to draw these ideas out to their logical consequences. (CEJL, IV, 502)

As for the passages of argument, Orwell strongly resisted a suggestion from an American publisher that they should be abridged.

> It would alter the whole colour of the book and leave out a good deal that is essential. (CEJL, IV, 483)

He made the same point in commenting on a draft blurb from his English publisher:

> It makes the book sound as though it were a thriller mixed up with a love story, and I didn't intend it to be primarily that. What

it is really meant to do is to discuss the implications of dividing the world up into 'Zones of influence' (I thought of it in 1944 as a result of the Teheran conference), and in addition to indicate by parodying them the intellectual implications of totalitarianism. (CEJL, IV, 460)

It is then from Orwell's own sense of the book that we can find support for taking this central structure of argument, this element of reasoned anticipation, as important. Moreover it is above all with this central structure that a re-reading in 1984 should be primarily concerned.

This is so in spite of some formal difficulties, which can be briefly noted. Writing under great difficulties, because of his illness, Orwell undoubtedly had problems in integrating these levels of argument. This is especially clear in the fact that the essay on 'The Principles of Newspeak' had to be put in as an appendix, though some of it is a more developed version of the description and examples he had included in the main narrative. It is one of Orwell's liveliest essays, but there is a problem of position, caused by its attachment to the story. Thus within the first two pages Orwell veers between a position as historian of Ingsoc and Newspeak—

It is with the final, perfected version, as embodied in the Eleventh Edition of the Dictionary, that we are concerned here (NEF, 305)

—and a position as contemporary essayist, contemplating the horrible projection—

Newspeak was founded on the English language as we now know it, though many Newspeak sentences, even when not containing newly created words, would be barely intelligible to an English-speaker of our own day. (NEF, 306)

This kind of uncertainty, in fact soon overcome by the interest of the examples, is repeated in a more serious way in the extracts from the Book. On the one hand, as will be shown, they are very close to some of Orwell's own political thinking at the time, and even closer to some of his more obvious sources. They are in any case presented as from the secret Book of the underground opposition, the Brotherhood, and as written by the reviled Goldstein. On the other hand, like so much else that at first sight appears hopeful and trustworthy, they are eventually presented as elements of the Party's total deception. The Inner Party torturer O'Brien says:

'I wrote it. That is to say, I collaborated in writing it. No book
is produced individually, as you know.'
   'Is it true, what it says?'
   'As description, yes. The programme it sets forth is nonsense.'
(NEF, 267)

The intricacies of deception and betrayal, and of the deliberate confusion of
truth and lies, are at this point so great that it is futile to ask which version
Orwell intended readers to believe. What matters much more is that the
extracts are there—whatever the plausibility of their use in an already
complete trap—because Orwell wanted to set out, in a consecutive
argument, his ideas of how the world was going and could go. The narrative
status of the Book becomes important only when we compare his fictional
projections, in the extracts and in the more general story, with what he was
writing in the same years without these special problems of form.

   Three themes predominate in this central structure on which, at the
level of ideas, the book is founded. First, there is the division of the world
into three super-states, which in shifting alliances are in a state of limited but
perpetual war. Second, there is the internal tyranny of each of these states,
with a specific version of the relations between social classes and a detailed
presentation of a totalitarian society which has been developed beyond both
capitalism and socialism. Third, there is the exceptional emphasis on the
control of a society through ideas and means of communication: backed up
by direct repression and torture but mainly operating through 'thought
control'.

   These three themes need to be considered in detail, both in Orwell's
presentation of them and in the actual history to which they offer to
relate. It is especially important to consider all three, and to see how
Orwell thought of them as essentially interrelated. Ironically, however, it
is only possible to consider them, with the seriousness that he expected, if
we isolate them, temporarily, from the actual structure of the novel, and,
in a more permanent way, from the resonance which, since its publication,
has surrounded it.

   It would be possible, for example, to run a silly kind of checklist on
the projections. Is there an Anti-Sex League? Is there a two-way
telescreen for spying on people in their homes? Is there a statutory Two
Minutes Hate? No? Well then it just shows, as some said at the time, that
the book is a wild kind of horror-comic, or at best stupidly exaggerated.
But these are elements of the parodic superstructure. The structure then?
Yet in the predominant political resonance which has surrounded the
novel we do not even have to look at these arguments, because their proof

is already given in the real world. 'This is where socialism gets you.' 'This is where it has already got, in Russia and Eastern Europe.' But Orwell was quick to separate himself from this interpretation, which accounted for much of the early success of the book and which is still offered as if it were beyond question.

> My recent novel is NOT intended as an attack on Socialism or on the British Labour Party (of which I am a supporter) but as a show-up of the perversions to which a centralised economy is liable and which have already been partly realised in Communism and Fascism. (CEJL, IV, 502)

'*Partly* realised', in the social orders directed by Stalin and Hitler. The full perversions are shown as going further. Moreover the easy response, to put down the book and look East, where 'it is all already happening', should be checked by Orwell's emphasis:

> The scene of the book is laid in Britain in order to emphasise that the English-speaking races are not innately better than anyone else and that totalitarianism, *if not fought against*, could triumph anywhere. (CEJL, IV, 502)

The point is more than one of local correction, against the use and abuse of the novel during the cold war. It is central to Orwell's arguments that what is being described, in its main tendencies, is not only a universal danger but a universal process. That is the true source of his horror. If the novel is absorbed into the propaganda of this or that state, as a basis for hating and fearing an enemy state, against which there must be preparation for war, there is the really savage irony that a citizen of Oceania, in 1984, is thinking as he has been programmed to think, but with the reassurance of the book to tell him that he is free and that only those others are propagandised and brainwashed. Orwell was offering no such reassurance. He saw the super-states, the spy states, and the majority populations controlled by induced ideas as the way *the world* was going, to the point where there would still be arbitrary enemies, and names and figures to hate, but where there would be no surviving faculty of discovering or telling the truth about *our own* situation: the situation of any of us, in any of the states and alliances. This is a much harder position than any simple anti-socialism or anti-communism. It is indeed so hard that we must begin by examining what he took to be its overpowering conditions, leading first to the super-states and to limited perpetual war.

II

Nineteen Eighty-Four is so often quoted as a vision of the worst possible future world that it may seem odd to say that in at least one respect Orwell notably underestimated a general danger. It is not often remembered that in the novel a war with atomic bombs has been fought in the 1950s. There are not many details, though it is mentioned that an atomic bomb fell on Colchester. This is one of several instances in which, read from the actual 1984, the novel can be clearly seen as belonging to the 1940s. Orwell was quick to comment on the importance of the new weapon. He wrote in *Tribune* in October 1945 that it was dangerous mainly because it made the strong much stronger; its difficult manufacture meant that it would be reserved to a few powerful societies that were already heavily industrialised. 'The great age of democracy and of national self-determination' had been 'the age of the musket and the rifle'. Now, with this invention,

> we have before us the prospect of two or three monstrous super-states, each possessed of a weapon by which millions of people can be wiped out in a few seconds, dividing the world between them. (CEJL, IV, 8)

This is not only the outline of the world of *Nineteen Eighty-Four*. It is also an intelligent recognition of the actual power of the new weapons. Yet still, after this, he included in his story a war with atomic weapons after which, though with its own kinds of horror, a relatively recognisable land and society survived. This is no discredit to Orwell. Again and again it has been almost impossible to imagine the true consequences of an atomic *war*, as distinct from the one-sided use of the bomb which has been the only actual event. Indeed there has been a familiar kind of *doublethink* about nuclear weapons, in which it is simultaneously if contradictorily known that they would lead to massive and in many cases absolute destruction and yet that, with sufficient political determination, of whatever kind, they could be absorbed and survived.

The idea of an atomic war in the 1950s was common enough in the middle and late 1940s. It was seen as virtually inevitable, once more than one state possessed atomic bombs, by several writers and especially by James Burnham, about whom Orwell wrote two substantial essays in the years in which he was writing *Nineteen Eighty-Four*. Orwell began his novel in August 1946 and completed the first draft in November 1947. His essay 'Burnham and the Managerial Revolution' was published in May 1946 and 'Burnham and the Contemporary World Struggle' in March 1947. The essays are full of the themes of the novel, and there are several close correspondences between them and the fictional extracts from the Book. On the other hand there are significant differences between Orwell's discriminating discussions of Burnham's theses and the relatively simplified presentation of closely comparable ideas in the Book.

Thus Burnham's argument in *The Struggle for the World* is that the United States, while in sole possession of the atomic bomb, should move to prevent any other nation ever acquiring it. Orwell comments that 'he is demanding, or all but demanding, an immediate preventive war against Russia' (CEJL, IV, 316), and indeed such proposals, to be preceded by ultimatum-like demands to abandon 'communism' or 'world-communism', were directly made by others. Against such arguments, Orwell in the later essay hoped that there would be more time than Burnham had supposed: 'perhaps ten years, but more probably only five' (CEJL, IV, 314). If there was indeed more time there would be better political directions than an American world order and an anti-communist crusade. He added that 'the more the pessimistic world-view of Burnham and others like him prevails, the harder it is for such [alternative] ideas to take hold' (CEJL, IV, 324).

It is strange now, when Burnham has been largely forgotten, and when *Nineteen Eighty-Four* is so much better known than Orwell's essays, to retrace the formation of the 'pessimistic world-view' of the novel. We can look again at the idea of the dominant super-states. In the novel it is as follows:

> The splitting up of the world into three great super-states was an event which could be and indeed was foreseen before the middle of the twentieth century. With the absorption of Europe by Russia and of the British Empire by the United States, two of the three existing powers, Eurasia and Oceania, were already effectively in being. The third, Eastasia, only emerged as a distinct unit after another decade of confused fighting. (NEF, 190)

This is more or less directly taken from Burnham:

> Burnham's geographical picture of the new world has turned out to be correct. More and more obviously the surface of the earth is being parcelled off into three great empires, each self-contained and cut off from contact with the outer world, and each ruled, under one disguise or another, by a self-elected oligarchy. (CEJL, IV, 8–9)

The idea is now so familiar, from the novel, that some effort is needed to realise the strangeness of Orwell's assertion, at that date, that the picture 'has turned out to be correct', and, further, that the empire nearest home—the American/British of the fictional Oceania—is, like the more frequently cited Soviet empire, 'ruled ... by a self-elected oligarchy'.

The next stage in Orwell's development of the idea, while he was in the middle of writing his novel, follows from his definition of three political possibilities: a preventive war by the United States, which would be a crime and would in any case solve nothing; a cold war until several nations have atomic bombs, then almost at once a war which would wipe out industrial civilisation and leave only a small population living by subsistence agriculture; or

> that the fear inspired by the atomic bomb and other weapons yet to come will be so great that everyone will refrain from using them. This seems to me the worst possibility of all. It would mean the division of the world among two or three vast super-states, unable to conquer one another and unable to be overthrown by any internal rebellion. In all probability their structure would be hierarchic, with a semi-divine caste at the top and outright slavery at the bottom, and the crushing out of liberty would exceed anything that the world has yet seen. Within each state the necessary psychological atmosphere would be kept up by complete severance from the outer world, and by a continuous phony war against rival states. Civilisations of this type might remain static for thousands of years. (CEJL, IV, 371)

This is, in effect, the option taken by the novel, though an intervening and less damaging atomic war has been retained from earlier positions. In his directly political writing, at this time, Orwell saw an alternative to all three dangers: the building of 'democratic Socialism ... throughout some large area ... A Socialist United States of Europe seems to me the only worthwhile political objective today' (CEJL, IV, 371). But in the perspective of the fiction this is entirely absent.

Obviously we must ask, in 1984, why none of Orwell's three (or four) possibilities has occurred. Yet we must do this soberly, since we shall not be released from any of the dangers he and others foresaw by the mere passage of a fictional date. It is not, in some jeering way, to prove Orwell wrong, but to go on learning the nature of the historical developments which at his most serious he was trying desperately to understand, that we have to ask what he left out, or what he wrongly included, in his assessment of the world-political future.

First we have to notice that what came through, in this period, were not unitary super-states or empires but the more complex forms of military superpowers and primarily military alliances. There are times, especially as we listen to war propaganda, when we can suppose that the Burnham/Orwell vision has been realised, in the monolithically presented entities of 'East' and 'West', and with China as the shifting partner of either. But the full political realities have turned out to be very different. There is, for example, a coexistent and different hierarchy of *economic* power, with Japan and West Germany as major forces. In significantly different degrees in 'East' and 'West', but everywhere to some extent, old national forms have persisted and continue to command the loyalty of majorities, though also in every such nation, including those of 'the West', there is a significant minority who are conscious agents of the interests of the dominant power in the military alliance.

At the same time, in ways that Orwell could not have foreseen, these elements of political autonomy and diversity—within very narrow margins in the Warsaw Pact, within broader margins in NATO which contains most kinds of political state from liberal democracies to military dictatorships—are radically qualified by the nature of modern nuclear-weapons systems. The atomic war of *Nineteen Eighty-Four* is damaging but not disastrous; in fact it is made to precipitate the 'perpetual limited war' which is a central condition of the novel, in which the super-states are unconquerable because their rulers cannot risk atomic war. The war actually being fought, with its distant battles and its occasional rockets, belongs technologically to the 1940s. But then it is not only that the effects of atomic war have been underestimated; it is that the military and political consequences of a relative monopoly of nuclear weapons have turned out to be quite different from anything that Orwell and most others supposed.

> Suppose—and really this is the likeliest development—that the surviving great nations make a tacit agreement never to use the atomic bomb against one another? Suppose they only use it, or the threat of it, against people who are unable to retaliate? In that case we are back where we were before, the only difference being that power is concentrated in still fewer hands and that the outlook for subject peoples and oppressed classes is still more hopeless. (CEJL, IV, 8)

Between the powers that have acquired atomic weapons there has been neither formal nor tacit agreement never to use the weapons against one another. On the contrary, the predominant policy has been one of mutual threat. Within this policy there has not, as Orwell thought, been technical stagnation, but a continual enlargement and escalation of weapons systems, each typically developed under an alleged threat of the superiority of the other side. And these have now reached the point at which national autonomies, within the alliances, contradict in one central respect the technical requirements of the most modern systems, which require instant response or even, some argue, preventive first use, if the other power is not to gain an early and overwhelming advantage.

It would be easy to argue from this, yet again, that the Burnham/Orwell kind of super-state, with the necessary unitary command, is inevitable, as a product of the new weapons. But to move to that kind of super-state, for all its strategic advantages, would be to provoke major political problems—especially, for example, in Western Europe—which would endanger and probably break the now fragile compromise between surviving political autonomies and loyalties and the military-strategic alliance which has been superimposed on them. Thus Britain, in 1984, both is and is not, in Orwell's phrase, Airstrip One. It is dense with its own and foreign air and missile bases but it is also—and crucially, by a majority, is valued as—an independent political nation. To force the question to the point where it would have to be one thing *or* the other would bring into play all the forces which Orwell recognised in his essays but excluded from the novel. For the agents of paranational military and economic planning Britain has become, in a true example of Newspeak, the UK or Yookay. But for the peoples who live on the actual island there are more real and more valued names and relationships and considerations.

It is in the exclusion of even these traditional elements of resistance to what might seem a logical new order that Orwell, in the novel though usually not in the essays, went most obviously wrong. But there is an even larger error in the exclusion of new forces of resistance: most notably the national-liberation and revolutionary movements of what he knew as the colonial world. The monopoly of nuclear weapons, in the major industrialised states, has not prevented major advances towards autonomy among the 'subject peoples' whose condition he predicted as more hopeless. This is the peculiar unreality of the projection, that the old world powers, newly grouped into super-states, are seen as wholly dominant, and that the rest of the world is merely a passive quarry of minerals and cheap labour. Again, however, what has actually happened is complex. There have been political liberations in this vast area that Orwell reduced to passivity, but there is a limited sense in which what he foresaw has happened: not in super-state wars for its control, but in a complex of economic interventions, by paranational corporations which have some of the technical attributes of super-states; of political interventions, manoeuvres and 'destabilisations'; of exceptionally heavy arms exports to what in the worst cases become client states; and of military interventions, in some cases, where heavy and bloody fighting still excludes the use or threat of use of the nuclear weapons which in the perspective of the 1940s had seemed decisive for either conquest or blackmail.

Thus there has been, in one sense, the 'perpetual war' that Orwell thought likely, but it has been neither of a total nor of a phoney kind. The complex political and economic forces actually engaged have prevented the realisation of the apparently simple extrapolations from technical necessity or political ambition. It is sometimes hard to say, at this world-political level, whether the real 1984 is better or worse than the projected Nineteen Eighty-Four. It is more complex, more dynamic, more uncertain than the singular nightmare. Many more people are free or relatively free than the projection allowed, but also many more people have died or are dying in continuing 'small' wars, and vastly more live in danger of annihilation by nuclear war. The rationed and manipulated shortages of the projection have been succeeded by an extraordinary affluence in the privileged nations, and by actual and potential starvation in extending areas of the poor world. It is then not for showing danger and horror that anyone can reproach Orwell. If there is to be reproach, it is for looking so intently in one direction, with its simplified and easily dramatised dangers, that there is an excuse for not looking at other forces and developments which may, in the end, prove to be even more disastrous.

III

War is Peace is one notable chapter of the Book. As a comment on a perpetual and normalised *state* of war its details may be wrong but its feeling is right. 'We are the peace movement,' a British Government minister said recently, supporting the next phase of rearmament.

Ignorance is Strength is the other main chapter. This eventually describes the purposes and methods of thought control, but it begins with an analysis of the social structure of the super-states, based on a sort of historical-political theory:

> Throughout recorded time, and probably since the end of the Neolithic Age, there have been three kinds of people in the world, the High, the Middle and the Low. They have been subdivided in many ways, they have borne countless different names, and their relative numbers, as well as their attitude

towards one another, have varied from age to age: but the
essential structure of society has never altered. Even after
enormous upheavals and seemingly irrevocable changes, the same
pattern has always reasserted itself ... (NEF, 206–7)

It is at points like this that the status of the Book, in relation to Orwell's own
thinking, is most problematic. Many examples could be quoted to show that
he understood history as change rather than this abstract recurrence. The
point is relevant again when the Book asserts:

No advance in wealth, no softening of manners, no reform or
revolution has ever brought human equality a millimetre nearer.
(NEF, 208)

This is, as written, such obvious nonsense that the status of the whole
argument becomes questionable. If this were really true, there would be no
basis for calling Ingsoc a 'perversion'; it would be yet one more example of
an inevitable, even innate process.

Clearly Orwell did not believe this, and neither did the author or the
authors of the Book, a page or two on. For what is there argued is that while
in earlier periods, because of the stage of development of the means of
production, 'inequality was the price of civilisation', in the twentieth century
'human equality had become technically possible' with the development of
'machine production'. However, just at that point, 'all the main currents of
political thought' stopped believing in equality and became authoritarian.

This level of argument is so perverse that one could indeed believe that
O'Brien had written it. But more significantly it is an imperfect composition
of three incompatible kinds of argument: one from Orwell, one from
Burnham and one from Marx. The Marxist proposition of the unavoidable
relations between the stages of development of the means of production and
the formation of class societies, with the orthodox communist gloss that fully
developed machine production would at last make equality possible, is
unmistakably present. The Orwell argument or reservation that much talk of
this kind, among its actual representatives, is just a cover for a new
authoritarian conspiracy, ending capitalism but then even more thoroughly
repressing and controlling the working class, is also evident. But the really
discordant element, though it becomes dominant, is from Burnham. As
Orwell summarises him in the first essay:

Every great social movement, every war, every revolution, every
political programme, however edifying and Utopian, really has

behind it the ambitions of some sectional group which is out to
grab power for itself ... So that history consists of a series of
swindles, in which the masses are first lured into revolt by the
promises of Utopia, and then, when they have done their job,
enslaved over again by new masters. (CEJL, IV, 176–7)

In the essay Orwell circles hesitantly and intelligently around these crude
propositions. He even comments:

> He ... assumes that the division of society into classes serves the
> same purpose in all ages. This is practically to ignore the history
> of hundreds of years. (CEJL, IV, 177)

And he goes on from this to the Marxist proposition, repeated in the Book,
on the relation of class society to methods of production.

At the level of Orwell's direct arguments, then, the eventual emphasis
of the Book is a known simplification. But it is the combination of this
simplification with his own, often reasonable, reservations and suspicions
about socialists or nominal socialists who are really authoritarians which
determines the social structure of *Nineteen Eighty-Four*. His own
contribution is then more specific than Burnham's. Burnham had foreseen a
'managerial revolution'. As Orwell summarises:

> Capitalism is disappearing, but Socialism is not replacing it.
> What is now arising is a new kind of planned, centralised society
> which will be neither capitalist nor, in any accepted sense of the
> word, democratic. The rulers of this new society will be the
> people who effectively control the means of production: that is,
> business executives, technicians, bureaucrats and soldiers, lumped
> together by Burnham under the name of 'managers'. These
> people will eliminate the old capitalist class, crush the working
> class, and so organise society that all power and economic
> privilege remain in their own hands. Private property rights will
> be abolished, but common ownership will not be established.
> (CEJL, IV, 160)

This is not, in any full sense, how things have actually turned out, though
there are elements that are recognisable. But Orwell did not call the new
social order Ingmana; he called it Ingsoc. Burnham's prediction, and the
wider argument of which it is a relatively simple instance, pointed as clearly
to Fascism and the Corporate State, or to what is now called a managed,

interventionist post-capitalism, as to an authoritarian communism. It was Orwell who specialised it to a development within the socialist tradition, which it was also betraying. We can then, in 1984, only properly assess the prediction if we pull back to its full context.

In one way it is easy to understand Orwell's narrowing specialisation. Fascism, when he was writing, had just been militarily defeated. Capitalism, he assumed, was finished and deserved to be finished. What then mattered was which kind of socialism would come through, and since his option was for democratic socialism what he had mainly and even exclusively to oppose was authoritarian socialism.

> The real question is not whether the people who wipe their boots on us during the next fifty years are to be called managers, bureaucrats or politicians: the question is whether capitalism, now obviously doomed, is to give way to oligarchy or to true democracy. (CEJL, IV, 165)

This makes strange reading in 1984, especially if *Nineteen Eighty-Four* is there to tell us to concentrate our attention on Ingsoc and the Party. It is true that within the countries of what is now called 'actually existing socialism' this is broadly how it has turned out. Indeed the only correction we have to make, in that area, is that 'the Party', in that singular ideological sense, has proved to be less significant than the actual combination of technicians, bureaucrats and soldiers which the political monopoly of the Party makes possible and legitimises. It was significant during the Solidarity crisis in Poland that the different fractions of this hitherto effective ruling group were shown, under pressure, to have crucially variable interests, and more generally the idea of the monolithic Party has been shown to be false by a continuing series of internal dissensions and conflicts. However, that 'actually existing socialism' is still the prime case (though closely followed by the 'nationalised' or 'publicly owned' industries of the capitalist democracies) of the prediction that 'private property rights will be abolished, but common ownership will not be established'.

This does not mean, however, that the Orwell prediction of oligarchy has to be specialised, as in the novel, to 'Oligarchical Collectivism'. There are and for a long time have been many other forms of oligarchy. The most important modern form depends on the centralisation of effective political and economic controls. This has been associated with state versions of socialism, and indeed, ironically, Orwell conceded and approved this association:

> Centralised control is a necessary pre-condition of Socialism, but
> it no more produces Socialism than my typewriter would of itself
> produce this article I am writing. (CEJL, IV, 18)

But so far from this idea of a centralised socialism being a modern
perversion, or likely to lead to it, it is in fact an old kind of socialism, of the
period of the Fabians as much as of the Bolsheviks, and it has been
increasingly rather than decreasingly challenged by new socialist ideas of
decentralised politics and economic self-management. Orwell, in that sense,
is behind even his own time.

Yet this is still to specialise the argument about oligarchy to socialism,
when what has really undermined the basis of Orwell's prediction has been
the phenomenal recovery of capitalism, which he had seen as 'doomed'. The
spectacular capitalist boom from the mid-1950s to the early 1970s falsified
virtually every element of the specific prediction. The real standard of living
rose for many millions of working people. The main socialist movements, in
the old industrial societies, moved steadily towards a consensus with the new,
affluent, managed capitalism. Political liberties were not further suppressed,
though their exercise became more expensive. The main motor of the boom,
in an extraordinary expansion of consumer credit, was a new predominance
of financial institutions, which gained in power at the expense of both
political and industrial forces. When the boom ended, in depression and the
return of mass unemployment, a new oligarchy was plainly in view. The
national and international monetary institutions, with their counterparts in
the giant paranational corporations, had established a both practical and
ideological dominance which so far from being shaken by the first decade of
depression and unemployment was actually reinforced by it. These were the
actual forces now 'wiping their boots on us', in the old industrial societies
and the new ex-colonial countries alike. Internally and externally they had all
the features of a true oligarchy, and a few people, at least, began to learn that
'centralisation' is not just an old socialist nostrum but is a practical process of
ever-larger and more concentrated capitalist corporations and money
markets. State power, meanwhile, though trying to withdraw from its earlier
commitments to common provision for social welfare, has increased at
military levels, in the new weapons systems, and in its definitions of law and
order and of security (backed up by some intensive surveillance). Thus it is
an obvious case of *doublethink* when the radical Right, now in power in so
many countries, denounce the state at the level of social welfare or economic
justice but reinforce and applaud the state at the level of patriotic militarism,
uniform loyalty, and control over local democratic institutions. To hear some

of the loudest of these double-mouthed people is to know what is meant, in Newspeak, by a *doubleplusgood duckspeaker*.

But then what about the *proles*? Here again the prediction was quite wrong, though there are a few disillusioned people thinking it might have been right. For the key feature of the new capitalist oligarchy is that it has not left 'eighty-five per cent of the population' to their own devices. On the contrary, it has successfully organised most of them as a market, calling them now not 'proles' but 'consumers' (the two terms are equally degrading). It is true that there is massive provision, by the newspapers and other media of the oligarchy, of the semi-pornography and gambling and mechanical fiction which the Party was supposed to provide. (This, incidentally, is one of Orwell's interesting errors about Soviet communism, where the Party has exercised its ideological controls *against* these mainly 'Western' phenomena.) But the real controls are different. A straight contract between disciplined wage-labour and credit-financed consumption was offered and widely accepted. Even as it became unavailable to the many millions who in depression became, in that cruel oligarchic term, 'redundant', its social and political hold, as the essence of any social order, was at first barely disturbed. Indeed the ideological response of the oligarchy was to act to make the contract more secure: by disciplining the trade unions which represent an independent element in its bargaining, beyond oligarchic control; and by identifying as public enemies, in its newspapers, dissenting political figures: not the 'proper official Opposition' but the 'unofficial' Reds, Wreckers, Extremists, who in good *Nineteen Eighty-Four* style are seen as either mad or guilty of *thoughtcrime*.

IV

It would be surprising if one kind of oligarchy could succeed, for long, in using the features of another to distract attention from its own. Yet *Nineteen Eighty-Four*, in 1984, is being primarily used for just this purpose, ironically by some of the same propaganda methods which it exposes and attacks. Because what Orwell wanted to show as a universal tendency became attached (by his choice, though he protested against it) to the practice of socialism, any anti-socialist movement can exploit it, even in ways which confirm its own deepest warnings. It is one thing for dissident and oppositional groups in Eastern Europe to say, as some of them do, that *Nineteen Eighty-Four* shows the underlying truth of their condition. I was asked by students, in one communist country, to lecture on Orwell, and I did so willingly, against some official disapproval, because I wanted to follow the whole argument through: not just what could be mocked or hated but what could still, genuinely, be believed. Beyond the obvious pyrotechnics of the projection there is, however qualified, a steady insistence on the value of thinking for oneself and of refusing the official simplifications which all ruling groups employ. The more there is to be mocked or hated, in any system, the more it is necessary to resist these feelings being used by others, for their own governing purposes. One scene in the novel sticks in my mind, in this later period, when the figurehead of the Opposition, Goldstein, appears on the screen—

> demanding the immediate conclusion of peace with Eurasia ... advocating freedom of speech, freedom of the Press, freedom of assembly, freedom of thought ... And all the while, lest one should be in any doubt as to the reality which Goldstein's specious claptrap covered, behind his head on the telescreen marched the endless columns of the Eurasian army... (NEF, 16)

This trick is now being played so often: certainly in official denunciations of unofficial peace, civil rights and workers' movements in Eastern Europe as 'Western-inspired'; but just as certainly in the West, as when the independent peace movements are directly accused of serving Russian interests, 'the endless columns of the Eurasian army'. Meanwhile anyone can see that the other side's Big Brother is a tyrant and a fraud, but the endlessly imposed ruling faces of one's own side are supposed indeed to be 'loved'.

It is interesting that what has really survived, from *Nineteen Eighty-Four*, is Orwell's understanding of propaganda and thought control. There have been changes of style and technology but certain basic methods of the oligarchy—endlessly repeated slogans, displacements of one kind of news by another, the regular institution of hate-figures—are still clearly recognisable. In 1946 Orwell wrote:

> In England the immediate enemies of truthfulness, and hence of freedom of thought, are the press lords, the film magnates, and the bureaucrats. (CEJL, IV, 64)

That familiar case still holds. But there is another key element in Orwell's diagnosis:

> But ... on a long view the weakening of the desire for liberty among the intellectuals themselves is the most serious symptom of all. (CEJL, IV, 64)

It was from this conviction that some of the most specific features of *Nineteen Eighty-Four* were composed. In a way what is most surprising about its tyrannical system is that it more or less neglects eighty-five per cent of the population and is concerned mainly with controlling the thoughts and the very memories of a minority.

It is difficult to follow this kind of anticipation through. There are no obvious objective events from which to assess it. But I have sometimes felt that almost the exact opposite has happened. I do not mean that there have not been time-serving and even lying 'intellectuals', together with a much larger executive group with conveniently selective memories. I mean that there is a case for saying that in the capitalist democracies there has been intense and continuous attention to the state of mind of the eighty-five per cent (or whatever the precise figure for majority popular opinion might be) and a relative indifference to what 'intellectuals'—already marked off as peculiar—believe or do. It is different, I know, in the 'actually existing socialist' societies, where there has been intense pressure, and worse, on just these minority groups. It can be reasonably argued that because the capitalist societies are electoral democracies attention to majorities is inevitable, while minorities can be disregarded and even sneered at or, obscurely, shown to be 'wrong' *because* they are minorities. Yet, beyond this difference of systems, and even after allowing for the fact that Orwell was parodying monolithic one-party societies, it is still the case that he thought that the state of mind of intellectuals would be decisive. And then there is indeed some basis for saying that we could wish that he had been right.

The point bears most closely on the notorious 'memory hole'. For if there is one thing that has not proved necessary, in manipulating majority opinion, it is systematically rewriting the past. On the contrary, the past in itself becomes a kind of memory hole, from which only a few scholars and researchers bother to uncover and recover the facts. Why were the first atom bombs dropped on Japan *after* its government had proposed the outline of a peace? What really happened in the Gulf of Tonkin? Which way and during what peace negotiations was the *General Belgrano* sailing? These are questions (none, in their whole context, with very simple answers) which with a thousand others, from the role of Trotsky in the Russian Revolution to the policy of Mao and the Red Guards in China, are still intensely inquired into by small minorities, while the dominant public stance, in one social order after another, is to go blithely on with the news of the day, leaving the past to the obsessive and to the dry-as-dust. General versions of the past, selected and packaged to show the present as inevitable and the ruling future as desirable, are of course deployed. But the detail, the two-and-two of the inquiry, can be there and not there: in the books and the monographs and the seminars but not in what is aggressively presented as 'the real world'. Orwell was right, of course, to attack the time-serving, submissive and lying intellectuals whom he had encountered and saw proliferating. But in *Nineteen Eighty-Four* there is another level, quite contrary to his own best practice, in which the scheming and the power-hungry are of this intellectual kind, and the only actual alternative to them are the stupid and ignorant, protected by stupidity and ignorance. And what then of the Party slogan, *Ignorance is Strength*?

It has not, on any reckoning, worked out like that. This is especially the case in what he saw as the worst danger: power-worship. There has been plenty of that, but not just from some intellectual habit. Militarism, chauvinism, tough policing, penal cruelty have been general epidemics. And the people in charge of them, in any social order, have not needed intellectuals to justify what they are doing, though in some systems they take care to employ hacks. The powerful and the fraudulent have been the powerful and the fraudulent. Their interests are their reasons; they do not need cogitators.

But this brings us to the hardest question in a reassessment of *Nineteen Eighty-Four*. Worried and fascinated by Burnham's arguments that power is the only political reality, whatever phrases may accompany it, Orwell observed:

> It is curious that in all his talk about the struggle for power, Burnham never stops to ask *why* people want power. He seems to assume that power hunger, although only dominant in comparatively few people, is a natural instinct that does not have to be explained. (CEJL, IV, 177)

It is fascinating that when Winston Smith comes to the point in his reading of the Book when this motive to power is to be explained he realises that Julia has been asleep for some time and puts the book away, still wondering what the secret could be. The question returns only during his torture by O'Brien, and O'Brien answers it:

> The object of persecution is persecution. The object of torture is torture. The object of power is power. Now do you begin to understand me? (NEF, 269)

'A natural instinct that does not have to be explained'? This is the terrifying irrationalism of the climax of *Nineteen Eighty-Four*, and it is not easy, within the pity and the terror, to persist with the real and Orwell's own question.

The point of Burnham's position is to discredit all actual political beliefs and aspirations, since these are invariably covers for naked power or the wish for it. But if this is so, there is not only a cancellation of history—as Orwell in his essay went on to observe. The real variations of what happened, as well as of what was said and believed, are flattened into a meaningless, degrading uniformity of human action. There is also a cancellation of inquiry and argument, and therefore of the possibility of truth, since whatever is said can be instantly translated into the base and cruel reality which it is known to cover. It is not necessary to deny the existence, even the frequent occurrence, of persecution and power and torture 'for their own sake' (meaning, for the private gratification of their executors, rather than for any objective cause) to go on resisting the cancellation of all links between power and policy. And this cancellation *must* be resisted, if only because it would then be pointless to try to distinguish between social systems, or to inquire, discriminatingly, where this or that system went good or went bad.

There is plenty of room for disagreement about the social and political systems which make arbitrary power, persecution and torture more or less likely. In the world of the actual 1984 there is so vast an extent of these practices, in social systems otherwise dissimilar—from Chile to Kampuchea, from Turkey and El Salvador to Eastern Europe, and with instances from as close to home as Belfast—that it is tempting to override the discriminating questions, to recoil from man become brute. Yet it is the two-plus-two kind of reckoning—obstinately factual and truthful, however complex the sums may become—that is then most at risk. There are reasons, as outside the fiction Orwell well knew, why there are systems and phases of systems in which, as throughout recorded history, opponents and even inconvenients are imprisoned, tortured and killed; just as there are other systems and phases of systems—nearly all of them modern; nearly all of them achieved by prolonged political argument and struggle—when these brutal short-cuts are lessened or brought under control. Of course Orwell is warning against a modern totalitarian system, developed beyond even Stalin or Hitler. But there is a totalitarian way of warning against totalitarianism, by excluding just those discriminating historical analyses, those veridical political distinctions, those authentic as distinct from assumed beliefs and aspirations, which are a much better protection against it than the irrational projection inspiring either terror or hate. It is useful to remember what he said of Burnham:

> Burnham is trying to build up a picture of terrifying, irresistible power, and to turn a normal political manoeuvre like infiltration into Infiltration adds to the general portentousness. (CEJL, IV, 170)

It can be the same with Ingsoc. As he again said in discussing Burnham's thesis:

> Power worship blurs political judgment because it leads, almost unavoidably, to the belief that present trends will continue. (CEJL, IV, 174)

Yet Orwell himself, always an opponent of privilege and power, committed himself, in the fiction, to just that submissive belief. The warning that the world could be going that way became, in the very absoluteness of the fiction, an imaginative submission to its inevitability. And then to rattle that chain again is to show little respect to those many men and women, including from the whole record Orwell himself, who have fought and are fighting the destructive and ignorant trends that are still so powerful, and who have kept the strength to imagine, as well as to work for, human dignity, freedom and peace.

BOOKLIST, REFERENCES, ACKNOWLEDGEMENTS

Books by Orwell

DOPL: *Down and Out in Paris and London*; London, 1933
BD: *Burmese Days*; New York, 1934
CD: *A Clergyman's Daughter*; London, 1935
KAF: *Keep the Aspidistra Flying*; London, 1936
RWP: *The Road to Wigan Pier*; London, 1937
HC: *Homage to Catalonia*; London, 1938
CUA: *Coming Up For Air*; London, 1939
IW: *Inside the Whale*; London, 1940
AF: *Animal Farm*; London, 1945
NEF: *Nineteen Eighty-Four*; London, 1949
CEJL: *Collected Essays, Journalism and Letters of George Orwell*; 4 volumes, edited by Sonia Orwell and Ian Angus; London, 1968

Page references, other than CEJL, are to the Uniform Edition. Acknowledgement of copyright in quotations to Sonia Brownell Orwell and to Secker and Warburg Limited, 14 Carlisle Street, London, W1. All books by Orwell mentioned above are available in Penguin paperback editions.

Some Books about Orwell

Aldrith, Keith *The Making of George Orwell*. London, Edward Arnold, 1969
Atkins, John *George Orwell*. London, Calder, 1954
Brander, Laurence *George Orwell*. London, Longman, 1954

Calder, Jennie *Chronicles of Conscience* (part). London, Secker & Warburg, 1968

Crick, Bernard *George Orwell: a Life*. London, Secker & Warburg, 1980

Greenblatt, S. J. *Three Modern Satirists* (part). New Haven, Yale, 1965

Gross, M. (ed.) *The World of George Orwell*. London, Weidenfeld & Nicolson, 1971

Hollis, Christopher *A Study of George Orwell*. London, Hollis & Carter, 1958

Lee, Robert A. *Orwell's Fiction*. Notre Dame, Indiana, 1969

Lief, Ruth A. *Homage to Oceania*. Ohio State University, 1969

Oxley, B. *George Orwell*. London, Evans, 1967

Rees, Richard *George Orwell—Fugitive from the Camp of Victory*. London, Secker & Warburg, 1961

Stansky, P. and Abrahams, W. *The Unknown Orwell*. London, Constable, 1972

Thomas, Edward M. *Orwell*. Edinburgh, Oliver & Boyd, 1953

Vorhees, Richard J. *The Paradox of George Orwell*. Lafayette, Indiana, Purdue University, 1961

Williams, R. (ed.) *Twentieth Century Views: George Orwell*. New Jersey, Prentice-Hall, 1974

Willison, J. R. *George Orwell: Some Materials for a Bibliography*. School of Librarianship and Archives, University of London

Woodcock, George *The Crystal Spirit*. London, Cape, 1967

SUE LONOFF

Composing Nineteen Eighty-Four:
The Art of Nightmare

My new book is a utopia in the form of a novel. I ballsed it up rather ...
but I think some of the ideas in it might interest you.

George Orwell to Julian Symons (1949)[1]

Check the commentary on *Nineteen Eighty-Four* and you will find support for Orwell's modest judgment. Indisputably, the book is a *dys*topia—a term that came into currency after, and partly because of, his narrative. But four decades of scholarly study have yet to yield consensus on its literary aspects: its genre, its consistency, its rendering of character, the quality of the execution. To some readers, it seems not to be a novel at all; it is a fantasy or satire or tract for the times, a history lecture done up as a prophecy.[2] Even those who place it in the novel tradition find flaws in every phase of execution. The segment on Goldstein's book interrupts the narrative. The characters are weak or "rudimentary." The third part is implausibly melodramatic. Room 101 projects a schoolboy's fantasies. Orwell's very language, the prose he took such pride in, has been attacked on the one hand for betraying signs of haste and on the other for revealing too much effort.[3]

You can do what Irving Howe did when he challenged its detractors—hold the book exempt from mere aesthetic judgment: "The last thing Orwell cared about when he wrote *Nineteen Eighty-Four*, the last thing he should, have cared about, was literature."[4] But Orwell would have disagreed—

From *The Revised Orwell*. © 1991 by Jonathan Rose.

31

emphatically: "... I could not do the work of writing a book, or even a long magazine article, if it were not also an aesthetic experience" (*CEJL*, 1:6). In *Animal Farm*, he had tried (successfully, he thought) "to fuse political purpose and artistic purpose into one whole" (*CEJL*, 1:7). He had hoped for fusion of this kind in its successor, but his final effort left him disappointed.

Yet as Bernard Crick notes, Orwell's discontent was chronic; *Animal Farm* alone met his high standards (*GO*, 384). And against his allegation that he "ballsed up" the writing, there is evidence of long-term care and craftsmanship: an outline done five years before the typescript was completed; notes toward a revision of the first draft; an interim manuscript, dense with corrections; and remnants which support Peter Davison's argument that Orwell composed the novel in six stages—seven, if you include the proofs.[5] Wretched health increased the burden of revision. He had to rush the last draft. He could not get a typist, so he did it in his bedroom over two or three weeks, fighting weakness and the constant threat of relapse. But if tuberculosis sapped his physical strength, it did not impair the vigor of his narrative. The adjectives repeatedly invoked to describe the book—"urgent," "haunting," "terrifying," "brilliant"—attest to its continuing power.

Does its power stem from the fusion Orwell thought he had failed to achieve, or is it powerful despite flawed execution? These questions lead backward and forward: back to versions that precede the final draft, and forward to speculation on its status now that 1984 is past. Strangely, the closer you get to answers, the more you become aware of paradox: this book that attacks totalitarian control is itself more controlled, rhetorically and structurally, than critics have been able to realize.[6] Even so, Orwell felt (with some justice) that he had not made his aims completely clear. If he had, though, he might also have reduced the complexity that takes the book so far beyond the topical. But before going further, I want briefly to consider what he meant when he talked about artistry.

Before he finished his first novel, *Burmese Days*, he spelled out what he thought a novel ought to do. The first and simplest thing was "to display or create character." The second was "to make a kind of pattern or design," as distinct from merely turning out a story. And the third, the one he seems to have cared most about, was "to produce *good writing*." Typically, he added an analogy: writing was to novels what the quality of brush-strokes, the "*texture*," was to really good painting (*CEJL*, 1:126).[7]

In the fifteen years between that book and *Nineteen Eighty-Four*, Orwell revised his priorities. The age, he felt, did not permit a leisurely pursuit of art; politics had to be paramount. Increasingly, he wrote to give insight into power, to examine political corruption. Ideas launched his efforts. He meant to move his audience. "All art is propaganda," he insisted, though "not all propaganda is art" (*CEJL*, 1:448). To crank out propaganda was to sacrifice integrity and publish work devoid of lasting value. Even as a pamphleteer, Orwell took pains. As for fiction, instead of giving up his old criteria, he meshed them with political objectives. Character became less important than subject—or rather, he subsumed the development of character under that of issue, theme, and message. Design remained significant. He cared about the plot as plot; beyond that, he cared about symmetry, tempo, the balance to be struck between dialogue and narrative, arrangement of episodes and images. Above all, he retained his pleasure in good writing and his faith in the potential of language. Barbarity and falseness threatened that potential, as they threatened human freedom and sound government.[8] In his own books, preeminently *Nineteen Eighty-Four*, he would attack those interlocking perils. Hence his need to control the words that paint a world in which control is inescapable and lethal.

The governing metaphor and palpable reality of *Nineteen Eighty-Four* is the nightmare. (The word runs consistently through Orwell's notes and drafts, from his first outline to his last response to critics.) It is not the kind of nightmare you associate with Kafka, whose characters and actions seem to emanate directly from the raw, chaotic force of the subconscious. Orwell's political and sexual distortions have a motive, an articulated logic. He does not consistently avoid extravagance or keep subconscious forces from intruding. But even at its most grotesque the novel keeps its balance. Its horrors mount in sequence; dreams and omens create patterns; the issues converge on one another. Most chilling and pervasive are the intricate connections between public and personal pathology. This attack upon a system evolves as one man's story; nothing private can exist that's not political. The point is made repeatedly, and even if it were not, its consequences would be obvious from the action.

Less plain is the extent to which "nightmare" is the key to the structure and progression of the narrative.[9] Perhaps that is because Orwell deliberately cast it "in the form of a naturalistic novel" (*CEJL*, 4:330). From the opening windblast to the last two tears on Winston's nose, this is a world made oppressively factual, too dustblown to be phantasmagoric. But as actual nightmares conflate disparate elements— memories, projections, sensations real and fantasied—so a book that approximates a nightmare can integrate elements drawn from any other mode: naturalism, satire, fable, parody, the Gothic. And since the term connotes two kinds of experience, terrifying dream and terrible reality, it tends to blur distinctions between them. "Nightmare situation" could describe Winston's daily life; the context—a society governed by the

Party; the real-world threat that drove Orwell to write; and the totalitarian ethos that he satirizes. If a single term can encompass all these elements then it is likely, as well, to offer clues to the literary aspects of the novel. Those are the aspects I want to consider now, exploring them in terms of Orwell's criteria—form and structure, character development, writing—to answer questions about fusion, control and the art of *Nineteen Eighty-Four*.

* * * * *

That Orwell planned to unify politics and artistry is evident from his preliminary outline for the book he called "The Last Man in Europe." Newspeak, the party slogans, Ingsoc, world geography, the Two Minutes Hate, the lonely hero and his diary—all were conceived by the start of 1944 and listed in the pages of his notebook. Big Brother was foreshadowed in the phrase "Leader-worship," doublethink in "Dual standard of thought" (*GO*, 407–9). The atmosphere of nightmare, the systematic lying, the altering of history, the torture, the insanity—these basic ingredients of *Nineteen Eighty-Four* were on his mind before he wrote a page of manuscript. But they were not just items in a memo. From the outset, he viewed them as components of a structure, which he held to with remarkable fidelity.[10]

The book he envisioned was to have two major parts: a "build up" in six "long chapters," a climax and denouement in three. Later, he divided his manuscript in three parts: a section that establishes the terms of Winston Smith's life, a section that develops his relationship with Julia, and a section after their arrest at Mr. Charrington's, in which O'Brien carries out the torture. But in some ways the book remains a two-part structure—first the build-up that culminates in Winston's arrest, then everything that happens to him after he is captured—with a hinge in the middle and an epilogue. The hinge is Goldstein's book, or rather, Winston's reading of it; the Newspeak Appendix is its complement.

Orwell's plan is at once complex and elegantly simple. In Part One, Winston is essentially alone, though we are made aware of Julia and O'Brien ("The writer's approaches to X & Y," Orwell had noted in his outline.) In Part Two, Winston's primary relation is with Julia, though O'Brien comes to the foreground in two chapters. In Part Three, Winston's primary relation is with O'Brien, though Julia comes to the foreground in two chapters. Not coincidentally, "*the book*" within the book is also divided into three parts, though Winston never gets to read its middle chapter. Even "The Principles of Newspeak" has three sections—on the A, B, and C vocabularies. But again, there are underlying patterns of two: Newspeak is explicitly contrasted with Oldspeak; its grammar has "two outstanding peculiarities"; words like "duckspeak" have two opposing meanings.

Could Orwell have played games or created balanced forms to gratify a sense of aesthetics? The very notion insults the spirit of his work. Yet intricate patterns, based on twos, threes, and even fours, proliferate in the text and in his notebooks:[11] three Party slogans comprised of linked opposites ("War is Peace, Freedom is Slavery, Ignorance is Strength"); three super-states, which form shifting alliances; three stages in Winston's "reintegration"; 101, an integer consisting of three numerals but hinting at a binary sequence. Symmetry can also be observed on the sentence level. Consider the openings of the first and last chapters:

It was a bright cold day in April, and the clocks were striking thirteen.

The Chestnut tree was almost empty. A ray of sunlight slanting through a window fell yellow on dusty tabletops. It was the lonely hour of fifteen.[12]

As Winston Smith enters his building (and the novel) he is isolated—in this draft, at any rate. An earlier version has him talking to "the aged prole who acted as porter and caretaker" (*Ms*, 3). But Orwell cut the caretaker, leaving Smith by himself except for the poster of Big Brother. Again, as the novel closes, Winston is alone, except for the internalized Big Brother. In between he travels a boomerang's course, from the solitude which leads to self-awareness to that which marks the loss of his identity.

But if the narrative follows a trajectory, how can it also be hinged? To answer, we might start by examining the changes between the outline and the finished novel. Most of those changes affect the story's politics, rather than its structure. Orwell dropped allusions to "the Trusts" and "Bakerism" and subdued the allusions to Jews and Roman Catholics;[13] in this dystopia, Ingsoc would supplant all other systems, as the worship of Big Brother would supplant all other faiths. He seems to have enlarged the role of X (O'Brien), but again, the change would not require a major shift in structure, since he had only to establish connections between two consecutive items in his outline: "Conversation with X" (I.vi) and "The torture and confession" (II.i).

Virtually, all the later structural changes—especially the revision from two parts to three—can be traced back to a single item in the first version of the layout: "The brief interlude of the love affair with Y" (I.i). This "interlude," subservient to the politics in outline, expanded to fill the middle section of the novel and run over into "torture and confession." Perhaps Orwell always meant to give Y (Julia) a larger role. Certainly, by filling in the details of their meetings, the contrasts in their outlooks, and the dangers that confront them, he added a romantic dimension to the plot—and a motive for Winston's rebellion. But more than that, he provided the book with a profounder, more engaging dialectic.

The outline and earliest versions of the manuscript suggest the basic terms of the conflict. On one side there is the Party, a nightmare system whose horrors include the worship of power, constant surveillance, denial of the past and of objective reality. On the other side there is Winston, fighting for sanity, for memory and truth, for self and sexual expression. But these are not the only forces in conflict. Another set of terms emerges in Part Two as Winston discovers the supreme importance of uncomplicated human love and loyalty.[14] This female side of *Nineteen Eighty-Four*—female in that its agents are Julia, Winston's mother, his sister, and the prole washerwoman— contrasts with the male side embodied in the Party and its agents, O'Brien and Charrington. In Part Three, the dialectic is predominantly male again; O'Brien's arguments counteract Winston's and tragically overcome them. But without the addition of love—in all its aspects—the ending would be less complete and chilling. Winston as "the last man" isn't nearly so alone before he forms the ties with Julia and recovers buried memories—his history, the truth about his own life. Enlightened, he can reach beyond himself, beyond Julia, to the woman in the yard and proles everywhere. Then he is literally arrested by the Thought Police and borne back to unalterable solitude. In a grim perversion of Hegelian synthesis, love becomes the proof of his subjection to Big Brother, loyalty becomes a constant shifting of belief, and sanity becomes untenable.

In America, the Book of the Month Club felt uneasy about the chapter I have called the hinge and sounded Orwell out on cuts and alterations. Orwell was adamant: "A book is built up as a balanced structure and one cannot simply remove large chunks here and there unless one is ready to recast the whole thing" (*CEJL*, 4:483). He had already done his recasting. He had drafted Goldstein's book (perhaps in 1946) and then thoroughly revised and rearranged it (*Ms*, xiv). He had made substantial alterations in the chapters that precede Winston's reading of the volume, frequently removing the transitional passages that smooth the narrative flow. For instance, in rough draft Winston puts on his overalls, tells Julia that he is going to O'Brien, and accepts her decision to accompany him. When they rejoin each other inside O'Brien's building, she takes charge of getting them admitted. After the encounter Julia leaves before Winston, but she violates O'Brien's orders and waits for Winston outside, where she embraces him and plans their next meeting (*Ms*, 130–75). All of this (except her exit) disappears from the final draft. The story cuts from Winston's thoughts, in the room above the junk-shop, to their entry in the room where O'Brien sits dictating; at the end of the encounter it cuts again, from Winston's thoughts about O'Brien's "interrupted" Party business to his weary walk to Charrington's, eleven days later, with the unopened book in his briefcase.

The removal of these episodes compresses the action; perhaps less positively, it reduces Julia's role and shifts the focus from her feminine affection to the specious understanding between men. But that, I think, was not Orwell's objective in revising, at least, not on any conscious level. Plot elaboration at these junctions is distracting—if you are writing a novel of ideas. He had already made the love affair sufficiently explicit; he had shown that, in this system, sex itself becomes political. By omitting transitions he could subtly emphasize the arbitrary, disconnected nature of his nightmare-state, where sudden shifts in policy and sudden disappearances are the very stuff of daily life.

On the other hand, he could not omit the explanation that would make these lives and policies plausible. He had to interpolate "*the book*." To maximize its impact on the narrative, he placed it between the aftermath of Hate Week and Winston's beatific vision at the window. In that position, even as it halts the story's progress, it works as an ideological pivot or hinge between the rising action and the denouement. Turning (or returning) to origins and causes, Goldstein's book suggests why Winston's story takes a tragic course and why his efforts are about to boomerang. Winston thinks he understands it but miscalculates its message—as he misconstrues O'Brien and Charrington. Because he fails to grasp the pervasive power of doublethink, the basis of the system's "controlled insanity," he also fails to realize that "*the book*" portends defeat and closure, rather than eventual liberation. ("Among ourselves we call it the Book of the Dead," O'Brien announces in the draft [*Ms*, 167]).

O'Brien, complex as a character and theorist, exemplifies the fusion of art and politics that Orwell wanted to achieve. He is doublethink made palpable. Dual in all aspects of language and behavior, he maintains schizoid standards with a singleness of purpose that demonstrates the madness of the system. His duality, evident in Winston's first impressions, becomes more pronounced with every subsequent encounter—and, at the same time, more insidious. O'Brien's form is "bulky" yet oddly graceful; his manner is "urbane" yet sympathetic. Powerfully constructed, manifestly intellectual, he reminds Winston of a prizefighter and nobleman, roles to which he adds those of ally and tormentor, rationalist and zealot, lethal guardian. His gestures—the way he manipulates his spectacles, the handshake so hearty that it crushes Winston's bones are singular as well as symbolic. Even his name suggests doubleness. "O'Brien" is both common and Irish, belying his high position in the Party and setting him apart from Smith, Syme, Charrington, and Parsons, whose names are all distinctly English. I am tempted to believe that Orwell knew those six letters could also be divided differently: "*ob*," the Latin preposition "from" or "out of," is followed by "*rien*," the French word for "nothing" whose root is the Latin "*rem*" or "thing."[15] In any case, the name is implicitly Catholic, and therefore consistent with the priestly role of this sinister apostle and betrayer.

O'Brien's words, above all else, convey his duality. Orwell carefully worked and reworked them, revising to emphasize the ironies implicit in O'Brien's ideology and actions. For instance, Orwell first had Winston dreaming that O'Brien says, "Sooner or later you will come to me" (*Ms*, 67). But he changed that phrase in draft to the luminous and vatic, "We shall meet in the place where there is no darkness" (*Ms*, 69). Later, the draft has O'Brien proposing a toast "to the day when two & two make four" (*Ms*, 167), words that Winston could hardly misinterpret or ignore as an allusion to his diary (*NEF*, 69). Perhaps for those reasons Orwell cut it from the novel, leaving the dialogue suitably ambiguous, so that when Winston proposes drinking "to the past," O'Brien agrees "gravely": "The past is more important" (*NEF*, 146). The impact of this statement only becomes clear when you see what Winston's future entails. Still later in the draft, Winston thinks he hears O'Brien say,

> For seven years I have watched over you, Winston. Seven years ago I saw the seed of evil in your face. I watered it & nursed it till it was a thriving plant. And now that it has reached full growth I tear it out by the roots, & you will be made perfect, even as I am perfect. (*Ms*, 257–59)

But Orwell removed the allusion to Blake,[16] as he removed superfluous details elsewhere; he also made the theology less blatant, so that while the lines retain their biblical aura, their irony is chillingly political:

> Don't worry, Winston; you are in my keeping. For seven years I have watched over you. Now the turning point has come. I shall save you, I shall make you perfect. (*NEF*, 201).

Rereading O'Brien's speeches, you discover the extent of their duplicity. Although he rarely lies to Winston and Julia, his words are designed to deceive them: "Do you understand that even if [Winston] survives, it may be as a different person?" (*NEF*, 143). You also get a sense of the convolutions entailed in reality control. Did he collaborate in writing Goldstein's book, as he claims, or is the claim another Party fabrication?

Against such pervasion and unshakable doublethink, Winston's integrity is futile. "What a man," Winston says to himself in the draft, as he leaves O'Brien's building in darkness (*Ms*, 175). In fact, as O'Brien and the early title indicate, Winston is the last remaining man in this dystopia, the only advocate of humanistic values in a system bent upon destroying them.[17] Despite Party pressures, he insists on his identity, insists on seeking answers to his questions; despite his anxieties, he moves toward integration, combining the "male" qualities he so admires—courage, independence, strength of conviction—with the "female" ones he often dreads as weakness. In contrast, O'Brien is both more and less than human. Textual allusions link him with a pantheon of powerful male figures: God, the devil, the Grand Inquisitor, a sadistic schoolmaster, a punishing father, the brother who turns on his sibling.[18] In any guise he is a character immune to doubt, exempt from fear. Not even morality dismays him.

O'Brien unmans Winston—in the text's words, gets inside him—by making him cast off his love and faith. Winston's ultimate torturers are literally man-eaters, "enormous rats" whose teeth and muzzles loom before the victim sitting strapped and masked and impotent before them. Orwell later conceded to Julian Symons that "the 'Room 101' business" was vulgar (*CEJL*, 4:502–3). But its "schoolboy" melodrama produces effects that are consistent with his aims throughout this section. The victims of Room 101 surrender the last vestige of control over reason and autonomy. As terror repressed by the conscious mind takes over, their nightmares become their realities. To bring that terror home, Orwell shifts away from plainstyle. Prose and sanity degenerate together.

Winston's loss (of self and Julia) can be seen as a regression that culminates in premature senility. When he first rebels against the system, he is driven by anger and defiance, characteristics traditionally connected to an adolescent phase of development. By the end of Part Two he has matured, but his maturity is hard-won and precarious. It is also contingent on recall of his younger self; through memory and dream, he has relived and come to terms with his betrayal of his mother and sister. When O'Brien exerts his power over Winston, he reverses the process of development. As he puts his victim through what he terms the learning phase—in other words, as Winston is relentlessly tortured—Winston becomes more and more like a child, still defiant, yet requiring approval. As he enters the phase O'Brien terms understanding—that is, as mind and body are totally degraded—he becomes as dependent as a baby. He is given a respite to recover flesh and strength; then, abruptly, to insure his acceptance, he is plunged into O'Brien's inversion of the primal scene, reduced to the helpless terror of an infant confronting "the worst thing in the world."[19]

The process of regression is depicted in language that itself lapses from maturity. Through Part Three, the dialogue resounds with stage effects; the physical descriptions are hideous:

> He seized one of Winston's remaining front teeth between his powerful thumb and forefinger. A twinge of pain shot through Winston's jaw. O'Brien had wrenched the loose tooth out by the roots. He tossed it across the cell.
>
> "You are rotting away," he said; "you are falling to pieces. What are you? A bag of filth." (*NEF*, 224)

Perhaps these sections got beyond Orwell's control, despite considerable efforts at revision. Or perhaps he believed that only extreme language could convey these extremes of experience. I think he meant to imitate aspects of pulp fiction, the kind he analyzes in "Boys' Weeklies," out of a conviction that such "blood-and-thunder stuff" retains a hold on those who think they have outgrown it (*CEJL*, 1:482, 484). But here, crude effects serve sophisticated ends; they give the reader a "bellyfeel" of totalitarian brutality.

There is also a political dimension to Orwell's choice of rats as Winston's torturers. The system that sustains them engenders human beings who resemble beetles, rodents, and vermin. The Party itself is a devouring monster, a Cronos determined to annihilate chronology by forcing the present into stagnant circles and continually altering the past. Winston feels he has been rescued from the horror when he hears the cage door closing. But as the narrator says, it "had clicked shut and not open" (*NEF*, 236), phrasing that drives Winston's destiny home "like the final tap to a nail."[20]

Orwell was as thoroughly committed to "good writing" as he was to history and politics. His narrative contravenes the principles of Newspeak, extending the reader's range of thought and experience through language that is neither as barren as his vision nor radically inconsistent with it. He renders the gritty greyness of a world that relentlessly assaults the pleasures of the senses in phrases which thrust impressions at the reader, impressions of smells and tastes and colors. Similes coexist with clinical analysis: promiscuity is both a symptom of revolt and "like the sneeze of a horse that smells bad hay" (*NEF*, 102). Strategic repetition of ominous phrases and graphic descriptions of the implements of tyranny conduce to "fantasmagoric effect[s]," an expression that recurs twice in his outline. He breaks up the narrative with nursery rhyme and doggerel, verse that is at once nostalgic and prophetic, a link to the past and the future. He modulates to lyric prose for scenes in the country and Winston's last reverie at the window. And of course he employs the satirist's arsenal: irony, invective, innuendo.[21]

Yet in reading the novel you are far more aware of consistency than of variation. It is unified, not just by his political vision, but also by the method and angle of narration, which he seems to have determined quite early. The "layout" of 1943 (or 1944) begins as an objective list of items; its perspective is implicitly omniscient:

PART I Build up of
  a. The system of organized lying...
  b. The ways in which this is done...
  c. The nightmare feeling caused by the disappearance of objective truth....

But even before this version concludes, the protagonist's consciousness is coming into prominence, and in the second version, which follows it directly, the standpoint shifts to the diarist:

[II ...]
  i. The torture & confession
  ii. Continuation of diary, mentally.
  iii. Recognition of own insanity. (*GO*, 408)

Orwell had mixed feelings about first-person novels. (Of his own six, only *Coming Up for Air* is narrated by its protagonist.) He knew the form was useful for getting at the inner mind, for treating emotion and sex honestly. But he felt it tied the author too closely to the teller and narrowed what the teller could plausibly perceive and feel.[22] Nonetheless, he needed a spokesman for his views, an individual who, in looking outward and inward, would illuminate the evils of a system. So although he kept the story in the third person, he wrote it from Winston's perspective.

Winston is the filter for nearly everything that happens in *Nineteen Eighty-Four*. His activities compose the action of the novel. He overhears or joins in the dialogue. The details are those that impress themselves upon him: the woman in the film, with the child held against her; the crimson of Julia's sash, tight about her waist; O'Brien waving four extended fingers while his other hand prepares to press the lever. Of course, he is not wholly distinct from his creator. He shares Orwell's propensities in small and large matters: his love of dace and bluebells, his hatred of Party lies, his need to set ideas down on paper. He has the same eye for telling bits of color: the rat's pink hands, the diary's creamy pages. He has the same memory for commonplace lyrics. Most important for the texture of the prose, he is given Orwell's compulsion to describe, or perhaps I should say he is the agent of impressions which the narrative ascribes to his consciousness.

Orwell also uses Winston to achieve flexibility within the larger context of confinement. Winston moves, not only through the streets and rooms of Airstrip One, but also through a kind of inner space. There is no question as to which provides more latitude: his dreams sustain connections that the Party would obliterate; his memories reanimate the past. Though he gains information piecemeal, his identity is constant—until it is destroyed in the last chapter. The narrative voice is correspondingly consistent, so long as it's identified with Winston. Orwell varies the style by including prole dialect, the songs, the journal entries, bits of Newspeak, Julia's idiom, and O'Brien's later tirades. Only in the pages given over to "*the book*" is there a shift to an omniscient perspective. To mark that change (and possibly, to imitate Trotsky's prose[23]), the words become more Latinate and the syntax becomes more convoluted. Yet even here, the limited perspective casts its shadow. Winston's choice of chapters determines what the reader sees; "*the book*" breaks off abruptly when he stops.

In important ways, however, the narrative dissociates Winston's perspective from the reader's. Orwell plays with time and continuity, moving freely in and out of Winston's consciousness, shifting between action and reflection. He also creates distance through parody and satire, enabling the reader to draw conclusions that are far beyond the reach of any character.

Both dissociation and the angle of narration contribute to the atmosphere of nightmare, an atmosphere sustained by his control of tone and image—in broader terms, the texture of the writing. Here, for example, the Party's men have just broken into the room above the shop:

> There was another crash. Someone had picked up the glass paperweight from the table and smashed it to pieces on the hearthstone.
>
> The fragment of coral, a tiny crinkle of pink like a sugar rosebud from a cake, rolled across the mat. How small, thought Winston, how small it always was! There was a gasp and a thump behind him, and he received a violent kick on the ankle which nearly flung him off his balance. (*NEF*, 183–84)

This is reportage, and yet each bit of observation draws you in and makes you feel for the observer. The words are terse and plain—a man like Winston would use them—but their plainness does not preclude complexity. Delicate images are balanced against harsh ones; the simile compounds the violation. Details stir the senses, while onomatopoeia intensifies the message of destruction: "crash," "smashed," "gasp," "thump," "flung." Psychologically as well, the text is complex. The paperweight had symbolized beauty and the past. Now, like Winston's world, it lies shattered. It is also metonymic, a sexual surrogate. The tiny pink crinkle is devalued and ruined as Julia writhes helpless on the floor. The ankle reference adds to the imagery of impotence; Winston has a varicose ulcer. Then there is the site of destruction, the hearthstone, an allusion that recalls both the couple's domesticity and Winston's lost mother, dispenser of chocolate. Counterpointing the elements of loss and invasion is a subtle undercurrent of detachment. Winston's reaction—"How small ... how small it always was!"—momentarily puts the terror at a distance, while two uses of the impersonal "There" and the inexplicit "Someone" generalize the agents of destruction.

That in fact such lucid prose was the product of great effort is clear from Orwell's letters and, more specifically, from remnants of earlier versions. Though less than half the text survives in manuscript facsimile, those pages suggest how the draft he called "a ghastly mess" developed into publishable writing (*CEJL*, 4:404). Predictably, he worked to cut away the fat, eliminating details not germane to the story and adjectives that cluttered his sentences. You can see these trends in the opening line:

>   the clocks
>   bright   ~~innumerable clocks~~
> //It was a / cold ~~blowy~~ day in ~~early~~ April, and ~~a million radios~~ ...

But economy—or even that broader goal, "good writing"—did not motivate all of the changes. Orwell seems to have corrected with several aims: to bring out ideas, tighten up the story, add items that would reinforce pattern and motif, and produce lean, vivid sentences. Sometimes, propaganda and art were at cross purposes; more often, the tension was productive.

Consider the draft of the section in which O'Brien first enters Winston's cell:

>   The shock of the sight had driven all discretion
> Winston sprang to his feet. ~~All discretion had gone~~ out of him.
> For the first time in years he forgot the presence of the telescreen.

"They've got you too!" he cried.
                long
"They got me ~~years~~ ago," said O'Brien. "My name is Watson.
                    by
Nosy Watson is the nickname ~~under~~ which you have been
taught to call
~~known~~ me, I believe."
    He stepped aside. The stumpy guard with the gorilla-like face
appeared from behind him.... (*Ms*, 241)

From this passage, you can understand why Orwell rarely bothered to save
his notes and drafts. He must have had some purpose for O'Brien's clumsy
alias. "The most hateful of all names in an English ear is Nosey Parker,"
he had written in "The Lion and the Unicorn" (*CEJL*, 2:59). He had also
noted that Holmes and Dr. Watson exemplify aspects of an "ancient
dualism," the split between soul and body (*CEJL*, 2:163). But whatever his
intentions, the nickname is a howler, and (like Julia's last name, Vernon) it
got cut:

> Winston started to his feet. The shock of the sight had driven
> all caution out of him. For the first time in many years he forgot
> the presence of the telescreen.
>   "They've got you too!" he cried.
>   "They got me a long time ago," said O'Brien with a mild,
> almost regretful irony. He stepped aside. From behind him there
> emerged a broad-chested guard with a long black truncheon in
> his hand.
>   "You knew this, Winston," said O'Brien. "Don't deceive
> yourself. You did know it—you have always known it." (*NEF*,
> 197)

The changes here suggest that Orwell wrote by the rules he set in
"Politics and the English Language." He hones his prose to give more point
to the encounter; the new lines add meaning, not filler. They also improve
the rhythm of the passage and the balance between dialogue and narrative.
Plain, short words of native origin predominate. Images gain particularity.
Now the barbarisms are intrinsic in the plot and not a byproduct of style or
execution. But the contrast isn't only in the polish. The second version
amplifies the power of the Party and the terror that lies in wait for Winston.
While the first guard is simply an atavistic brute, his successor wields an
instrument, a black one. O'Brien too becomes more sinister. His "mild,

almost regretful irony" signals the change in his relations with his victim yet preserves his consistent duality. He admits—indirectly—to deceit and entrapment, yet his very confession is accusing: Winston knew. And Winston assents to the charge of self-deception: "Yes, he saw now, he had always known it."

How are we to take this statement? It fits into a pattern; all through the novel there are references to doom and fatality. "The end was contained in the beginning," Winston says in resolving to visit O'Brien. "We are the dead," each major character repeats, before the "iron voice" confirms the allegation. Winston and Julia cannot make love without remembering that someday they will be destroyed. But Julia, the hedonist, makes light of retribution until she is tortured and converted. Winston is more complex. He rebels against the system yet virtually invites it to destroy him. Why, when he hopes "to keep the inner heart inviolate," does he boast to O'Brien, "I have not betrayed Julia"? Why, as he undergoes O'Brien's vicious baiting, does he think, "Perhaps one did not want to be loved so much as to be understood"? Is this part of Orwell's satire? Or part of something else that the narrative could not contain or fuse?

There may be several answers, several ways of construing the recurrent allusions to fatality. Viewed as part of the design, they are fully consistent with the circular structure of the narrative. For in a way, Winston's first rebellion is his last, the determinant of everything that follows. From the time he purchases the diary and pen—for seven years, if you reckon from his first dream of O'Brien—he moves inexorably toward the Chestnut Tree Cafe and the "victory over himself." Images of dust and water reinforce the theme of inescapable defeat and dissolution. Dust invades all surfaces: the cracks of people's faces, the floor of the belfry where Julia draws her map, the tabletop where waiters set his liquor. Water both sustains and engulfs him. He feels like a wanderer at the bottom of the sea, "lost in a monstrous world where he himself was the monster" (*NEF*, 25); he dreams of his mother, "drowning deeper every minute," yet continuing to gaze at him through "darkening water" (*NEF*, 135). Finally, he sinks his consciousness in alcohol. Victory Gin becomes "the element he swam in"; its scent pervades his penitential tears (*NEF*, 241).

Orwell also provides him with a background that makes an obsession with death plausible. The absence of his father, his mother's disappearance, the whole thrust of the system toward acceptance and conformity, suggest that when he does rebel each impulse toward fulfillment will exact its toll in self-recrimination. Long before O'Brien gets him, Winston tortures Winston: "It was as though [he and Julia] were intentionally stepping nearer to their graves" (*NEF*, 116). He hopes only to postpone the day of capture, and after that, to die with hate intact. Instead, he abandons even his hatred in his "blissful" surrender to Big Brother.

A few critics have complained that there is something spurious in Winston's reactions under pressure.[24] While no one says the story should have ended optimistically, Winston's masochism strikes some readers as exaggerated, willed by Orwell for propaganda purposes instead of evolving from the action. It also tends to erode the opposition between enforced compliance and autonomy. Orwell postulates a system that is closed and a "lost man" who searches for an opening. If the character himself is predestined or preprogrammed, what becomes of this crucial antithesis?

I would answer that Orwell chose to undercut it, to increase the sense of nightmarish reality. "*I understand HOW*" Winston writes in his diary. "*I do not understand WHY*." O'Brien tells him why the Party is so obsessed with power, why it thinks it has control over reality and history, and why it is so sure that it's invincible. Winston knows these "reasons" are profoundly irrational, but knowing just exacerbates the torture. He himself is confident of few things. One is that the forces of destruction lie in wait for him. Another is that sanity, which never was "statistical," can only be maintained by stubborn vigilance. If he were convinced that he was always sane and rational, the novel's oppositions would be simpler. But the forces of unreason inhere within him, too. They contravene his efforts to maintain his independence; they complement the madness of the system. And certainly, that is part of Orwell's message. Decency is always being menaced, he lets us know, threatened from without and from within. Even Winston kicks a hand into the gutter.

Above all, Winston's fatalism sets in relief the issue Orwell cared most about: survival. It was a subject he knew something about—after Paris and pneumonia, Spain and a bullet wound, increasingly severe tuberculosis. I do not mean to read the author's fate into the character's; Orwell's letters on his illness, and reports from those who knew him, make it plain that he expected to recover.[25] But he was pessimistic about the fate of Europe and desperate to make his contemporaries realize what totalitarianism might portend. Gravely ill and driven, he was writing with two purposes: to warn the world and leave *his book* in testament.

Nineteen Eighty-Four concludes by satirizing the conventions of the comic ending: love, reunion, happiness. Winston is no longer "a flaw in the pattern." Big Brother has won out, and Winston loves him. There is a terrible rightness about the conversion scene, a rightness about the whole last chapter. Though Winston's life is shattered and his mind reduced to fragments, the narrative is strikingly coherent. Scarcely a facet of life in Oceania, scarcely a motif or significant image, is not reinvoked and set in place. The sequence of the book's three parts is also recapitulated in this section. First there are the details of Winston's life, its ambiance. Then his thoughts move back to Julia and his mother, though he dismisses both as faulty memories. Finally, he is left with the "enormous face" above him and the prospect of a bullet in his brain.

Thus in formal terms the novel ends in closure, its loose threads tied, its hero's future settled. In other terms, however, it stays open. Its political vision is still trenchant. The horror story grips new generations. That which is slated for oblivion within its boundaries haunts the reader's memory beyond them. This, I think, is proof that Orwell did not botch the task he found so urgent. As he himself said (in an analysis of Dickens), "There are no rules in novel writing, and for any work of art there is only one test worth bothering about—survival."[26]

NOTES

1. *CEJL*, 4:475; see also *CEJL*, 4:448.

2. The classifications into parody, satire, fantasy, and so forth have appeared in so many articles and chapters that attributing them to single sources seems pointless—though attention should be paid to Bernard Crick's long argument on the book's "Seven Satiric Thrusts" (George Orwell, *Nineteen Eighty-Four*, ed. Bernard Crick [Oxford: Clarendon, 1984], 55–92); to Denis Donahue's assertion that the book is a political fable ("*Nineteen Eighty-Four* Politics and Fable," in *George Orwell and Nineteen Eighty-Four*, [Washington, D.C.: Library of Congress, 1985], 59–60); and to Irving Howe's claim, following Northrop Frye, that the book is a Menippean satire ("The Fiction of Anti-Utopia," in *Orwell's Nineteen Eighty Four. Text, Sources, Criticism*, ed. Irving Howe [New York: Harcourt, Brace, 1963], 197). More recently, Howe has modified that definition, suggesting that the book is "a mixture of genres, mostly Menippean satire and conventional novel, but also bits of tract and a few touches of transposed romance" ("1984: Enigmas of Power," in *1984 Revisited*, ed. Irving Howe (New York: Harper, 1983], 7–8). The mixed genre position has also been taken by Lynette Hunter in her reader-oriented study of the narrative (*George Orwell: The Search for a Voice* [Milton Keynes: Open University Press, 1984], 192 and, more broadly, chap. 7).

3. For a summary of arguments as to whether or not the book is a novel, see Robert A. Lee, *Orwell's Fiction* (Notre Dame: University of Notre Dame Press, 1969), 129–30. For an early listing of the novel's flaws, see Bruce Bain, "After the Bomb," *Tribune*, 17 June 1949, 17–18. By 1956, Howe finds it necessary to refute the "complaint one often hears ... that there are no credible or 'three-dimensional' characters in the book" ("Orwell: History as Nightmare," in *Politics and the Novel*, 2d ed. [New York: Avon, 1970]), 241. Julian Symons is among the critics who label the third part melodramatic ("Power and Corruption," *Times Literary Supplement*, 10 June 1949, 380). V. S. Pritchett also criticizes the torture scenes and the Ministry of Love ("Books in General," *New Statesman and Nation*, 18 June 1949, 646, 648). To some extent, these assumptions remain current; see, for example, Michael Orange, "*Nineteen Eighty-Four* and the Spirit of Schweik," in *George Orwell*, ed. Courtney T. Wemyss and Alexej Ugrinsky (New York: Greenwood Press, 1987), 51–54 (although Orange seems to respect "the intertextual density of [*NEF*'s]

texture," 56). Isaac Deutscher (whose comments have often been disputed) accuses Orwell of a narrow imagination, derivative plotting, and "crude" symbolism ("*1984*—The Mysticism of Cruelty," reprinted in *Twentieth-Century Interpretations of 1984*, ed. Samuel Hynes [Englewood Cliffs, N.J.: Prentice-Hall, 1971], 30). There has been astute and favorable work on the literary aspects, as my notes will suggest. Still, opinion persists that *Nineteen Eighty-Four* is not well written. Consider Alfred Kazin's comment: "Orwell was an efficient novelist not particularly interested in fiction; he used it for making a point" ("'Not One of Us,'" in *George Orwell and Nineteen Eighty-Four*, 71). Bernard Crick has consistently maintained that the novel does not represent Orwell's best writing. But unlike the critics who think he dashed it off, Crick thinks Orwell tried too hard for effect and created conflicting layers of satire (*Nineteen Eight-Four*, 132–33).

4. Since Howe first made this judgment in 1956 ("Orwell: History as Nightmare," 230), he has moved steadily toward an appreciation of Orwell's craftsmanship: "Reading through these four large volumes [of *CEJL*] has convinced me that Orwell was an even better writer than I had supposed .... He was, I now believe, the best English essayist since Hazlitt, perhaps since Dr. Johnson" (*Harper's Magazine*, quoted on the back covers of the HBJ/Harvest edition). See also his analysis of "formal means" in "The Fiction of Anti-Utopia," 180. But he seems still to prefer the essayist to the novelist. Hugh Kenner makes more accurate comments on the strategic effects of Orwell's fictive language; see the conclusion to "The Politics of the Plain Style" in *Reflections on America, 1984: An Orwell Symposium*, ed. Robert Mulvihill (Athens, Ga.: University of Georgia Press, 1986), 64–65.

5. The outline, now in the Orwell Archive, has been printed as Appendix A in Crick's *George Orwell* (407–9) and his edition of *Nineteen Eighty–Four* (137–38). The notes toward revision (1948), from a notebook also in the Orwell Archive, have been printed as Appendix C in his *Nineteen Eighty-Four* (141–43). Davison's introduction to the facsimile establishes the evidence for the six stages. And several of Orwell's own letters suggest the amount of effort he put into the book—for instance, "a novel has to be lived with for years before it can be written down, otherwise the working-out of detail, which takes an immense amount of time and can only be done at odd moments, can't happen" (*CEJL*, 4:497).

6. Hunter (*Search for a Voice*, 212–14) is the only other critic I have found who connects the creator's control over his fiction with the party's control within it.

7. As Ian Watt notes, Orwell's "attitude to language is old-fashioned" (as are many of the views on art I cite here). Nonetheless, it was genuine and "central" ("Winston Smith: The Last Humanist," in *On Nineteen Eight-Four*, ed. Peter Stansky [New York: W. H. Freeman, 1983), 111).

8. The obvious source is "Politics and the English Language," especially the second half (*CEJL*, 135–140). On links between art and propaganda, see also *CEJL*, 2:126, 130, and 240–41. Orwell's comments on aesthetics are scattered through *CEJL*. See especially "Why I Write," "Charles Dickens," "Inside the Whale," "Politics vs. Literature," "The Prevention of Literature," and his reviews of Henry Miller's, Jack London's, and George Gissing's work.

9. Mark Crispin Miller takes a similar position: While the book has lost its topical immediacy, it will keep its grip on readers because it is "a work ... that deliberately evokes the state of perfect nightmare" ("The Fate of 1984" in *1984 Revisited*, ed. Irving Howe, 22; see also 19–46). Though Jeffrey Meyers challenges the "cliché" that *Nineteen Eighty-Four* is a "nightmare vision," in reading it realistically he demonstrates connections between craft and idea (*A Reader's Guide to George Orwell* [London: Thames and Hudson, 1975], chap. 8).

10. Joseph Slater comments incisively on the novel's form in "The Fictional Values of 1984," in *Essays in Literary History Presented to J. Milton French*, ed. Rudolf Kirk and C. F. Main (New Brunswick, N.J.: Rutgers University Press, 1960), 254–57. Langdon Elsbree also discusses its structure in "The Structured Nightmare of 1984," *Twentieth Century Literature* 5 (October 1959): 135–41; but I do not accept his argument that its form is a function of its "subrational" elements—its dreams, reveries, and symbols.

11. For instance, here are some of the entries under "Chap. VI" in "Notes of 1948 Towards a Revision of the First Manuscript..." (Crick's *Nineteen Eighty–Four*, 141–43):

The war, & the Eurasian advance in W. Africa, 3 times (4?)
Gin (3 times at least)
Two or three refs. to the _____ (never named)?
Picture of B.B. (3 or 4 times, & introduce early).

12. Miller (see n. 9) indicates another kind of symmetry. In its revised form, "the sentence (nearly) breaks apart into a neat pair of old-fashioned trimeter phrases" reminiscent of an English ballad; but "thirteen" disrupts the rhythm, as it disrupts our expectations (22–23).

13. Though they are less blunt than they would have been if Orwell had followed his outline, references to Catholics and Jews remain. For analyses of them, see Crick's *Nineteen Eighty–Four*, 39–41; Melvyn New, "Orwell and Antisemitism: Toward 1984," *Modern Fiction Studies* 21 (Spring 1975): 81–105; and, for a larger perspective, John Rodden, "Orwell on Religion: The Catholic and Jewish Questions," *College Literature* 11 (1984): 44–58.

14. My interpretation implicitly takes issue with Daphne Patai's (*The Orwell Mystique* [Amherst: University of Massachusetts Press, 1984], 239ff.). Patai is astute about the games that Orwell plays (220–38), but too one-sided about his "Androcentrism." A more objective assessment of Orwell's attitude toward women is Leslie Tender's "'I'm Not Literary, Dear': George Orwell on Women and the Family," in *The Future of Nineteen Eighty-Four*, ed. Ejner J. Jensen (Ann Arbor: University of Michigan Press, 1984), 47–63. On the connection between mother-love and feeling, it is also useful to compare this version with the more emphatic passage in the early draft, *Ms*, 129–31.

15. In 1931–1932, Orwell sought work as a translator, claiming that he could manage modern and old French—"at least anything since 1400 A.D." (*CEJL*, 1:78).

16. The implications and the phrasing of the cancelled lines recall "A Poison Tree" (*Songs of Experience*). Orwell knew Blake's work from early childhood; he suspected that his own first poem, dictated at age four or five, was plagiarized from Blake's "Tiger, Tiger" (*CEJL*, 1:1).

17. Watt makes a strong case for Winston's humanism (*On Nineteen Eighty-Four*, ed. Stansky, 107–8); he also takes account of its limits and the charges that Orwell failed at characterization (ibid., 110–13). Patrick Reilly also considers its defeat in "*Nineteen Eighty-Four*: The Failure of Humanism," *Critical Quarterly* 24 (Autumn 1982): 19–30. An argument that contradicts Watt's (and mine) is James Connors, "Do It to Julia," in *Nineteen Eighty-Four to 1984*, ed. C. J. Kuppig (New York: Carroll & Graf, 1984), 231–41. Connors assembles textual evidence to show that Orwell makes Winston "a shadow-man" in service to the party, rather than a full "human being"; if space and time permitted, I would argue that he misreads the evidence, ignoring the subtler shadings of the passages that bring out Winston's humanistic values.

18. Allusions to these roles recur throughout Part Three, in chaps. 2, 3, and 5. Additionally, O'Brien functions as a surgeon, a perverse healer of the spirit. He is capable of containing Winston, mirroring his thoughts, and getting inside him, acts whose erotic implications Paul Robinson explores ("For the Love of Big Brother: The Sexual Politics of *Nineteen Eighty-Four*" in *On Nineteen Eighty-Four*, 155–58).

19. Philip Rahv makes more politically oriented comments on "the psychology of capitulation" ("The Unfuture of Utopia," *Orwell's Nineteen Eighty-Four*, ed. Howe, 313). For more intensive studies of the novel's psychoanalytic and mythic aspects, see Marcus Smith, "The Wall of Blackness: A Psychological Approach to *1984*," *Modern Fiction Studies* 14 (1968): 423–33; Richard I. Smyer, *Orwell's Development as a Psychological Novelist* (Columbia: University of Missouri Press, 1979), 142–59—speculation that goes too far; and Alex Zwerdling, "Orwell's Psychopolitics," in *The Future of 1984*, ed. Jensen, 87–110.

20. *CEJL*, 4:221. In this passage from "Politics vs. Literature," Orwell cites the effect of ore of Swift's sentences; more broadly, he argues that the literary quality of *Gulliver* cannot be divorced from its world-view. On possible sources for Orwell's rat episode, see Crick's *Nineteen Eighty-Four*, 442–43. Meyers traces other allusions in his work (*Reader's Guide*, 149–50). Judith Wilt, implicitly refuting the "schoolboy" charges, analyzes Orwell's use of rats and its modernist implications ("Behind the Door of *1984*," in *Modernism Reconsidered*, ed. Robert Kiely and John Hildebidle (Cambridge: Harvard University Press, 19831, 247–62).

21. I have omitted from this hasty summary allusions to techniques that have already been analyzed—for example, Orwell's use of the boot image. Slater (see n. 10) deals briefly yet cogently with style, dialogue, interior monologue, imagery, and Orwell's use of lyrics (a subject that warrants closer study).

22. For samples of Orwell's comments on point of view, see *CEJL*, 1:126–28, 154–55, 495, and *CEJL*, 4:512. The impact of this perspective becomes clearer when you contrast it with the omniscient narration of Huxley's *Brave New World* and the first-person narration of Zamyatin's *We*.

23. Deutscher (in *Twentieth Century Interpretations*, ed. Hynes) was one of the first to make this claim, which Meyers also supports (*Reader's Guide*, 146–47).

24. For instance, Symons and Pritchett. While Patai does not claim that they are spurious, she views Winston's reactions as symptomatic of Orwell's flawed values (*Orwell Mystique*, 232–33, 263).

25. In many letters from this period he talks about his illness, but as frequently he talks about recovery. He qualifies the sole allusion to his death, which appears in a letter to his publisher, Warburg: "If anything should happen to me I've instructed Richard Rees, my literary executor, to destroy the MS without showing it to anybody, but it's unlikely that anything like that would happen. This disease isn't dangerous at my age, and they say the cure is going on quite well, though slowly...." (*CEJL*, 4:404).

26. *CEJL*, 1:455, and cf. *CEJL*, 4:302. John Rodden, to whose comments on this article I am deeply indebted, points out that Orwell never fully acknowledged the effect of extra-literary factors on a book's reputation: "Survival is an institutional and political matter, as much as a literary/aesthetic one."

ERIKA GOTTLIEB

The Demonic World of Oceania:
The Mystical Adulation of the 'Sacred' Leader

Unlike Bernard Crick, Richard Rees finds Orwell's consistent analogy between the Church and the Party essential to the satire in *Nineteen Eighty-Four*, but he does not contemplate the possibility that Orwell may be parodying the "secular religion" of totalitarianism from the point of view of the secular humanist. According to Rees, in creating analogy between political and religious concepts, "Orwell's purpose is satirical. He infuses religious metaphors into a completely secular context to suggest the corruption of the system, the perversion of eternal values by the ephemeral demands of politics. The transference of belief to Big Brother is profane— but inevitable in a world in which no sacred equivalents remain" (148).

Of course, Rees is right in pointing out the perversions of the religious ideal in Oceania, where it is a human being who demands to be worshipped as Divinity and who rules quite openly through Hate and not through Love. Rees assumes, however, that the topsy-turvy world of Oceania, the inverted world of parody, would reveal the satirist's hidden standard, if only we could turn this world back straight, right side up again. But would Orwell want to return to what Rees calls the eternal values of the sacred, the values of Christianity, the values of religion?

There is actually a far more interesting question here that Rees seems to overlook entirely. By juxtaposing religious and political spheres so

From *The Orwell Conundrum: A Cry for Despair or Faith in the Spirit of Man?* © 1992 by Carleton University Press Inc.

consistently, does Orwell use religion to make fun of totalitarianism, or does he use totalitarianism to make fun of religion?[1] My suggestion based on the 'Catechism scene' is that Orwell the secular humanist parodies aspects of a mentality he sees as common to both. At the most universal level of the satire, in "blackwhite" Orwell sets out to parody three characteristics of this mentality: first, an insistent tendency towards polarization, towards splitting the entire world into the opposites of "them" and "us," black and white; second, the projecting of our "shadow" upon "them," the mutual name calling that Orwell shows to be absurd and confusing; and finally, the tendency for all distinctions to collapse in a 'mystical' oneness, a coalescence or coincidence of opposites.

The Two Minutes Hate, the daily ritual of public worship, is clearly predicated on such polarization. It is by attributing satanic powers to Goldstein, the Prime Enemy, that Big Brother, who admittedly had started his career as a mere mortal, could imperceptibly arrogate to himself the power of supernatural goodness, the power of the Sacred. "All that is needed is that a state of war should exist," states *Goldstein's Book* (168), revealing the meaning of the paradox "War is Peace."

But the "imposture" of war (173) the Party engineers in the political arena is also corollary to the psychic battle it engineers between 'sacred' and 'satanic,' so that Big Brother may continually reveal his more than human power by scoring new victories over the inexhaustible supply of invariably satanic opponents. Thus who or what belongs to the satanic at any given moment may change, but the category of the satanic is unchangeable, indispensable to the psychological apparatus of totalitarianism. (It is due to the experience of the communal ecstasy of hate directed at the satanic Goldstein; that the true believer is "uttering a prayer" to Big Brother, the "Saviour!" (19).)

So far Orwell's parody implies a direct parallel between the Party and the Church Militant. But as Chapter 7 on Doublethink indicates, there is a point where the Party goes beyond the Church: to add to the tension of polarizing the entire world in terms of 'sacred' and 'satanic,' the Party arrogates to itself the power to switch the enemy at will, and then to deny that a switch has taken place. The people of Oceania are trained from childhood to be vigilant in detecting and persecuting evil, yet they are also prevented from relying on their own judgement or memory in identifying evil: As a result, they succumb to a state of mind the Party chooses to call the "love" of Big Brother, the same state of mind *Goldstein's Book* defines as "controlled insanity" or Doublethink. To have any sense of good and evil, the people of Oceania have to be ruled by, indeed become one with, the will of Big Brother, and Big Brother chooses to reveal his will through the Law of

Contradiction: "War is Peace, Freedom is Slavery, Ignorance is Strength" (92). The cadence is a convenient reminder of both the obscure, paradoxical language of religious revelation and the oracular pronouncements of dialectical materialism. (Orwell shows obvious irritation, when referring to the paradox "the expropriation of the expropriators" [*RWP* 229], or to thesis, antithesis, and synthesis as those "mysterious entities" [*RWP* 176], or "the *sacred* sisters" [*RWP* 229].) What is just as important to note, for the majority of Oceania the triple slogan, which they accept as the very essence of Big Brother's Being, remains the language of *unresolved* paradox, unresolved contradiction.

In his analysis of "Triplethink," Professor Rohatyn raises the interesting questions of whether it is possible to believe in the Law of Contradiction, to act upon it, to elevate it to the level of an abstract principle (3). My answer would be yes on all three counts. It is possible to make people *believe* in contradiction if the purpose is to emphasize belief as a psychological state perceived to be the opposite, contrary to Reason. This kind of language and this kind of emphasis is familiar from the accounts of mediaeval mystics when they want to draw attention to the fact that their ecstasy, the peak experience of their spiritual journey, is inexpressible through the classical logic of the language of communication. Using the mystical logic of the "coincidentia oppositorum" embodied in the language of oxymoron and paradox—a code in itself—the Inner Party attempts to draw attention to a power beyond the realm of Reason, and to generate faith in this power. In effect, the greater the logical dichotomy, the greater the psychological intensity of faith.

Making the people abnegate Reason by accepting the unresolved triple paradox is just as effective in generating fervour of faith as exposing them to the omnipresent icon with the hypnotic eyes—indeed, the Party uses both strategies interchangeably, or simultaneously.

In the first scene of the book, when we meet Winston, he feels he is being watched by Big Brother's eyes from every direction, showing the sense of what scholars of mysticism call the mysterium, the tremendum, and the fascinans that a human being experiences when faced with the numinous, the more than human (Otto). The tremendum: Winston is in awe and fear; the fascinans: he is drawn to it, like a magnet; the mystery: he is intrigued by the secret behind Big Brother's expression.

Appropriately, in Part 1 Winston raises three questions. In stating that he understands "how" but not "why," he questions the motivating force behind the Party's unceasing scapegoat hunts and witch trials. His second question deals with a nameless horror awaiting him in the future. That he will be captured, tortured, and executed he accepts as inevitable. "Why then," he asks, "did that horror which altered nothing, have to lie embedded in future time?" (92). Part 1 ends with his third question. Both the political puzzle of "why" and the personal puzzle of the "nameless horror" are intertwined with the puzzle proposed by Big Brother's mask, the essential, hidden nature of the Godhead: "The face gazed up on him, heavy, calm, protecting: but what kind of a smile was hidden beneath the dark moustache?" (92).

At the end of Part 1 we leave Winston contemplating his future, musing over the baffling riddle of the triple paradox, which echoes his own three questions: "Like a leaden knell the words came back to him: WAR IS PEACE FREEDOM IS SLAVERY IGNORANCE IS STRENGTH" (92). Winston's questions are triple aspects of the same mystery, and he will find his answer by probing into the triple paradox, the Word through which Big Brother chooses to reveal himself.[2]

In effect, one may approach the structure of the novel in terms of the three paradoxes Winston is compelled to understand one by one and in the right sequence. Exploring these riddles forms a spiritual journey O'Brien describes to Winston as "Learning, Understanding and Acceptance," which I suggest is Orwell's parody of the spiritual journey undertaken by many a mediaeval mystic, consisting of the three stages of Purgation, Illumination, and Union.

The stage of Learning for Winston begins with his reading about the first paradox in *Goldstein's Book*: War is Peace. This, by the way, is the only paradox he will begin to understand by reading about it. The next phase of his learning takes place in the Ministry of Love, where, to begin with, he is made to deny that he remembers the photograph of Aaronson, Rutherford, and Jones—clearly an allusion to what the mystics describe as "purgation through recollection" (Underhill 310). Next, Winston is made to admit that two and two make five; this is a parody of the mystic's "purgation through the senses"—that is, "the cleansing of the self to reach humility and perfect intention" (Price 73). Winston reaches this stage when he no longer wants to deceive O'Brien, but genuinely wants to see the four fingers as if they were five (216).

After his Purgation (O'Brien calls it Learning), Winston is ready to achieve Understanding, a stage bearing resemblance to the mystic's Enlightenment or Illumination. Winston's first moment of "luminous certainty" is his first glimpse at the "absolute truth" that "two and two could have been three as easily as five" (222). This stage culminates in O'Brien's revelation that explains the mystery of "why" the Party engineers its scapegoat rituals: "The Party seeks power entirely for its own sake.... The object of persecution is persecution. The object of torture is torture. The object of power is power" (227). This is the ultimate intellectual revelation in Winston's journey, offering explanation for the "why," the motivation behind the "perpetuum mobile" of terror, the self-perpetuating witch-hunts, denunciations, trials, and executions. This revelation is also a prerequisite for his understanding of the second paradox: Freedom is Slavery. Since God is the Eternal power of the Party, and the individual is powerless because he is mortal, he may "free" himself of the burden of mortality and powerlessness by becoming a "slave" to the Party—that is, by giving up the freedom of the autonomous individual in order to become a mere cell in the collective. This is as far as Winston is allowed to go in what the mystics have called the accumulating of knowledge about God, which comes through reason and study (Price 46).

The last stage, according to accounts of mysticism, involves both knowing and loving God perfectly, until the soul experiences "total self-abandonment" (Underhill 388), a sense of oneness in which, according to the mystic, "My *me* is God: nor do I know my selfhood except in God" (Underhill 396). It is this stage O'Brien calls Acceptance and it is clearly concerned with Winston's ability to love. The climactic scene here takes place in Room 101, where Winston is expected, though never told so directly, to break his emotional bond with Julia: To "love" Big Brother, to become one with him, is tantamount to betraying any human bond. Although Room 101 is the climactic scene in the novel, Winston's conversion is not complete until "the final, indispensable, healing change" (256) takes place in the last scene, when, like the prodigal son, Winston is ready to return from the individual's "self-willed exile from the loving breast" (256) in the spirit of repentance. To "love" Big Brother in the spirit of true Acceptance means to become one with the essential nature of the Godhead revealed as the brutal, treacherous God of Power. It is the God of Power that was hiding in "the smile ... beneath the dark moustache" (92). Returning to the "loving breast," Winston is ready to admit this Divinity into his own breast and loses the "spirit of Man" irretrievably.

By the end of the novel, Winston has explored the meaning of the triple paradox. He has learned that War is Peace—the machinery of unceasing wars is an imposture to allow the world dictators to have absolute power over their own enslaved populations. Yet now, when listening to the war bulletin, Winston undergoes the same sense of orgiastic triumph as the rest of the people around him. He has also learned the meaning of "Freedom is Slavery"; yet now, he joins the masses, his individuality enslaved like everyone else's. Then, when for the last time he is haunted by a scene of his childhood, a memory of his old self, he learns to reject the scene as a "false memory" (255).

War is Peace, Freedom is Slavery, Ignorance is Strength—he has learned it all, but only now does he learn that Acceptance, the final stage after Learning and Understanding, is the ability to ignore, to forget, to *unlearn* all the knowledge he has accumulated throughout his journey. It is only now that he can practise the most mysterious third paradox for which he could have received no explanation: his new "strength" to become part of the cheering masses depends on his self-imposed "ignorance" of his old self, of the world of reality. Like all the others around him, finally he has learned to practise Doublethink. It is only now that, in the words of the mystic, "the individual drop had reached the ocean"[3] (Price 45): the heretic's atonement is complete; he is truly *at one* with Big Brother.

Orwell's allusions to the concepts of mysticism are surprisingly detailed and consistent;[4] indeed, I would like to suggest that these allusions form one of the most significant satirical undercurrents to the naturalistic texture. Winston's journey in the Ministry of Love through Learning, Understanding, and Acceptance is worked out in fine detail to parallel the religious mystic's journey towards Divine Love through Purgation, Illumination, and Union. Orwell also makes several allusions to the pervasive light imagery associated with mystics' accounts of their experience ("a blinding flash of light"; "luminous certainty"; "the place where there is no darkness"; etc.), and to the imagery of Pilgrimage, Spiritual Alchemy, and Spiritual Marriage scholars identify as the most important symbols in describing the mystic's journey (Underhill).

When O'Brien announces that "we shall squeeze you empty, and then we shall fill you with ourselves" (220), there is more than an echo here from "'Solve et coagula'—break down that you may build up," the principle of "the Spiritual Alchemist ... who is to burn away the dross before he can reach the Perfection of alchemical gold from which comes the Magnum Opus: deified or spiritual man" (Underhill 146).

Images of the Pilgrimage and Spiritual Marriage are even more readily recognizable: Winston's feeling for O'Brien right from the beginning is an allusion to the mysterious attraction that Underhill describes as a fundamental doctrine of mysticism, where the symbol of mutual desire is often mingled with the images of pilgrimage. And if we keep in mind that the attraction between the human soul—traditionally represented as female—and the Absolute—traditionally represented as the pursuing male—is mutual, we may see the hide-and-seek between O'Brien and Winston in an entirely new light.

Winston and O'Brien's relationship is a problematic and controversial one, often approached by Freudian critics as paranoid (Sperber), homosexual or sadomasochistic (Fiderer). More recently, critics have approached it as a sign of Winston's preference for the male bond, and hence an expression of Winston's—or Orwell's—latent misogyny (Patai). What both the Freudian and the Feminist critic overlook, however, is that in the novel O'Brien is the representative of Big Brother, the cold, cruel intelligence behind the smiling icon. In terms of Orwell's consistent allusion to mystical symbols, the hide-and-seek between Winston and O'Brien is like the mystical "Game of Love," described, for example, by Francis Thomson in the *Hound of Heaven*, which "shows to us the inexorable onward sweep" of God, this "tremendous Lover ... hunting the separated spirit rushing in terror from the overpowering presence of God, but followed, sought, conquered in the end" (Underhill 135). Such a description is quite appropriate to Winston's journey both in the course and in the concluding scene of his "tour aboli," his torture pilgrimage leading to the "love union" with O'Brien. (In *Keep the Aspidistra Flying* Orwell draws a similar analogy between God pursuing the human soul and the Money God pursuing Gordon Comstock: "Sometimes your salvation hunts you down like the Hound of Heaven," Gordon remarks ironically [719].)

To read Winston and O'Brien's mutual attraction in terms of the mystical symbol of Spiritual Marriage does not fly in the face of the naturalistic level of the novel. As discussed in Chapter 8, Orwell makes it quite clear that by depriving the people of sexual fulfillment the Party provokes hysteria, an emotional energy it will channel first into the fanatical hatred of the enemy and then into the equally fanatical worship of the leader.

But where Orwell makes most effective use of the mystical symbol is in the image of the pervasive eye, a fundamental concept of mysticism being that the human Soul is always in the presence of God. Big Brother's hypnotic gaze, which penetrates all minds of Oceania, is a parody of this concept, and it points to the greatest danger inherent in the totalitarian mentality. At the beginning Winston is horrified by the all-seeing eye and would like to hide from it. Looking at a coin with Big Brother's face on it, he feels that "even from the coin the eyes pursued you" (27). At the end of Part 1, "just as he had done a few days earlier, he slid a coin out of his pocket and looked at it. The face *gazed up at him*, heavy, calm, protecting" (92, my italics). Then, in the Ministry of Love, after he is broken intellectually, he feels "swallowed up" (209), absorbed by the mysterious eye. Finally, in the last scene, "*he gazed up* at the enormous face ... [and] loved Big Brother" (256). By now he emerges with a new consciousness so that he could say with the mediaeval mystic: "The eye by which I see ... is the same as the eye by which God sees me." Not satisfied with mere obedience, the Party makes the individual internalize the censoring eye of the punitive authority; by the end Big

Brother has penetrated Winston's Superego, and the Thought Police has taken internal—that is, total—command over the Self.

Reading Orwell's essays, it becomes clear that he was sceptical of the mystic's search for confrontation with the sacred and associated the self-abandonment of mysticism with the relinquishing of personality, judgement, and responsibility—the prerogatives of the autonomous individual.[5] It is no wonder that what Orwell presents as Winston's "union" with the Godhead is equivalent to a psychotic breakdown, the disintegration of the personality. Winston's journey in the Ministry of Love—both a bureaucratic Ministry and the Ministry of Priesthood where he is taught to love and 'minister to' the ruling Divinity—is a cruel, bitter parody of the mysticism inherent both in the religious and in the totalitarian mentalities—ultimately a savagely bitter comment on man's miscarried search for the sacred.

This does not mean, however, that Orwell would take the materialist's contemptuous or condescending attitude to the human being's search for the spiritual. We feel great sympathy for Winston, who is a seeker, a pilgrim on the journey to Truth, a man with an undeniably spiritual dimension. As a matter of fact, Winston is doing well as long as he is in search of the "good" on his own terms, through his relationship to other human beings. When we meet him in the first chapter, he is on his way up a staircase, and throughout Parts 1 and 2 we should picture him ascending the 'ladder' of love, self-expression, and liberation. Part 3, which takes place almost entirely in the Ministry of Love, is the parody, the reversal of this process. He is broken down step by step, until in Room 101 he has, reached "as deep down as it was possible to go" (244). In the hands of O'Brien he undergoes the spiritual experience of conversion, until he is remade into the image of Big Brother, and made to live up to the Party's superhuman, and therefore inevitably *inhuman*, standard of the "good." In his essays, and indirectly in *Goldstein's Book*, Orwell reproaches his contemporaries, particularly his Adversary, the Leftist intellectual, for making a ludicrous mistake. Trying to get away from the 'non-scientific' ideals of religion, he is unaware of the psychological vacuum left behind, and falls into the trap of fanaticism and mysticism while giving his soul to the political dictator.[6] Orwell would therefore insist that what Richard Rees called the eternal values of the sacred should be redefined as human, anthropo-centred values, depending on the human being's relationship to another human being, and not to a standard that is transcendent, superhuman—whether this standard is Hitler's Law of Nature, Stalin's Law of History (Berger 86–87), or what the Church has defined as the transcendental realm of the sacred.

ORWELL'S "SPIRIT OF MAN" AND
THE "HUMAN FORM DIVINE"

As a parody of the totalitarian mentality, *Nineteen Eighty-Four* is also a warning against a system based on the mystical adoration of the 'sacred' leader and the fanatical hatred of the 'satanic' enemy. But in addition to this warning, has the satirist anything positive to suggest about our attitude to good and evil? Unlike his Existentialist confreres, Orwell feels we are in need of spiritual, moral values that are universally acceptable, that Man "is not likely to salvage civilization unless he can evolve a system of good and evil which is independent of heaven and hell" (v. 3, 127).

The question remains as to how Orwell would define the spiritual without recourse to the religious dimension. I believe there is a sequence of three significant scenes in the novel that allude to the biblical concept of Man being created in the image of his Maker, where Orwell the secular humanist explores the spiritual dimension in relation to the "spirit of Man," a force in us capable of creating an image of God according to what is highest in the human being, the ideal of the highest self. In this context, Orwell's concept of "the inner heart, whose workings were mysterious even to yourself, [and that] remained impregnable" (148) to external forces, is not unlike Blake's "Divine Image" that resides in our heart, in "the human form divine."

In the first of these three scenes Winston ponders the connection between three mysteries to be revealed in the future: his own essential self, the meaning of the Party slogans, and Big Brother's essential nature, so far concealed by the "smile ... beneath the dark moustache" (92).

> The past was dead, the future was unimaginable. What certainty had he that a single human creature now living was on his side? And what way of knowing that the dominion of the Party would not endure *for ever*? Like an answer, the three slogans on the white face of the Ministry of Truth came back to him:

> War is Peace
> Freedom is Slavery
> Ignorance is Strength

> He took a twenty-five cent coin out of his pocket. There too, in tiny clear lettering, the same slogans were inscribed, and on the other face of the coin the head of Big Brother. Even from the coin the eyes pursued you (27).

The second scene exploring this image is the one at the end of Part 1, where Winston repeats the same gesture: "just as he had done a few days earlier, he slid a coin out of his pocket and looked at it. The face gazed up at him, heavy, calm, protecting: but what kind of smile was hidden beneath the dark moustache? Like a leaden knell the words came back at him: War is Peace ... Freedom is Slavery ... Ignorance is Strength" (92). What is implied in these two scenes with the coin is the concept of Man being created in the image of his Maker, an allusion to the parable where Christ explains the difference between worldly and spiritual powers to his disciples: "Shew me a penny. Whose image and subscription hath it? They answered and said, Caesar's. And he said unto them, Render therefore unto Caesar the things which be Caesar's, and unto God the things which be God's" (Luke 20: 21–25). While the coin has the "image and subscription" of Caesar, Man, being created in the image of his Maker, has the "image and subscription" of God. Therefore Man's first allegiance is to God, to his spiritual self, and not to the worldly powers of Caesar.

The image Winston sees on the coin is the image of Big Brother, a Caesar who demands to be worshipped both as a worldly and a spiritual authority. In order to remain true to the "spirit of Man," Winston should be able to pay his dues to Caesar and keep his "incorruptible inner self" (v. 4, 402), his "inner heart" (148) that is the core of his spiritual being, intact. The point in these two scenes is that when Winston ponders his essential being in relation to the image of his Maker, he does, in fact, ponder about Man making God in his own image, his choice of the highest good he is going to model himself upon. The perversion of Oceania derives from humanity's mistaken choice to accept God as Power (a divinity who shows remarkable resemblance to Carl Jung's "God of Terror which [also] dwells in the human soul" [*Civilization* 235]). In the second scene with the coin Winston still resists the image of Caesar gazing at him from the coin: he refuses to admit into his heart the God of Power because his own essential, highest self, his "inner heart," is still intact.

Finally, in the third scene in this sequence, which is also the last scene in the novel, Winston comes to the recognition that he has been made over into the image of Caesar, that he is unable to maintain his inner self. We realize that this was the "nameless horror ... embedded in the future," a loss that follows from the essential nature of Big Brother, revealed as the cruelty and treachery of the God of Power. In the last scene Orwell brings to a conclusion Winston's original questions about his essential self and its reflection in the Divine Image in his breast, as Winston gazed up at the enormous face. Forty years it had taken him to learn what kind of smile was hidden beneath the dark moustache. O cruel, needless misunderstanding. O stubborn, self-willed exile from the loving breast! Two gin-scented tears trickled down the sides of his nose. But it was all right, everything was all right, the struggle was finished. He had won the victory over himself. He loved Big Brother. (256)

To "love" Big Brother means to admit Caesar, who demands to be worshipped as the God of Power, into the "inner heart": Winston's "victory" over his old self is tantamount to the defeat of the "human form divine," of his highest self which made him "the last guardian of the human spirit," of the "spirit of Man."

In his essays Orwell warns repeatedly that the modern world's worship of the God of Power leads to the breakdown of all the moral values essential for the salvaging of our civilization. But how would Orwell define these universal values, without recourse to an absolute good or the sacred? It is probably in his delightful essay on Gandhi that he comes closest to revealing the norm or standard often hinted at, yet left hidden, in works of satire. Here he emphasizes that the "other worldly" and the "humanistic ideal" are incompatible. As a humanist, he is suspicious of Gandhi's "non-attachment" as merely "a desire to escape from the pain of living, and above all from love, which sexual or non-sexual is hard work" (v. 4, 528). Like Camus at the end of *The Plague*,[7] Orwell concludes that it takes greater courage to attempt to be human by participating in the "process of life" than to give it all up by aspiring to sainthood: "Many people genuinely do not wish to be saints, and it is probable that some who achieve or aspire to sainthood never felt the temptation to be human beings" (v. 4, 528). Although Orwell expresses personal appreciation for Gandhi, he is ironic about Gandhi's pursuit of the sacred: "No doubt, alcohol, tobacco and so forth are things a saint must avoid, but sainthood is also something human beings should avoid" (v. 4, 527).

A study of Orwell's essays and fiction should indicate that he was far from being obsessed by the demonic. In *Nineteen Eighty-Four* he parodies the totalitarian mentality precisely for *setting up* the category of the 'satanic' for the opponent in order that it could set up the category of the 'sacred' for the leader. Isaac Deutscher is quite off the mark, then, when blaming Orwell for presenting the world in terms of black and white and frightening the reader with the bogeyman of a demonic enemy ("1984"). Orwell in effect parodies Big Brother for doing so. *Goldstein's Book* reveals that Orwell, the secular humanist, condemns the "secular religion" of the totalitarian mentality because surreptitiously it re-introduced the categories for sacred and satanic. Having set out to "indicate by parodying them, the intellectual implications of totalitarianism (v. 4, 520), Orwell presents us with an unforgettable image of a world that assumes its demonic dimensions through a system where the mystical adulation of the 'sacred' is balanced by the cruel persecution of the 'satanic.' Orwell's image of the demonic world of Oceania contains a secular humanist's acute analysis and forceful condemnation of the totalitarian mentality.

NOTES

1. Christopher Small, in *The Road to Miniluv*, touches upon this problem when he raises the question "what actually is being parodied: Is it a parody of religion in terms of the totalitarian State, or of the State in terms of religion?" (165).

2. According to the seventeenth-century Protestant mystic, Jacob Boehme, "From God flows his will which is revealed through the Word and God is made known to us as the Trinity ..." (qtd. in Price 73).

3. Orwell's attitude to this image of the "oceanic" is similar to Freud's, who acknowledges that the "oceanic feeling ... of something limitless, unbounded" is the "source of religious energy which is seized upon by the various Churches and religious systems." He concludes, however: "I cannot discover this feeling in myself" (v. 21, 64).

4. In spite of his admission that he was no theologian, Orwell was familiar with the images associated with mysticism. For example, in his book review of Karl Adam's *The Spirit of Catholicism*, Orwell juxtaposes Adam's open emphasis on the mystical aspects of religious faith with the more rational emphasis advocated by Father Martindale's *The Roman Faith* (v. 1, 102–105, 109).

That the one-to-one relationship between the human soul and the Infinite occupied Orwell's mind is witnessed by *A Clergyman's Daughter*, where the narrative culminates in the heroine's loss of religious faith. In previous scenes Dorothy discusses mysticism with her father's assistant (292) and ponders over the difference between religious worship and the pantheistic "nature mysticism" her clergyman father frowns upon.

Orwell's perception of the mystical is also illustrated in his book review discussing Edith Sitwell's approach to Pope's poetry. Orwell expresses surprise that "Miss Sitwell comes to Pope for the same enchantment as one finds in people like Francis Thomson or Gerald Manley Hopkins" (v. 1, 45). There is a clear sense of Orwell's own position; he would regard Pope's classicist sensibilities dictated by the Age of Reason as diametrically opposed to the religious-mystical sensibilities of Thomson or Hopkins. That Orwell admired the enchantment offered by the latter is made clear in his BBC broadcast of 1941, when he offered careful exegesis of a poem by Hopkins, based on the poet's religious vision of reality (v. 2, 157–161). As for Francis Thomson, the other poet he associates here with mysticism, Orwell was undoubtedly familiar with *The Hound of Heaven* (which describes man's relationship to the Infinite as a love chase—one of the best examples of mystical poetry for the imagery of Spiritual Marriage). Gordon Comstock, for example, refers to the Hound of Heaven ironically (*KAF* 719).

5. Orwell's essays offer evidence that he considered the relinquishing of the self in mysticism reprehensible. He says, for example, that Henry Miller "performed the essential Jonah act of allowing himself to be swallowed, remaining passive, accepting .... It is a

species of quietism, implying either complete unbelief or else a *degree of belief amounting* to mysticism" (v. 1, 572). He also blames his Adversary for relinquishing his freedom as "an autonomous individual" when identifying with a "nation or other unit in which he has chosen to sink his own individuality" (v. 3, 411).

6. Orwell comments on this several times in his essays: "All the loyalties and superstitions that the intellect had seemingly banished could come rushing back under the thinnest disguises. Patriotism, religion, Empire, military glory—all in one word, Russia.... God—Stalin. The devil—Hitler. Heaven—Moscow. Hell—Berlin" (v. 1, 565). He also points out that the Communist Party was "simply something to believe in. Here was a Church, an army, an orthodoxy, a discipline" (v. 1, 565).

7. In *The Plague* Camus compares Taroux's ambition to become a saint and Rieux's desire for "simply being a man." He concludes that "heroism and sanctity" are indeed "less ambitious" than "simply being a man" (209).

WORKS CITED

1. All references to George Orwell's *Nineteen Eighty-Four* are to the novel's 1984 Penguin edition. Page references are indicated in brackets immediately after the quotation.

2. References to Orwell's other novels are to *The Penguin Complete Novels of George Orwell*, 1983.

3. All quotations from George Orwell's essays, articles, and letters refer to *The Collected Essays, Journalism and Letters of George Orwell* in 4 volumes, ed. Sonia Orwell and Ian Angus, Penguin Books, in association with Secker and Warburg, 1970. Page references are indicated in brackets immediately after the quotation, and include both volume and page number.

Arendt, Hannah. *The Origins of Totalitarianism*. New York: Harcourt, Brace and World, 1951 (originally *The Burdens of Our Times*; London: Secker and Warburg, 1951).

Armytage, A.G.H. "Orwell and Zamyatin." *Yesterday's Tomorrows: An Historical Survey of Future Societies*. London: 1963.

Arnold, Matthew. "Culture and Anarchy." *Selected Poetry and Prose*. New York: Rinehart, 1952.

Ashe, Geoffrey. "The Servile State in Fact and Fiction." *Month* 4 July 1950, 57–59.

Auden, W.H. "George Orwell." *Spectator* 16 Jan. 1971, 86–87. Baruch, Elaine Hoffman. "The Golden Country: Sex and Love in *1984*." *1984 Revisited*. Ed. Irving Howe. New York: Harper and Row, 1983.

Beadle, Gordon. "George Orwell and the Death of God." *Colorado Quarterly* 23 (1974), 51–63.

Beauchamp, Gorman. "Of Man's Last Disobedience: Zamyatin's *We* and Orwell's *1984*." *Comparative Literature Studies* 10 (1973), 285–301.

Berger, Harold. *Science Fiction and the New Dark Ages*. Bowling Green: Bowling Green University Popular Press, 1976.

Bettelheim, Bruno. *The Informed Heart: Autonomy in a Mass Age*. New York: Free Press, 1960.

Billington, Michael. "A Director's Vision of Orwell's '1984' Draws Inspiration from 1948." *New York Times 3* June 1984, 19 and 29.

Birrell, T.A. "Is Integrity Enough? A Study of George Orwell." *Dublin Review* 224 (Autumn 1950), 49–65.

Bonifas, Gilbert. *George Orwell: L'Engagement*. Paris: Éditions Didier, 1984.

Borkenau, Franz. "Communism as an International Movement." *World Communism*. New York: Faber, 1939.

Bracher, Karl Dietrich. "The Disputed Concept of Totalitarianism." *Totalitarianism Reconsidered*. Ed. Ernest Menze. Port Washington, New York: Free Press, 1981.

Buitenhuis, Peter, and Ira Nadel, eds. *George Orwell: A Reassessment*. London: Macmillan, 1988.

Burgess, Anthony. *The Novel Now*. New York: 1970.

Byron George Gordon. *Byron: A Self-Portrait: Letters and Diaries 1798–1821*. Ed. Peter Quennell. London: Murray, 1967.

Calder, Jenni. *Chronicles of Conscience: A Study of George Orwell and Arthur Koestler*. London: Seeker and Warburg, 1968.

Camus, Albert. "The Failing of the Prophecy." *Existentialism versus Marxism: Conflicting Views on Humanism*. New York: Dell, 1966.

———. *Notebook 1942–1951*. Trans. Justin O'Brien. New York: Knopf, 1966.

———. *The Plague*. Trans. S. Gilbert. Harmondsworth: Penguin, 1948.

Carrère d'Éncausse, Hélène. *A History of the Soviet Union 1917–1958*. Trans. V. Ionescu. London: Longman, 1970.

Carter, Michael. *George Orwell and the Problem of Authentic Existence*. London: Croom Helm, 1985.

Caute, David. *The Fellowtravellers: A Postscript to the Enlightenment*. London: Weidenfeld and Nicolson, 1973.

Claeys, Gregory. "Industrialism and Hedonism in Orwell's Literary and Political Development." *Albion* 18.2 (Summer 1986), 219–245.

The Collapse of Communism. By Correspondents of *The New York Times*. Ed. Bernard Gwertzman and Michael Kaufman. New York: Random House, Times Books, 1990.

Comfort, Alex. "1939 and 1984: George Orwell and the Vision of Judgment." *On 1984*. Ed. Peter Stansky. New York: Freeman, 1983.

Connelly, Mark. *The Diminished Self*. Pittsburgh: Duquesne University Press, 1987.

Connolly, Cyril. "George Orwell." *The Modern Movement: 100 Key Books from England, France and America, 1880–1950*. London: 1965.

Coombs, James. "Towards 2084." *The Orwellian Moment*. Ed. Robert Savage, James Coombs, and Dan Nimmo. Fayetteville: University of Arkansas Press, 1989.

Coppard, Audrey and Bernard Crick, eds. *Orwell Remembered*. London: B.B.C. Ariel Books, 1984.

Crick, Bernard. "Critical Introduction and Annotations to George Orwell's *Nineteen Eighty-Four*." *Nineteen Eighty-Four*. By Orwell. Oxford: Clarendon Press, 1984.

———. *George Orwell: A Life*. London: Secker and Warburg, 1980.

Deane, Herbert A. "Harold Laski." *The International Encyclopedia of the Social Sciences*, vol. 9, 30–33. New York: Macmillan and Free Press, 1968.

Deutscher, Isaac. "The Ex-Communist's Conscience." *Heretics and Renegades*. London: Hamish Hamilton, 1955. (Originally "Review of *The Gods that Failed*" in *The Reporter* [New York], April 1950.)

———. "*1984*—The Mysticism of Cruelty." *Heretics and Renegades*. London: Hamish Hamilton, 1955.

Devroey, Jean Pierre. *L'Âme de cristal: George Orwell au present*. Bruxelles: Éditions de l'Université de Bruxelles, 1985.

Dickerson, Mark, and Thomas Flanegan. *An Introduction to Government: A Conceptual Approach*. Toronto: Nelson Canada, 1990.

Dutsher, Alan. "Orwell and the Crisis of Responsibility." *Contemporary Issues* 8 (1956), 308–316.

Eckstein, Arthur. "Orwell, Masculinity, and Feminist Criticism." *The Intercollegiate Review* 21.1 (Fall 1985), 47–54.

Edel, Leon. *The Modern Psychological Novel*. Gloucester, Mass.: Peter Smith, 1972.

Edwards, Paul, ed. *The Encyclopedia of Philosophy*. 8 vols. New York: Macmillan and Free Press, 1967.

Ehrenpreiss, Irwin. "Orwell, Huxley, Pope." *Revue des langues vivantes* 23 (1957), 215–230.

Eliade, Mircea. *Occultism, Witchcraft and Cultural Fashions*. Chicago: University of Chicago Press, 1976.

Elliott, George. "A Failed Prophet." *Hudson Review* 10 (1957), 149–154.

Elliott, Robert. "Satire." *Princeton Encyclopedia of Poetry and Poetics*. Ed. O. Preminger. Princeton: Princeton University Press, 1965.

———. *The Shape of Utopia: Studies in a Literary Genre*. Chicago: University of Chicago Press, 1970.

Faulkner, Peter. "Orwell and Christianity." *New Humanist* 89 (Dec. 1973), 270–273.

Fiedler, Leslie. Keynote address. *1984 Forum*. Seneca College, Toronto. February 27, 1984. Verbatim.

Fiderer, Gerald. "Masochism as Literary Strategy: Orwell's Psychological Novels." *Literature and Psychology* 20 (1970), 3–21.

Fink, Howard. "Orwell versus Koestler: *Nineteen Eighty-Four* as Optimistic Satire." *George Orwell*. Ed. C. Wemyss and Alexej Ugrinsky. Contributions to Study of World Literature #23. Westport: Greenwood, 1987.

Forster, E.M. "George Orwell." *Two Cheers for Democracy*. New York: Harvard, 1951, 60–63.

Frankel, Viktor. *Man's Search for Meaning*. New York: Washington Square Press, 1963.

Freud, Sigmund. *Complete Works*. Trans. James Strachey. 29 vols. London: Hogarth Press, 1955.

Freud: The Hidden Nature of Man. Dir. George Kaczender. The Learning Corporation of America, 1970.

Friedrich, Carl, and Zbigniev Brzezinsky. *Totalitarian Dictatorships and Autocracy*. New York: Praeger, 1956.

Frye, Northrop. *Anatomy of Criticism: Four Essays*. Princeton: Princeton University Press, 1957.

———. "The Authority of Learning." Lecture delivered at the Empire Club, Toronto, Jan. 19, 1984.

Fyvel, T.R. "A Writer's Life." *World Review*. June 1950, 7–20.

Geller, Mikhail, and Aleksandr Nekrich. *Utopia in Power: The History of the Soviet Union from 1917 to the Present*. New York: Summit Books, 1986.

Gerber, Richard. *Utopian Fantasy: A Study of English Utopian Fiction since the End of the Nineteenth Century*. London: 1955.

Golding, William. *Lord of the Flies*. London: Faber, 1954.

Good, Graham. "Orwell and Eliot: Politics, Poetry and Prose." *George Orwell: A Reassessment*. Ed. P. Buitenhuis and I. Nadel. London: Macmillan, 1988.

Goodey, Chris. "The Abyss of Pessimism." *GRANTA* 69 (25 April 1964), 7–9.

Gorfman, Bernard. "Pig and Proletariat: *Animal Farm* as History." Delivered at Southwest Political Science Association, Houston, Texas. April 12–15, 1978.

Gorfman, Bernard, and Jonathan Pool. "Language as Political Control: Newspeak Revisited." Delivered at *George Orwell: A Reassessment*. Vancouver, B.C. Nov. 23–24, 1984.

Gottlieb, Erika. "Orwell in the 1980's." *Utopian Studies* 3, No. 1 (1992), 108–120.

———. "Review of Daphne Patai's *The Orwell Mystique: A Study in Male Ideology*." *Dalhousie Review* (Halifax) 64.4 (1984–1985), 807–811.

Greenblatt, Stephen. *Three Modern Satirists: Waugh, Orwell and Huxley*. New Haven: Yale University Press, 1965.

Griefenhager, Martin. "The Concept of Totalitarianism in Political Theory." *Totalitarianism Reconsidered*. Ed. Ernest Menze. Port Washington, New York: Free Press, 1981.

Gulbin, Suzanne. "Parallels and Contrasts in *Lord of the Flies* and *Animal Farm*." *English Journal* 55 (1966), 86–90.

Hamilton, Alice. "The Enslavement of Woman." *Nazis: An Assault on Civilization*. Ed. P. Van Paassen and James Waterman Wise. New York: Harrison Smith and Haas, 1934.

Handelman, Stephen. "30 Political Parties in One Opposition Group." *Toronto Star* October 22, 1990, 13.

Heller, Peter. *Dialectics and Nihilism: Essays on Lessing, Nietzsche, Mann and Kafka*. Amherst: University of Massachusetts Press, 1966.

Hilferding, Rudolf. "State Capitalism or Totalitarian State Economy." *The Modern Review* June 1947, 266–271.

Howe, Irving, ed. *1984 Revisited*. New York: Harper and Row, 1983.

Huxley, Aldous. *Brave New World*. Harmondsworth: Penguin, 1955.

———. "Brave New World Revisited: Proleptic Meditations on Mother's Day, Euphoria and Pavlov's Pooch" from "The Study of Aldous Huxley." *Esquire* July 1956.

Inge, W.R. *Christian Mysticism*. New York: Meridian, 1956.

Jung, Carl. *Civilization in Transition*. Trans. R.C. Hull. 2d ed. Bollingen Series. Princeton: Princeton University Press, 1970.

———. "The Undiscovered Self" (1957). *The Essential Jung*. Sel. and introd. Anthony Storr. Princeton: Princeton University Press, 1983.

Kamenka, Eugene. *The Portable Karl Marx*. New York: Viking, 1983.

Keats, John. *The Letters of John Keats*. Ed. Hyder Edward Rollins. Cambridge: Harvard University Press, 1958.

Kirkpatrick, Jeane. *Dictatorship and Double Standards: Nationalism and Reason in Politics*. New York: Simon and Schuster, 1982.

Klaits, Joseph. *The Age of Witch Hunts*. Bloomington: Indiana University Press, 1981.

Koestler, Arthur. *Darkness at Noon*. Tr. Daphne Hardy. New York: Macmillan, 1941.

———. Foreword. *Stalin's Russia*. By Susan Labin. London: Gollancz, 1949.

———. "A Rebel's Progress." *Observer* 29 (January 1950), 4–5. (Reprinted as "In Memory of George Orwell" in *Bricks to Babel: Selected Writings and Comments by the Author*. London: Hutchinson, 1980.)

———. *The Yogi and the Commissar*. New York: Macmillan, 1945.

Labedz, Leopold. "Will George Orwell Survive 1984? Of Doublethink, and Double-Talk, Body-Snatching and Other Silly Pranks." *Encounter* 63 (July/August 1984), 25–34.

Labin, Susan. *Stalin's Russia*. Trans. Edward Fitzgerald. Foreword Arthur Koestler. London: Gollancz, 1949.

Lamont, Corliss. *The Philosophy of Humanism*. 5th ed. New York: Ungar, 1965.

Lee, Robert. *Orwell's Fiction*. Notre Dame, Indiana: University of Notre Dame Press, 1969.

Leites, Nathan. "Psychology of Political Attitudes." *Psycho-Political Analysis: Selected Writings of Nathan Leites*. Ed. Elizabeth Wirth Marvick. New York: John Wiley, Sage Publications, 1977.

Lewis, C.S. "Donne and Love Poetry in the Seventeenth Century." *Seventeenth Century English Poetry*. Ed. W.J. Keast. New York: Oxford University Press, 1962.

Lifton, Robert Jay. "Death and History: Ideological Totalism: Victimization and Violence." *Totalitarianism Reconsidered*. Ed. Ernest Menze. Port Washington, New York: Free Press, 1981.

Loewenthal, Karl. *Hitler's Germany*. New York: Macmillan, 1939.

Lottman, Herbert. *Albert Camus: A Biography*. New York: Doubleday, 1979.

Mann, Golo. "1984." *Frankfurter Rundschau* 5 Nov. 1949, p. 6.

Mann, Thomas. "Mario and the Magician." *Death in Venice and Other Works*. Trans. H.T. Lowe-Porter. London: Secker and Warburg, 1979.

Marcuse, Herbert. *Eros and Civilization*. New York: Vintage, 1955.

May, Rollo. *Love and Will*. New York: Norton, 1969.

McGill, Arthur. "Structure of Inhumanity." *Disguises of the Demonic*. Ed. A.M. Olson. New York: Association Press, 1975.

Menze, Ernest, ed. *Totalitarianism Reconsidered*. Port Washington, New York: Free Press, 1981.

Meyers, Jeffrey, and Valerie Meyers. *George Orwell: An Annotated Bibliography of Criticism*. New York: Garland Publishing, 1977.

Mills, Wright. *The Marxists*. New York: Dell, 1962.

Milosz, Czeslaw, quoted by Edward M. Thomas in *Orwell*. Edinburgh: Oliver and Boyd, 1965.

More, Thomas. *Utopia*. Trans. Paul Turner. Harmondsworth: Penguin, 1961.

Moreno, Antonio. *Jung, Gods and Modern Man*. London: Notre Dame Press, 1970.

Muggeridge, Malcolm. "Muggeridge's Diaries." *Orwell Remembered*. Ed. Audrey Coppard and Bernard Crick. London: B.B.C. Ariel Books, 1984.

Nasty Girl. Dir. Michael Verhoeven. With Lena Stolz. 1989.

Nelson, John. "Orwell's Political Myths and Ours." *The Orwellian Moment*. Ed. Robert Savage, James Coombs, and Dan Nimmo. Fayetteville: The University of Arkansas Press, 1989.

1984. Dir. Michael Anderson. With Edmund O'Brien, Jan Sterling, and Michael Redgrave. 1955.

1984. Dir. Michael Radford. With John Hurt and Richard Burton. 1984.

Novack, George, ed. *Existentialism versus Humanism: Conflicting Views on Humanism*. New York: Dell, 1966.

Novoe Vremya, 1 Jan. 1984.

Olson, A.M., ed. *Disguises of the Demonic: Contemporary Perspectives on the Power of Evil*. New York: Association Press, 1975.

Olson, Robert G. *An Introduction to Existentialism*. New York: Dover, 1962.

Otto, Rudolf. *The Idea of the Holy*. Trans. J.W. Harvey. London: Oxford, 1923.

Patai, Daphne. "Gamesmanship and Androcentrism in Orwell's *Nineteen Eighty-Four*." *PMLA* 97 (1982), 856–870.

———. *The Orwell Mystique: A Study in Male Ideology*. Amherst: University of Massachusetts Press, 1984.

Price, Robert, and Kenneth Noble. *Damascus and the Bodhi Tree: Ancient Wisdom and Modern Thought*. Toronto: Thistle Printing, 1981.

Rahv, Philip. "The Unfuture of Utopia." *Partisan Review* (16 July 1949), 743–749.

Rai, Alok. *Orwell and the Politics of Despair*. Cambridge: Cambridge University Press, 1988.

Rees, Richard. *Fugitive from the Camp of Victory*. London: Secker and Warburg, 1961.

———. "George Orwell." *Scots Chronicle* 26 (1951), 11 (quoted by Rodden 401).

Reich, Wilhelm. *The Mass Psychology of Fascism*. Trans. V.R. Carfagno. New York: Farrar, Strauss and Giroux, 1970.

Reilly, Patrick. *George Orwell: The Age's Adversary*. London: Macmillan, 1986.

Repentance (Pokayaniye). Dir. Tengiz Abuladze. With Avlandi Makhaladze. 1984.

Rieff, Philip. *Freud—The Mind of the Moralist*. Garden City, New York: Doubleday Anchor Books, 1961.

Roazan, Paul. "Orwell, Freud and 1984." *Virginia Quarterly Review* 54 (1978), 675–695.

Robbins, R.H. *The Encyclopedia of Witchcraft and Demonology*. New York: Crown, 1960.

Roberts, Stephen. *The House that Hitler Built*. London: Methuen, 1937.

Rodden, John. *The Politics of Literary Reputation: The Making and Claiming of 'St. George' Orwell*. New York: Oxford University Press, 1989.

Rohatyn, Dennis. "Triplethink." Delivered at the American Historical Association Conference, Orwell Session, Honolulu, Aug. 14, 1986.

Roubiczek, Paul. *Existentialism: For and Against*. Cambridge: Cambridge University Press, 1966.

Russell, Bertrand. [George Orwell] *World Review* Jan. 1950, 5–7.

Russell, Francis. *Three Studies in Twentieth Century Obscurity*. London: Dufour Editions, 1959.

Sandison, Alan. *The Last Man of Europe: An Essay on George Orwell*. London: Macmillan, 1974.

Sartre, Jean-Paul. "Existentialism is a Humanism." *Existentialism versus Marxism: Conflicting Views on Humanism*. Ed. George Novack. New York: Dell, 1966.

———. "The Wall." *The Best Short Stories of the Modern Age.*, Ed. D. Angus. Greenwich, Conn.: Fawcett, 1962.

Savage, Robert, James Coombs, and Dan Nimmo, eds. *The Orwellian Moment*. Fayetteville: University of Arkansas Press, 1989.

Schapiro, Leonard. *Totalitarianism*. New York: Praeger, 1972.

Schuman, Frederic. *The Nazi Dictatorship*. New York: Knopf, 1935.

Seligman, Kurt. *The History of Magic and the Occult*. New York: Harmony Books, 1948.

Shelden, Michael. *Orwell: The Authorized Biography*. London: Heinemann, 1991.

Simecka, Milan. "Introduction to the Czech Samizdat Edition of 1984." Published by *Index on Censorship*, quoted by Labedz in "Will George Orwell Survive 1984?" *Encounter* 63 (July/Aug. 1984), 30.

Simms, Valerie, J. "A Reconsideration of Orwell's 1984: The Moral Implications of Despair." *Ethics* 84 (1973–74), 292–306.

Sinyard, Neil. *Filming Literature: The Art of Screen Adaptations*. London: Croom Helm, 1986.

Slater, Ian. *Orwell: The Road to Airstrip One*. New York: Norton, 1985.

Small, Christopher. *The Road to Miniluv: George Orwell, the State and God*. London: Gollancz, 1975.

Smith, Marcus. "The Wall of Blackness." *Modern Fiction Studies* 14 (1968–69), 423–433.

Smyer, Richard. *Primal Dream and Primal Crime: Orwell's Development as a Psychological Novelist*. Columbia: University of Missouri Press, 1979.

Solzhenitsyn, Aleksandr. *The Gulag Archipelago*. New York: Harper and Row, 1973.

Sperber, Murray. "Gazing into the Glass Paperweight: The Structure and Philosophy of Orwell's *Nineteen Eighty–Four*." *Modern Fiction Studies* 26 (1980), 213–216.

Stansky, Peter, ed. *On 1984*. New York: Freeman, 1983.

Stansky, Peter, and William Abrahams. *Orwell: The Transformation*. London: Constable, 1979.

Steiner, George. *Portage to San Cristobal*. New York: Simon and Schuster, 1979.

Steinhoff, William. *George Orwell and the Origins of 1984*. Ann Arbor: University of Michigan Press, 1975.

Sterny, Vincent. "George Orwell and T.S. Eliot: The Sense of the Past." *College Literature* 14 (Spring 1987), 85–100.

Stunia, Melor. *Izvestiya* 15 January 1984.

Swift, Jonathan. *Gulliver's Travels*. Ed. Louis A. Landa. Riverside Editions. Cambridge, Mass.: Houghton Mifflin, 1960.

Talmon, J.L. *The Origins of Totalitarian Democracy*. London: Secker and Warburg, 1955.

Thomas, Edward M. *Orwell*. Writers and Critics Series. Edinburgh: Oliver and Boyd, 1965.

Thomas, Norman. *Socialism Re-examined*. New York: Norton, 1963.

Tolstoy, Nikolai. *Stalin's Secret War*. London: Cape, 1981.

Trilling, Diana. *Nation* 25 June 1949.

Trilling, Lionel. *New Yorker* 16 June 1949.

———. "Introduction to *Homage to Catalonia*." *Homage to Catalonia*. By Orwell. Boston: Beacon Press, 1952.

Ulanov, Ann B. "The Psychological Reality of the Demonic." *Disguises of the Demonic*. Ed. A.M. Olson. New York: Association Press, 1975.

Underhill, Evelyn. *Mysticism*. London: Methuen, 1930.

Wain, John. "Del diagnostical la pesadilla." *Revista de Occidente* 33–34 (1984), 95–109.

———. "The Last of George Orwell." *20th Century* 155 (Jan. 1954), 71.

Warnock, Mary. *Existentialism*. London: Oxford University Press, 1970.

Weintraub, Stanley. "Homage to Utopia." *The Last Great Cause: The Intellectuals and the Spanish Civil War*. New York: 1968.

Wemyss, Courtney, and Alexej Ugrinski, eds. *George Orwell*. Contributions to Study of World Literature #23. Westport: Greenwood, 1987.

Williams, Raymond. *George Orwell*. Modern Masters Series. London: Fontana, 1970.

Wilson, Edmund. "Grade-A Essays: Orwell, Sartre and Highet." *New Yorker* 26 (13 Jan. 1951), 76.

Woodcock, George. *The Crystal Spirit: A Study of George Orwell*. New York: Shocken, 1982.

Zamyatin, Yevgeny. *We*. Tr. Mirra Ginsburg. New York: Avon, 1972.

Zwerdling, Alex. *Orwell and the Left*. New Haven: Yale University Press, 1974.

LAURENCE LERNER

Totalitarianism:
A New Story? An Old Story?

There are three alcoholic drinks in *1984*, corresponding strictly to class distinction: the Proles drink beer, the Outer Party drinks gin, and the Inner Party wine. The first two are both disgusting. Victory gin, at its first mention, is described as giving off "a sickly oily smell, as of Chinese rice-spirit" (p. 8);[1] Winston gulps it down like a dose of medicine, turns scarlet, and water runs out of his eyes: Swallowing it, "one had the sensation of being hit on the back of the head with a rubber club" (p. 8), and only later does its (very mildly) cheering effect begin to be felt. Virtually every time gin is mentioned, we are reminded of its unpleasantness. Drinking it in the canteen, Winston "paused for an instant to collect his nerve, and gulped the oily-tasting stuff down" (p. 43); in the Chestnut Tree cafe it is served with saccharine and cloves, which seem to make it even worse: "The stuff was horrible. The cloves and saccharine, themselves disgusting enough in their sickly way, could not disguise the flat oily smell [...]" (p. 231).

Beer is not in itself as nasty as this, but there is plenty of disgust associated with it. When Winston enters a pub, "a hideous cheesy smell of sour beer hit him in the face" (p. 73)—is cheese, one wonders, worse than beer, or is it rather that the displacement of one smell by another, in Orwell's perception, gives us the worst of both? The pub itself is "a dingy little pub

From *Telling Stories: Studies in Honour of Ulrich Broich on the Occasion of his 60th Birthday*, edited by Elmar Lehmann and Bernd Lenz. © 1992 by B.R. Grüner.

whose windows appeared to be frosted over but in reality were merely coated with dust" (p. 72). The drunken woman he meets in the prison cell, obviously full of beer, vomits it copiously onto the floor—a procedure she seems to find not unpleasant, but she herself is almost as repulsive as the prostitute with streaks of white in her hair and no teeth who haunts Winston's memory. In contrast to this, the wine that O'Brien offers Winston and Julia in his apartment is a dark-red liquid that "seen from the top [...] looked almost black, but in the decanter it gleamed like a ruby" (p. 139). (We are not invited to wonder how Winston, in Airstrip One, has ever seen a ruby.) Winston finds the taste disappointing, but the experience of being offered it is deeply moving because of the memories and associations it stirs. Another substance reserved for the Inner Party, this time one which does not disappoint, is coffee: "The smell was already filling the room, a rich hot smell which seemed like an emanation from his early childhood [...]" (p. 115).

These pleasures offer an interesting glimpse of Orwell's tastes: wine, coffee, sugar, and cigarettes that do not spill their tobacco. This is the Orwell who was so put off by the image of Gandhi ("home-spun cloth, 'soul forces' and vegetarianism"), to which he confessed feeling an "aesthetic distaste."[2] That distaste reveals preferences that are conventional and rather Philistine: Cigarettes should come properly rolled in factories, not incompetently rolled by hand, wine is posh but not actually very nice, and the complete lack of sympathy for what keeps the body healthy and the environment unpolluted makes that sensibility seem dated and even, today, rather quaint.

There are two other pleasures in *1984*, and only two. One is sex, which is given an ideological function: Though Orwell is (to us) curiously coy in describing the sexual act, even italicising it as *'that'*, he considers it extremely important because of its concentration on pure pleasure. Julia is an anarchic element in Ingsoc because of her lack of interest in ideology, even in subversive ideology: Her intense hedonism is a rejection of the whole society, and Winston's sexual embrace with her therefore becomes, we are told, a political act. Fittingly, therefore, when she has been beaten down into submission, her body loses its erotic quality.

The other pleasure, and perhaps the most interesting, is nostalgia. The attempt to recover the past is a constantly recurring obsession with Winston, not only because of its direct political significance (he has seen a photo that proves Jones, Aaronson and Rutherford were innocent of the crime they were accused of), but more interestingly for the way physical objects surviving from the past retain an aura of complex, sensuous experience. Mr Charrington's antique shop is the site of virtually all these objects: It is there Winston buys his diary, and later the glass paperweight containing coral, with "a peculiar softness, as of rainwater, in both the colour and texture of the glass" (p. 79). Its nostalgic significance is quite explicit: "What appealed to him about it was not so much its beauty as the air it seemed to possess of belonging to an age quite different from the present one" (p. 80). In Mr Charrington's shop too, he sees the print of St Clement Dane's and then—the physical object leading to an act of verbal memory—hears the first fragment of the nursery rhyme that haunts him, as an almost recoverable element of the past.

Not a very long list of pleasures, and all of them threatened. For Ingsoc is a society dedicated to the abolition of pleasure. O'Brien explains to Winston that the physiologists are working towards the elimination of the orgasm, so that the sexual act, used for the sole purpose of procreation, will no longer offer the subversiveness of being enjoyed for its own sake. Ingsoc, in fact, though Orwell does not seem to have noticed it, has here reverted to the doctrine of the medieval church, derived from Jerome and Augustine, for whom sexual pleasure was excusable—no more!—as long as it was not excessive, and did not interfere with the times that should be given to prayer.[3] The Inner Party, if we are to judge from what we see of O'Brien, seems to do without sex altogether. As for the objects in Mr Charrington's shop, their function is as bait: They are there to trap Winston, and once they have served that purpose they can be destroyed, as the paperweight is smashed when he and Julia are arrested. If the print is not also destroyed, that would only be because it might be useful as bait for the next victim (if there is to be a next victim—a point I shall come to shortly).

The few pleasures remaining in *1984*, then, are marked for destruction; and it is this rejection of pleasure that distinguishes *1984* from almost all other anti-Utopias, most obviously from Huxley's *Brave New World*, which is built on the contrast between freedom and happiness: Its inhabitants cannot be allowed to think independently, they cannot, as in *1984*, be given access to the great books of the past, but for the opposite reason: Freedom of thought would destabilise a society that is built, not on drabness, but on contentment. Structurally, there are close parallels between the rituals of the two societies, but functionally they are opposites: Where one has petting parties, the other has the Two Minutes Hate; where one has the Feelies, the other has the terrifying telescreen; where one uses the anodyne of sleep-inducing drugs, the other uses torture. Ten years before he wrote 1984, Orwell too believed that the unfree society of the future would at any rate provide happiness: "[...] the slave-state, or rather the slave-world", which he envisaged as the probable outcome if Fascism triumphed, "would probably be a stable form of society, and the chances are, considering the enormous wealth of the world if scientifically exploited, that the slaves would be well-fed and contented."[4] By 1948 he had sunk into deeper gloom.

The contrast between freedom and happiness derives from the tale that lies behind all modern anti-Utopias, Dostoyevsky's fable of the Grand Inquisitor, who "claims it as a merit for himself and his church that at last they have vanquished freedom, and have done so to make men happy."[5] There are moments in 1984 when O'Brien is equated with the Grand Inquisitor:

> He knew in advance what O'Brien would say. That the party did not seek power for its own ends, but only for the good of the majority. That it sought power because men in the mass were frail cowardly creatures who could not endure liberty or face the truth [...]. That the choice for mankind lay between freedom and happiness. (p. 210)

But this is not what O'Brien says, and after Winston is given an electric shock for attributing such a sentimental opinion to him, O'Brien explains, quite explicitly, that the Inner Party has no ultimate goal in retaining power. "The Party seeks power entirely for its own sake. We are not interested in the good of others; we are interested solely in power. Not wealth or luxury or long life or happiness: only power, pure power" (p. 211). It seems a fair guess that when the physiologists succeed in eliminating the orgasm, the Inner Party will give up wine.

II

How new is all this? The central difficulty, in the writing both of Utopias and of Dystopias, concerns newness. Since they describe non-existent societies, the account must draw on the actual history which they have abolished: That is why nostalgia, in a Utopia, is so idle a diversion, and in a Dystopia so crucial a pleasure. Looking for crucial elements of continuity with the past in Orwell's Dystopia, we can begin with the Proles.

If there is any hope, Winston says to himself several times, it must lie in the Proles; and it is difficult to know if this is a cry of despair, or a serious possibility. It is true that the "solid, contourless body, like a block of granite, and the rasping red skin" (p. 174) of the old woman hanging out washing, which suddenly strikes Winston as beautiful, is placed just before the arrest, and could therefore be seen as especially significant. But the Proles are neither the real victims in Ingsoc, nor potential rebels. It is not they who turn up in the Ministry of Love to be tortured; nor, apparently, are they a possible locus of revolt, for all we see in them is petty squabbling, superstition and greed. At one point, Winston is bitterly conscious of this. If there is hope, it must lie in the Proles: "When you put it in words it sounded reasonable: it was when you looked at the human beings passing you on the pavement that it became an act of faith" (p. 72).

This ambivalent view of working people runs right through Orwell. A deep disgust at the sordidness of proletarian life fuels the unforgettable, shocking account of the Brookers' boarding house,[6] and sits oddly with his faith in the reliable decency of the English working man as a kind of bulwark against extremism.

We are told that even when the Proles "became discontented, as they sometimes did, their discontent led nowhere, because being without general ideas, they could only focus it on petty specific grievances" (p. 61). Whether Orwell realised it or not, this is a historical commonplace. Roland Mousnier records how "fureurs paysannes" ('peasant outbreaks') in the 17th century usually failed to perceive the consequences of their particular demands, wanting tithes to be spent locally and used for welfare purposes without reflecting that this would dismantle the whole superstructure of the church; and how such uprisings, frequent and bloody though they were, did not attack monarchy, or feudalism, or religion, but a particular lord, or the king's evil counsellors, or at most the remote 'they' of central government. They did not, that is, throw up new political ideologies.[7]

The Proles of *1984* have reverted to a time before the French Revolution, to a condition without general political ideas. And so when Winston once heard a great formidable cry of anger and despair from a group of two or three hundred women and thought 'it's started', and then saw the anger fizzle out into a squabble between individuals over saucepans, his disappointment was at the failure to raise anger to the level of political consciousness—just like Galileo's frustration when listening to the little monk talking about the patience and piety of his parents: "Zum Teufel, ich sehe die göttliche Geduld Ihrer Leute, aber wo ist ihr göttlicher Zorn?"[8] That non-riot which Winston witnessed could have taken place in the 17th century.

The Proles are not the only element in 1984 that actually belongs to the past: another is war. Emmanuel Goldstein's book is an important text whose status is not easy to be sure about: It was written, evidently; as bait, yet its analysis of the political situation is meant to be correct. It too seems to describe an earlier state of affairs: "[...] by becoming continuous a war has fundamentally changed its character. In past ages, a war, almost by definition, was something that sooner or later came to an end, usually in unmistakable victory or defeat" (p. 159). This is clearly Orwell's own account of what things have come to be like in 1984, and it is more or less the opposite of the truth. The Hundred Years' War, the Thirty Years' War, the Anglo-French wars of the 18th century—all these earlier wars were more or less endemic, and came to half-hearted and inconclusive ends; whereas it is the Napoleonic Wars and the two World Wars of our century, more global, more ideological, that ended in clear-cut victory or defeat.

Even the concentration of property into the hands of institutions rather than individual capitalists can be seen as a reversion to the past, as is virtually admitted in the observation that "adoptive organizations such as the Catholic Church have sometimes lasted for hundreds or thousands of years" (p. 168). What then is new about *1984*?

III

To find the answer we must begin from the total rejection of pleasure that gives the book its brilliant, nightmarish quality. Because pleasure is an individual experience, its elimination is necessary to the elimination of individuality; because pleasure is naturally desired, the state needs constantly to intervene and frighten its members away from the quest for pleasure, and in order to do this successfully it must peer into and control every detail of private life. The name for this relentless, efficient interference is, of course, terror.

The great theorist of terror in our time is Hannah Arendt, and her monumental study of *The Origins of Totalitarianism*, written only a year or two after *1984*, can be seen as a systematic account of the view that informs Orwell's vision. Terror, according to Arendt, exists for its own sake: So far from being a means for the elimination of opposition, it is unleashed in its full fury only when opposition has been eliminated (p. 393).[9] The fact that there are actually no opponents left to spy on (p. 421) is a precondition of its total operation: The purpose of power, as O'Brien said, is power. The aim of the concentration camps was "not only to exterminate people and degrade human beings" (p. 438) but also "to eliminate, under scientifically controlled conditions, spontaneity itself as an expression of human behaviour" (p. 438): an uncannily accurate description of what is done to Winston and Julia. There are even organisational details in which Arendt's picture corresponds to Orwell's, such as the limitations in number of the Inner and Outer Party (p. 413).

Yet there are also very striking differences between Arendt's version of totalitarianism and Orwell's. One concerns the identification of victims. According to Arendt, the ultimate aim of totalitarian terror is that anyone could be a victim: The state will choose only "objective enemies", that is to say, categories which it has arbitrarily decided should be eliminated, with no reference whatever to the actions or even the thoughts of those it arrests.

"The category of the suspect thus embraces under totalitarian conditions the total population" (p. 430). In one way, this is what we see in 1984: Winston might meet anyone in the cellars of Miniluv, even Parsons, who in his mindless subservience had seemed the exact example of someone who would never be vaporised. But in another and more important way, *1984* rejects this view: Julia and Winston are not chosen arbitrarily, they really are subversives. "I'm good at spotting people who don't belong" (p. 100), says Julia, and she was right in spotting Winston: The whole point of *1984* is that they are pursued because of their total inner repudiation of the system.

This is easily explained: If the victims were merely random members of the population, the novel would lose interest. *1984* with Parsons as the central character would never engage much attention, for there would be no counter-consciousness, no resistance for O'Brien to overcome, no grief or outrage on our part. It is essential to: have, protagonists who commit sex as an act of political defiance, who, drink coffee, buy antiques, and build a human microcosm that we then see destroyed. From this we can draw either of two conclusions, depending on how seriously we take literature. First, that this is a technical matter concerning the writing of fiction: There are certain prerequisites for the creation of a convincing hero and heroine, and Orwell was a competent enough craftsman to realise this. Or second, that literature is the test of theory, that a vision of society which cannot produce a convincing hero is no longer describing a recognisable human situation. Without Winston and Julia, Ingsoc is just an anthill.

This point, too, I shall return to. Meanwhile, there is another difference between Arendt's version of totalitarianism and Orwell's. Power in totalitarian society, according to Arendt, is not monolithic. Not only is there a dual structure of authority, the party and the state (p. 395), but there is an elaborate process of duplication and division of authority, a constant shift of the locus of power from one institution to another (pp. 398–401), that contrasts with Orwell's simple picture of the all-powerful party. The real centre of power in Arendt is the leader, and there is no ruling clique (p. 408); whereas in Orwell we are encouraged to think that the leader is a fiction created by the Inner Party (does Big Brother actually exist?). The explanation for this apparent discrepancy, I suggest, is that there is a discrepancy in Arendt's own study. *The Origins of Totalitarianism* is a meticulous and scholarly work, based on extensive research and dealing with the full complexities of totalitarian society; yet it is also an apocalyptic vision, announcing the arrival of a form of politics that is totally and disastrously new, and culminating in a vision of how men will be made superfluous, a vision of "the transformation of human nature itself". This apocalyptic strain sometimes seems to brush aside the careful analysis we have earlier been given. In the crucial chapter on Totalitarianism in Power", Arendt speaks of "some radical evil previously unknown to us" (p. 443). There is "no parallel" to life in the concentration camps (and the concentration camp is the central institution of the totalitarian state, to which all society aspires). No "ordinary tyrant" in the past "was ever mad enough to discard all limited and local interests—economic, national, human, military—in favour of a purely fictitious reality in some indefinite distant future" (p. 412). (I find the word 'ordinary' revealing: It is a feature of claims to radical newness that they tend to smooth out the variety and complications of the past into ordinariness— as post-structuralist literary theory likes to talk of 'traditional literary criticism' as if it was one thing.)

It is this apocalyptic strain in Arendt that provides the parallel with *1984*, and for which Orwell created a series of images that have become part of the very language of politics: Big Brother, the huge face on the ubiquitous posters with their caption, "Big Brother is watching you"; the four ministries, Minipax, Miniluv, Minitrue and Miniplenty—the Ministry of Peace concerning itself with war, the Ministry of Love which maintains law and order, and so on; and then that culminating, chilling image for the future, "a boot stamping on a human face—for ever" (p. 215). This is the apocalyptic vision shared by Orwell and Arendt.

IV

But what gives the vision its tremendous power also robs it of plausibility: Its imaginative strength is also its great weakness. Take, for instance, that last image: Will there be, we can ask, a steady supply of faces for the boot to stamp on? The answer may seem obviously to be yes, for will not nature go on producing them? Only if nature, as we have known it, still operates; and it is therefore necessary to ask what *1984* presents as natural and normal, and what as exceptional. The answer to this is very tricky.

We can begin with Katherine. (Since Katherine is not very memorable, let me recall that she is Winston's estranged wife.) Winston remembers her as having "without exception the most stupid, vulgar, empty mind that he had ever encountered. She had not a thought in her head that was not a slogan [...]" (p. 57). But it is hard to see Katherine as any emptier, or stupider, than the rest of the Outer Party: Julia has no difficulty in recognising her clichés, and the brief account we are given of her seems to correspond exactly to what Ingsoc is designed to produce. The superlatives seem to derive from Winston, rather than to be an objective account of her. Or next, memory. "Was he, then, *alone* in the possession of a memory?" Winston wonders (p. 50), and the question is never answered; yet it is perhaps the most important

question of all. Winston's ordinariness is so central to the story that we
cannot attribute unusual powers to him, and the reason we know about his
memory is simply that he is the central consciousness of the novel—that is,
his is the one memory we have access to, but there is no reason to consider
it unusual. (The unusualness of Bernard Marx's unorthodoxy in *Brave New
World* is at least given an explanation, the error in the quantity of alcohol
administered in his foetus when in the test tube.) And next, corruption. What
are the possibilities of corruption in Ingsoc—of Julia's form of corruption,
for instance, "accepting the Party as something unalterable, like the sky, not
rebelling against its authority but simply evading it, as a rabbit dodges a dog"
(p. 108). This is a question Winston asks himself, and even asks her:

> 'Have you done this before?'
> 'Of course. Hundreds of times—well, scores of times anyway.'
> 'With Party members?'
> 'Yes, always with Party members.' (p.103)

Where are these scores of Party members? As the story proceeds, the
uniqueness of Winston and Julia seems to grow more and more marked, yet
why should they be unique if they are so ordinary?

Naturam expellas furca, tamen usque recurret. Is the natural normal in
1984? It looks as if Orwell is trying to have his cake and eat it—or perhaps
the image should be, trying to have his cake and sick it up. The answer to the
question, will there be a continuing supply of human faces to stamp on, is
both yes and no. There is one face, or the boot could not stamp on it; but if
there is one face here, could there not be another there—even in the Inner
Party, even on the wearer of the boot? If nature goes on producing faces,
Ingsoc is not as stable as O'Brien asserts.

The society of *1984* spares no effort to catch Winston and Julia. The
trap is baited with astonishing elaborateness, and the resources used on them
are tremendous. Since the slightest false move can land one in trouble, there
is really no need for the elaborate cat and mouse game played on them: Mr
Charrington could have arrested Winston the first time he came to the shop,
O'Brien could have arrested him the first time he came to his apartment, or
even the first time he hesitated to destroy the photograph, and no doubt
there were, or could have been, cameras watching Julia pass him the note
that began it all. Of course we'd then have no story; but though the long-
drawn-out illusion of successful surreptitious happiness is necessary for
narrative purposes, it still presents a problem when related to how
totalitarianism is represented. What the elaborate cat and mouse game
suggests is that there is a shortage of mice: Every cat in Airstrip One is

brought in to play with this mouse, so that the Thought Police and the Ministry of Love can—at last—have someone to keep them busy.

The contradiction is actually made explicit by O'Brien. Immediately after he produces the image of the boot he continues: "And remember that it is for ever. The face will always be there to be stamped upon. The heretic, the enemy of society, will always be there, so that he can be defeated and humiliated over again" (p. 215). Yet on the next page but one he tells Winston: "[...] you are the last man. Your kind is extinct [...]" (p. 217). This is not a passing carelessness, but a pointer to the central contradiction of the book.

V

Since I do not believe that the conditions of writing a successful story are of merely technical interest, since I consider literature does not merely illustrate but also tests ideas, I conclude by claiming that *1984* can be seen as a refutation of *The Origins of Totalitarianism*—or rather of one strand in it. Orwell's vision belongs wholly with the apocalyptic strain in Arendt: I have already shown that it ignores the complexities of her historical analysis, but fits perfectly with her picture of totalitarianism as completely unprecedented.

The myth of unprecedented catastrophe is always tempting. Arendt claimed in *Eichmann in Jerusalem* that the Jews, familiar with anti-Semitism, made the mistake of seeing an old enemy in Nazism instead of a new one. In *The Origins of Totalitarianism* she writes of "the seemingly absurd disparities between cause and effect which have become the hallmark of modern history" (p. 131), without pausing to ask how far such disparities lie scattered through all of our often absurd history. Succumbing to what seems too neat an analogy, she introduces an explicitly chiliastic image by comparing the DP camps to Hades, the Soviet Union's labour camps to Purgatory, and the concentration camps of the Nazis to Hell: "Hell and Purgatory, and even a shadow of their perpetual duration, can be established by the most modern methods of destruction and therapy" (p. 446). That shadow has to be seen as very faint; for the terror of the totalitarian camps has shown far less power of endurance than the age-old pogroms, tortures and cruelties of "ordinary tyrants".

Anyone can be forgiven, in the twentieth century, for wondering if humanity has ever before sunk to such degradation; and in answering, 'Yes, it has, and often', one must be careful not to argue with complacency. The fact that for so much of history humanity lacked discerning judgement and life was nasty, brutish and short, does not make these horrors any more acceptable in our time. But, with this admission, we can still go on to claim that we do not live in darker times than our ancestors. This claim can be based on historical study, or, as in this essay, by pointing out that precisely those elements that make *1984* so powerful and so unforgettable a rendering of the nightmare future are those that undermine its claim to perpetual duration, to newness, even to plausibility.

NOTES

1. All quotations from George Orwell's *1984* (published 1949) are taken from the Penguin edition (Harmondsworth 1954, repr. 1977) and referred to by page numbers.

2. "Reflections on Gandhi", in: *The Penguin Essays of George Orwell*, Harmondsworth 1984, pp. 465–472, here: pp. 465 and 472.

3. The wise man, according to Jerome, should "control the excess of voluptuousness, and not allow himself to be carried away precipitately during intercourse. Nothing, is more infamous than to love one's wife like a mistress" (*Against Jovinien*, 149).

4. George Orwell, *The Road to Wigan Pier*, in: *The Complete Works*, vol. 5, London 1986, p. 200.

5. Dostoyevsky, *The Brothers Karamazov*, transl. by Constance Garnett, London 1912, Bk. V, Ch. 5., p. 258.

6. Orwell, *The Road to Wigan Pier*, p. 3–14.

7. *Fureurs paysannes: les paysans dons les revoltes du 17iéme siècle*, Paris 1967.

8. Bertolt Brecht, *Leben des Galilei*, in: B.B., *Werke*, ed. by Werner Hecht et al., 20 vols, Berlin 1988, vol. 5, pp. 187–289, here: p. 246.

9. *The Origins of Totalitarianism* (Meridian Books), New York 1958 (1951). All references to page numbers are according to this edition.

ROBERT PLANK

The Ghostly Bells of London

The plot of *1984* is deceptively simple. The author presents the picture of an execrable regime which by the year 1984 has overrun England and indeed the world. He does so by showing the fate of one man who is inexorably crushed by the system. It is hardly possible to doubt, from the very beginning of the action, that he must fail. There is little suspense.

If *1984* were a utopia like any other, that would be all. However, every page, every sentence reveals to us new details that form the picture of this horrendous imagined society, simultaneously reverberating with resonances from the protagonist's inner life, with echoes from his past. We may leave open for the moment the problem of the extent to which we can speak of a past that actually was, or of a past that Smith never experienced. On the level of the manifest action of the novel (it is of such monotonous simplicity that we can hardly call it a plot), every step results inexorably in the next. On the less obvious level of the novel's real emotional content, each step is vibrant with the resonances of memories and fantasies, and with the symbols and relics of a strange world dredged up from the unconscious, a world that in a sense becomes the real novel; it never fails to shine through the rigid frame of its external events, as an interpreted dream. Thus, *1984* is really two novels: the manifest one that is grist for the mills of the political apologist, and the hidden one that provides a psychological case study of its

From *George Orwell's Guide Through Hell: A Psychological Study of 1984.* © 1994 by The Borgo Press.

protagonist. The official Chinese interpretation of the book as nothing but a satire on Stalinism, or at most on the Cultural Revolution and perhaps the "Gang of Four," concerns the manifest novel; interpretations such as the one penned by Anthony West soon after *1984* was published, which treats the work as an exudation of the "hidden wound" which had warped Orwell's character—and with it his judgment—refer to what we have called the hidden novel. It is true in both areas that some interpretations are correct or at least reasonable, and that others are merely bizarre or even outrageously false. In my view, the Chinese interpretation makes no more sense than does West's, but it is useful to keep in mind that the Chinese version considers aspects which we need not deal with here further, while we cannot completely avoid dealing with West's critical views, since they have been quoted by many later critics.

To do so, we must find some way to gauge Orwell's emotional involvement in his novel. Our assumption or conclusion that Orwell depicted in Smith the person he thought he would have been had he actually lived in Oceania, is only a beginning, no more. Orwell's emotional involvement in the book needs to be studied further.

Orwell could not get a typist to come to his hermitage on the secluded Scottish island of Jura. He could not seem to get the point across that the trip from London took only forty-eight hours if connections were good, and that, although his house was isolated, one could quite easily walk eight miles to the nearest store or a restaurant. So he typed much of *1984* himself, most of it in bed. His letters are full of complaints about his poverty, the pernicious weather, the poor food, his bad health, and the difficulties of writing in such an environment. It is almost as if he had sought such a refuge to imbue his growing manuscript with the grimness of his surroundings, and the knowledge of his deteriorating health. One can imagine that the writer would thus press the last ounce of strength out of his fingers in a desperate race against the Grim Reaper, so as to give form to something of such overriding emotional importance to him that he would not be able to depart from this Earth in peace before he had written it. A book reviewer friend of mine recently told me that he shared the opinion of many, including C. S. Lewis,[1] that *Animal Farm* is a better book than *1984*, but added that "I still can't deny the power that *1984* has over me, a malevolent intensity few books have."[2] It may be more reasonable to assume that this power results from the wrestling with death than from a hidden wound suffered long, long before.

One thing that Winston Smith cannot complain of is a lack of problems or worries. From the moment on that April day when the clocks are striking thirteen,[3] when he embarks on his self-destructive career of "thoughtcrime," to that other afternoon when we take our leave from him in the Chestnut Tree Café, when he can no longer hope for anything but for the bullet to enter his brain,[4] he suffers. He is not always a passive sufferer: though he does nothing to resist his fate, he has a knack for bringing down disaster on his own head, which he does to perfection.

All sorts of practical difficulties beset him, from the rustiness of his razor blades to the neighbors' intolerable brats. These difficulties, attacks, and humiliations wear him down; but they would be tolerable were it not for the choking atmosphere that pervades the world of *1984*: the constant surveillance, the ever-present intimation of being swept, utterly, helpless, toward some preordained destruction. Winston is a sufferer, but unlike Homer's Odysseus, the "divine sufferer" who becomes a tragic figure, Smith remains merely pitiable.

He cannot change the course of events, except to bring the final catastrophe closer. He himself knows this, though at times he deceives himself about this and many other things. There is no comfort for him in the present, no hope in the future. The only defense left to Winston is to dredge up the past and to find gratification in exploring it. It does not matter whether these chunks of his earlier life are jewels or rubbish, real or imagined. The only time he minds is when the dredge fails to bring up anything. We hear about this as early as the third page of the novel:

> He tried to squeeze out some childhood memory that should tell him whether London had always been quite like this .... But it was no use, he could not remember: nothing remained of his childhood except a series of bright-lit *tableaux*, occurring against no background and mostly unintelligible.[5]

Sometimes his search is rewarded, but only with illusion:

> All the while that they were talking the half-remembered rhyme kept running through Winston's head: Oranges and lemons, say the bells of St. Clements, You owe me three farthings, say the bells of St. Martins! It was curious, but when you said it to yourself you had the illusion of actually hearing bells, the bells of a lost London that still existed somewhere or other, disguised and forgotten. From one ghostly steeple after another he seemed to hear them pealing forth. Yet so far as he could remember he had never in real life heard church bells ringing.[6]

He will not shrink from any absurdity if only he can complete his knowledge of those nursery rhymes. He is told the end:

Here comes a candle to light you to bed,
Here comes a chopper to chop off your head,

but he heeds no warning:

> ... there must be another line after the bells of Old Bailey. Perhaps it could be dug out of Mr. Charrington's memory, if he were suitably prompted.[7]

One of the great turning points of the novel comes when Winston and Julia visit O'Brien to join "the Brotherhood," the allegedly secret underground organization that fights the Party. Eventually we discover that the Brotherhood probably does not exist. The deceit initiating Winston and Julia into the nonexistent opposition is the deadliest part of the trap that will be sprung on them. But since the characters do not know this (neither does the reader), this does not detract from the somber solemnity of the occasion. Winston and Julia declare their willingness to do practically anything in the service of the Brotherhood: to murder, to spread venereal disease, to throw acid into the faces of children, to commit suicide—and all that without ever having seen any results of their struggle, which will at best bear fruit in a hundred years.

At the end O'Brien asks whether there is anything they want to say before they go, any message, any question? Winston ponders this, then asks:

> Did you ever happen to hear an old rhyme that begins: Oranges and lemons, say the bells of St. Clements?

It undoubtedly takes O'Brien's considerable self-control to complete the stanza "with a sort of grave courtesy," and to add nothing more critical than, "And now, I am afraid, it is time for you to go."[8]

Winston has taken a step from the sublime to the ridiculous with the bravura of an innocent child. It is virtually a *cliché* to speak of a face so ugly that only a mother could love it, and since we might think of an author as the parent of the characters he invents, we might well wonder whether Orwell could have continued to love Winston Smith (if he ever did) when he engaged in antics such as this. The poetry of the ghostly bells, though somewhat removed from reality, gives Winston a gloriole; the insistence on getting every one of these rhymes, however inappropriate to the occasion, takes it away. The question here is not whether persons who go so far to satisfy their obsession exist in reality—if they don't, the reality of *1984* could conceivably have brought them into existence, or Orwell could have erroneously imagined that it would have. This is not what could have engaged Orwell's willingness to sacrifice his last bit of strength. Its intensity also could not have come from his interest in Winston Smith. However close Winston may have come in some context to representing his author, he remains too small a man, without the spark of fire necessary to inflame anyone's—even the author's—passionate interest. That intensity could only have come from Orwell's deep feeling against the system. The hatred of the government whose operations are conducive to the development in the otherwise-not-very-interesting Winston of such folly, that dislike must have been the severe driving force that made Orwell write the way he did—that, rather than any empathy with Winston, however much he may in certain respects have been Orwell's merely somewhat distorted self-portrait. For if there is one thing we can be sure of, it is that Orwell was not in love with any portrait of himself. Thus we can dispose of West's theory of the "hidden wound."

Because Winston is the person that Orwell felt he would have been if he had had to live in his *1984*, Smith is a distorted self-portrait of himself. And because of this distortion, Orwell could not live in peace with it. He must continually improve its traits, providing more and more of a nonexistent past to give Smith a more convincing identity. So Winston is compelled to dig up anything which can serve as his past. He does not enjoy this quest, but he has to do it.

There are people, both in reality and in fiction, who live in peace with their memories; their reflections arise spontaneously, offering themselves for their owners' enjoyment. There are others who do not so much own their memories as are owned by them. They are compelled to regenerate them, but they cannot enjoy the results of their efforts, which can at best be useful to them. Some can dredge up such memories themselves, others need the help of a psychoanalyst. If their memories come up unbidden or are brought up without proper skill and peace of mind, they degenerate into the psychological equivalent of painful ulcers. So Winston keeps searching for the missing rhymes, but fording them does not relieve his tension. He is not happier when he fords the missing lines from the nursery rhyme. His search leads nowhere, but it must go on.

The reason that such an obsession is plausible in *1984* when it might not be as plausible in the real world, is that in *1984* the search for the individual past and the historic past coincide. We live in a world where the history of an individual's emotional development is often hidden from his awareness by repression, while the external events of his environment and the facts of his own existence remain accessible to his memory and can be reconstructed by him from physical records or from what he learns from others. It is the peculiarity of the regime that Orwell imagined for *1984* that the general, collective past is concealed by amnesia; its reconstruction is "thoughtcrime," the most heinous crime of Orwell's imagined world. The citizens of that regime are first prohibited, and then effectively prevented, from knowing or remembering what happened in the world during their lifetime.

The system works only too well, as Winston finds out when he tries to explore what things were like before the revolution by the seemingly simple device of asking his elders.[9] The passages recording the dismal failure of "oral history" are remarkable for two reasons: they beautifully parody such endeavors, incidentally showing, as had *Animal Farm*, what delicious humor Orwell could write when his passions did not block its flow. The beauty of the parody is much enhanced by the absence of rancor: the people parodied include himself, for he had engaged in such interviewing on his trip to the North of England some years previously, and the report of that research, combined with a second part that was autobiographical and polemical, formed his 1936 book, *The Road to Wigan Pier*.[10] Secondly, the passage establishes the connection, deep in the unconscious, between guilt and punishment. In trying to unearth the past, Winston has, by the standards of *1984*, sinned. So what happens when circumstances compel him to terminate his sinful escapade? He "hardly noticed when his feet carried him out into the street again."[11] Promptly they carry him to where his unconscious directs them: "He seemed to know the place. Of course! He was standing outside the junk shop where he had bought the diary."[12] He "had sworn never to come near the place again." It is the place where he will buy the paperweight, where he will rent the room, where he will be arrested. He has sinned and he will make sure that he is punished. It is notable, though, that the sin this time does not consist of an infraction of rules accepted by him: he has transgressed against a rule set up by the power of the state; he has defied an authority that ruled over him before he even had a chance to internalize its demands.

These laws are no less strong for that, and their violation brings a feeling of guilt that cannot be ascribed to reason. Thus, only meaningless and severely distorted fragments of the past can emerge from Winston's subconscious, like those capitalists with their top hats; and it is only natural that Winston's personal childhood memories are equally fragmented. Hence his complaint that his efforts to remember his childhood produce nothing but "a series of bright-lit tableaux, occurring against no background and mostly unintelligible."[13]

One of the more brightly-lit *tableaux* is that of the murderous fight for a piece of chocolate. He was ten or twelve at the time, his sister two or three (Orwell had a sister five years his junior). He remembers "above all, the fact that there was never enough to eat."[14] One day his father disappeared. This is evidently as usual in Oceania as it was in Argentina during the military regime, a regime with which, former President Reagan noted, we shared certain values. So her husband's disappearance does not surprise Winston's mother, but it does dispirit her. "For hours at a time she would sit almost immobile on the bed, nursing his young sister," who was ailing, "with a face made simian by thinness."[15] "It was evident even to Winston that she was waiting for something that she knew must happen,"[16] and when she took Winston into her arms and pressed him against her for a long time, which happened only "very occasionally," he knew "that this was somehow connected with the never-mentioned thing that was about to happen."[17]

It eventually did happen, under unusual circumstances. The mother's tendency to be more giving to the young sister did not extend to food. "She took it for granted that he, 'the boy,' should have the biggest portion; but however much she gave him he invariably demanded more .... One day a chocolate ration was issued .... Winston heard himself demanding in a loud booming voice that he should be given the whole piece."[18] After a long and of course fruitless argument, his mother made the more than Solomonic decision that he would get three quarters of the piece, the little girl one-quarter, and she herself nothing. This did not help. "Then with a sudden swift spring he had snatched the piece of chocolate out of his sister's hand and was fleeing for the door."[19] A futile exchange of words and gestures ends with the mother drawing her arms around the girl and pressing the girl's face against her breast. "Something in the gesture told him that his sister was dying."[20] When he came home a few hours later "his mother had disappeared" (so had his sister, but in the resume of the events that he gives to himself and to Julia he does not mention this). At the time he remembers all this, he has no way of knowing whether they are alive or dead, but has every reason to presume the latter.

The story is brought into Winston's consciousness by a dream, but we are not told anything about the dream except that Winston woke up from it "with his eyes full of tears."[21] He tried to tell Julia, who was sleeping beside him, about it but found it too complex, especially because "a memory connected with it had swum into his mind in the few seconds after waking."[22] This, of course, is the memory of the chocolate episode. He associates with the final gesture of his mother pressing his sister to herself another gesture "made again thirty years later by the Jewish woman he had seen on the news film, trying to shelter the small boy from the bullets, before the helicopters blew them both to pieces."[23] He introduces the chocolate story to Julia with a somewhat cryptic remark: "'Do you know,' he said, 'that until this moment I believed I had murdered my mother?'"[24]

We are not told whether it was the dream or something else that disabused him, but it was in any event a change toward rationality. As he tells the story, it seems apparent that his mother would have disappeared anyway and his sister would have died anyway. But the turn toward rationality does not go deep: the guilt remains, with the result that Winston feels that the punishment which he eventually suffers is in some way deserved. This, and the fact that this fragment of Winston's memory is very "bright-lit" indeed, may well lead us to the hypothesis that we are here dealing with one of Orwell's own memories. It seems likely that he is recalling something he did as a child to his mother and his younger sister which lent itself to imaginative reworking into a memory of Winston. We do not know enough of Orwell's childhood to verify or refute our hunch or to specify what that event may have been. If it was anything similar to the chocolate episode, the similarity certainly must have been limited. Orwell's mother did not disappear— whatever happened in Orwell's childhood happened in England in the early part of the century, not in Argentina in its later part—and his younger sister survived him.

If there is a genuine memory of Orwell's behind the memory of Winston, it is a screen memory, a memory of something which happened but was not in itself of emotional importance, and which derived its apparent emotional significance from some even earlier event so laden with emotion that it had to be repressed. Working his own screen memory into Winston Smith's significant memory, Orwell the author not only changed the facts in a way that we can no longer trace them, but endowed them, along with similar events, with the power of setting the future apart from the past. Orwell heard the church bells—for Winston they are the ghostly bells of a vanished London.

When Winston and Julia visit O'Brien to join the (fictitious) Brotherhood, wine is brought in, a drink quite familiar to O'Brien but unknown to his guests, and O'Brien opens the proceedings by toasting the equally fictitious Emmanuel Goldstein. The completion of the "initiation" is to be sealed by a second toast. O'Brien tentatively proposes several possible toasts.

"What shall it be this time?" he said, still with the same faint suggestion of irony. "To the confusion of the Thought police? To the death of Big Brother? To humanity? To the future?"

Winston does not hesitate: "To the past," said Winston.[25] This is in character for Winston, but in a sense also for Orwell.

As Winston and Julia leave, O'Brien gives them small whitish pills to counteract the aroma of the wine, so no one will be able to smell it and draw dangerous conclusions. This is rational enough under the circumstances, but critics have also noted, probably correctly, that the solemn consumption of red wine and a white tablet mimics the transubstantiation, the crucial event of the Mass. It would be altogether erroneous to think of this as a parody. Orwell's attitude toward religion and specifically toward Christianity was complex and ambivalent, but by no means truly negative. He had seen in Spain a powerful church throwing its support squarely to the side of Fascism. In some of his essays, and indeed in those into which he put most of his intimate thinking, he had contrasted the attitude of saints who stress the future life and thus devalue earthly life with the "humanist" attitude that was his own, and which he found best embodied in Shakespeare. Yet he believed that the lowering of morality and standards which he thought characteristic of his age, as so many people find it characterizes ours, was due to the gradual loss of the belief in individual immortality among growing numbers of people. This was a typical middle-class complaint in the early part of the century. The usual middle-class and upper-class answer was that the mass of people (the lower classes) must be kept enthralled by religious principles (the "educated," naturally, did not need religion). Orwell does not seem ever to have considered such a solution.

He wrote about the problem explicitly in two articles, both included in Volume 3 of *The Collected Essays, Journalism and Letters of George Orwell*, from his regular column "As I Please" in the British journal *Tribune*, of March 3 and April 14, 1944 (#s 24 and 31 in the *Collection*). The latter article contains a reply to a Catholic writer who had maintained that a public opinion poll would show an overwhelming majority of Englishmen still believing in personal immortality. Orwell points out that while people indeed might tell an interviewer that they believed in life after death, the quality of that belief wasn't what it had been for our forefathers:

> Never, literally never in recent years, have I met anyone who gave me the impression of believing in the next world as firmly as he believed in the existence of, for instance, Australia ... have you ever met a Christian who seemed as afraid of Hell as he was of cancer?[26]

So, what was to be done about it?

> I do not want the belief in life after death to return, and in any case it is not likely to return. What I do point out is that its

disappearance has left a big hole, and that we ought to take notice of that fact.... [Man] is not likely to salvage civilization unless he can evolve a system of good and evil which is independent of heaven and hell.[27]

There is little doubt that the modern cult of power worship is bound up with the modern man's feeling that life here and now is the only life there is.[28]

We either get the new ethics that takes this into account, or we get *1984*. Having written the novel which did all it could to prevent the horrendous alternative, Orwell was able to think of his soul. On his deathbed he requested that he be buried in a churchyard according to the rites of the Church of England. And so it was done.

NOTES

1. Lewis, C. S. "George Orwell," in *Time and Tide* (January 8, 1955). Reprinted in Lewis's *On Stories*.
2. *Ibid.*
3. Orwell, *1984*, p. 1.
4. *Ibid.*, p. 300.
5. *Ibid.*, p. 5.
6. *Ibid.*, p. 99.
7. *Ibid.*, p. 47.
8. *Ibid.*, p. 179.
9. *Ibid.*, p. 87–93.
10. Barron, Neil. Personal communication.
11. Orwell, *1984*, p. 92.
12. *Ibid.*, p. 93.
13. *Ibid.*, p. 5.
14. *Ibid.*, p. 101.
15. *Ibid.*, p. 162.
16. *Ibid.*
17. *Ibid.*
18. *Ibid.*, p. 163.
19. *Ibid.*, p. 164.
20. *Ibid.*
21. *Ibid.*, p. 160.
22. *Ibid.*, p. 161.
23. *Ibid.*
24. *Ibid.*
25. *Ibid.*, p. 177.
26. *CEJL*, Vol. 3, p. 122.
27. *Op. cit.*, p.103.
28. *Ibid.*

ROGER FOWLER

Newspeak and the Language of the Party

Newspeak is a fallacy, and Orwell knows it. There is a myth about *Nineteen Eighty-Four* to the effect that Orwell predicts a future in which thought can be controlled by an artificial language. Although, as we have seen, Orwell does understand that there are vital relationships between language and thought, and he does believe that clear thought can be helped or hindered by language choices, he does not suggest that orthodoxy can be imposed by a government-controlled invented language. In fact, the tone of the Newspeak Appendix—which I suspect is rarely read carefully, or not in the context of the other styles of the novel—is quite clearly satirical, more reminiscent of Swift than anything else in the book. Newspeak seems rather to be presented as the implausible fantasy of an overconfident regime. We will return to these issues, but first let us examine the critique of the political and bureaucratic language usages that are actually represented in the book.

What might be called the language of the Party is manifested in a number of interrelated varieties which are described, referred to briefly, or quoted; as usual in this novel (cf. Cockney), the actual amount of speech in the category is small, but the samples are strikingly exaggerated parodies, hence memorable. There is political oratory, for instance Goldstein (pp. 15–17), the style of Big Brother (p. 44), and the orator in Hate Week (pp. 160, 161). There is what Orwell calls 'Duckspeak', evidenced not only in

From *The Language of George Orwell*. © 1995 by Roger Fowler.

public announcements such as the victory announcement on the telescreen, pp. 255–6, but also in the canteen 'conversation' of an anonymous Party member (pp. 48, 50–1). There is the lying optimism of the 'News' (p. 54). There is the 'hybrid jargon of the Ministries' illustrated in the instructions Winston receives at work (pp. 37, 42) and in a memorandum dictated by O'Brien (p. 150). Finally there is Newspeak itself, said not yet to be spoken by Party members as a whole language (as opposed to the use of Newspeak words within English), but used for editorials in *The Times*. Winston can write Newspeak, but it is not illustrated as such in the main body of the novel, though the 'jargon' consists almost entirely of Newspeak words.

At this point it is worth recalling the list of faults which Orwell found in official English (Chapter 3, pp. 29–30): *dead metaphors, borrowings, archaisms, jargon, meaningless words*, and *ready-made phrases*. All will be seen in the extracts quoted below, though there is no space for a complete analysis here. Of Orwell's six types, the last, 'ready-made phrases', is of immediate relevance to *Nineteen Eighty-Four*:

> 'long strips of words which have already been set in order by someone else' (*CEJL*, IV, p. 163).

The stylistic effect of this prefabricated language is conveyed in the account of Goldstein's 'rapid polysyllabic speech which was a sort of parody of the habitual style of the orators of the Party' (*Nineteen Eighty-Four* p. 16), or the speaker in the canteen, 'someone was talking rapidly and continuously, a harsh gabble almost like the quacking of a duck' (p. 48), whose phrases 'jerked out very rapidly and, as it seemed, all in one piece, like a line of type cast solid' (p. 51). The rapidity and fluency are made possible by the fact that the speaker is simply uttering strings of orthodox jargon and is in no sense choosing words in relation to intended meanings or to some state of affairs in the world. Thus language neither springs from consciousness (the speaker is not thinking), nor has any relation to truth. A striking example of the dissociation of language from thought and from facts is the speech of the orator on the sixth day of Hate Week:

> His voice, made metallic by the amplifiers, boomed forth an endless catalogue of [Eurasian] atrocities, massacres, deportations, lootings, rapings, torture of prisoners, bombing of civilians, lying propaganda, unjust aggressions, broken treaties.

In mid-speech he is handed a piece of paper which informs him that the enemy is now not Eurasia, but Eastasia; Eurasia is now an ally:

He unrolled and read it without pausing in his speech. Nothing altered in his voice or manner, or in the content of what he was saying, but suddenly the names were different. (p. 160)

Winston later reflects that:

'the speaker had switched from one line to the other actually in mid-sentence, not only without a pause, but without even breaking the syntax' (p. 161).

In a sense then it does not matter what the speaker is saying: his utterances are just an orthodox gesture and in no sense an account of a real state of affairs. It is just automated speech, the utterance of a machine. Orwell analyses the process in 'Politics and the English Language':

When one watches some tired hack on the platform mechanically repeating the familiar phrases—*bestial atrocities, iron heel, blood-stained tyranny, free peoples of the world, stand shoulder to shoulder*—one often has a curious feeling that one is not watching a live human being but some kind of dummy: a feeling which suddenly becomes stronger at moments when the light catches the speaker's spectacles and turns them into blank discs which seem to have no eyes behind them ... A speaker who uses that kind of phraseology has gone some distance towards turning himself into a machine. The appropriate noises are coming out of his larynx, but his brain is not involved as it would be if he were choosing his words for himself. If the speech he is making is one that he is accustomed to make over and over again, he may be almost unconscious of what he is saying, as when one utters the responses in church. And this reduced state of consciousness, if not indispensable, is at any rate favourable to political conformity. (*CEJL*, IV, pp. 166–7)

Orwell had parodied this kind of speaker some years earlier, in *Coming Up for Air*, when George Bowling listens to a 'well-known anti-Fascist' at a Left Book Club meeting:

his voice came across to me as a kind of burr-burr-burr, with now and again a phrase that caught my attention.
     'Bestial atrocities.... Hideous outburst of sadism.... Rubber truncheons.... Concentration camps.... Iniquitous persecution of the

Jews.... Back to the Dark Ages.... European civilization.... Act before
it is too late.... Indignation of all decent peoples ...' [etc.]
      You know the line of talk. These chaps can churn it out by the
hour. Just like a gramophone. Turn the handle, press the button,
and it starts. (p. 145)

Here we have the same idea of the political speaker as a machine working
without consciousness, and, interestingly, the phrases George catches are
excellent examples of the jargon, stock phrases and meaningless words which
Orwell attacks in the essay, including one, 'bestial atrocities' which is actually
used in the essay. The 'gramophone' metaphor for political speaking is
earlier found in *Wigan Pier*, p. 190.
      Returning to *Nineteen Eighty-Four*, Orwell follows the passage from the
essay in describing Winston's perception of the speaker in the canteen, even
to the metaphor of 'two blank discs instead of eyes'.

it was almost impossible to distinguish a single word ... And yet,
though you could not actually hear what the man was saying, you
could not be in any doubt about its general nature ... Whatever it
was, you could be certain that every word of it was pure
orthodoxy, pure Ingsoc ... Winston had a curious feeling that this
was not a real human being but some kind of dummy. It was not
the man's brain that was speaking, it was his larynx ... it was a
noise uttered in unconsciousness, like the quacking of a duck. (pp.
50–1)

'Duckspeak' may be a suitable Newspeak word for describing the gabbling
style (though too humorous and metaphorical for Newspeak really), but the
real evil being attacked is conceptual, the idea of speech which issues
mechanically without reference to thought or to truth. When, at the end of
the novel, the telescreen announces, in Duckspeak, 'the greatest victory in
human history' (passage quoted on p. 206 above), or when 'an eager, youthful
voice' claims that 'We have won the battle for production!' (p. 54; passage
quoted above, Ch. 2, p. 17), the reader knows that it is immaterial to wonder
whether this is true or not, and we know that the telescreen announcer is not
even thinking about what he says. Orthodox feelings are being
communicated and invoked, and that is about all one can say.
      A second version of the language of the Party which appears briefly
but strikingly in the novel is a clipped bureaucratic jargon, 'the hybrid
jargon of the Ministries'. Winston's working instructions are written in
this mode:

times 17.3.84 bb speech malreported africa rectify

times 19.12.83 forecasts 3 yp 4th quarter 83 misprints verify
    current issue

times 14.2.84 miniplenty malquoted chocolate rectify

times 3.12.83 reporting bb dayorder doubleplusungood refs
    unpersons rewrite fullwise upsub antefiling (p. 37; Oldspeak
    translation of the fourth order on p. 42)

O'Brien dictates into his 'speakwrite' a memo phrased in a variant of this style:

'Items one comma five comma seven approved fullwise stop suggestion contained item six doubleplus ridiculous verging crimethink cancel stop unproceed constructionwise antegetting plusfull estimates machinery overheads stop end message.' (p. 150)

What we have here are exaggerations of a clipped, bureaucratic style which (ignoring for a moment the Newspeak vocabulary) is familiar in office or institutional practice and also resembles telegrams. There is an absence of capitalisation and punctuation; a fondness for shortening words—'4th', 'refs'—and phrases—'bb' (= Big Brother), 'yp' (= year plan); omission of inflections on the ends of words—'bb's'—and of articles, linking verbs, auxiliaries and prepositions—'*the* suggestion *is* ridiculous', 'refs *to* unpersons'. The style has affinities to the language of telegrams, which is stripped of low-information words to save cost. More specifically, the elliptical style of Newspeak and of the memoranda in *Nineteen Eighty-Four* has been linked to what was known as 'cablese'; the abbreviated style in which reporters used to send in their stories to the newspapers and radio.[17] The media associations of cablese would have been significant to Orwell given his concern in the novel with the suspect veracity of public accounts of events; and we should note in this connection the notoriously compressed conventional style of newspaper headlines. Insofar as media language is a deformation of language, a deviation from ordinary or demotic speech, it becomes an unclear, unanalytical, representation of reality: the compression of headlines, for example, has an inherent potential for ambiguity or double meaning.[18]

It might be claimed that these clippings and ellipses are done for speed and efficiency, or to save space when fitting headlines in narrow newspaper columns, but it is more likely that their function is to *symbolise* speed and efficiency, and power (note that Winston's instructions, and O'Brien's memo, are packed with verbs of command), on the part of the person who communicates in this abbreviated mode. Let us for a moment pursue the office or institutional association, rather than the media connection, since the texts quoted above are more like office memoranda than news stories. (It should be noted that we need to think about the traditional, pre-information technology, institutional practices which would have been known to Orwell. These have only recently been revolutionalised—but by no means completely—by word-processing, the storage of massive amounts of data on small computers and its ready accessibility—even to managers—, networking, electronic mail, fax, etc. No doubt these facilities have transformed the structure and style of institutional and media communications.) If a manager or head of department scribbles 'refs pse asap' on some candidate's application form before passing it down to the secretary who has to send out for the references, he (more likely a man) is communicating busy-ness and authority: I do not think this style can be used 'upwards': a secretary (most likely a woman) would be more likely to address her boss in polite, full sentences on one of those ubiquitous sticky notelets: 'Mr Brown: would you please confirm that this candidate's qualifications are appropriate before I send out for her references'. The manager using the brusque abbreviations is requiring the addressee to work out, by reference to institutional conventions, what the full form of the shortened message would be: putting the onus on the inferior addressee. It is the use of a code, and of a code symbolising membership of an élite in-group.

Jargon, in institutional settings, works in the same way; Orwell had already recognised that jargon is a property of (intellectual) élites:

> English is peculiarly subject to jargons. Doctors, scientists, businessmen, officials, sportsmen, economists, and political theorists all have their characteristic perversion of the language, which can be studied in the appropriate magazines from the *Lancet* to the *Labour Monthly*. ('The English People,' written 1944, *CEJL*, III, p. 43)

The Newspeak words in the orders quoted above are themselves a form of jargon—specialised words in technical contexts, emanating from the powerful who somehow own the register and have the power to make judgement through it: 'malreported', 'malquoted', 'doubleplusungood'. There are also ordinary technical jargon phrases in these messages, for example 'machinery overheads'. If jargon symbolises privilege through specialised knowledge, it also tends to prefabrication: the jargon of a profession is a vocabulary of stock words known in advance of utterance; in

'The English People' Orwell connects it with ready-made phrases, which as we have seen are an enemy of thought. Similarly, jargon can lead to euphemism and lying; and to doublethink. A nice example is 'verify' in Winston's second instruction: he is told to check a 'misprint' in an old edition of the *Times* by referring to the current issue, and restore the truth by correcting the misprint. Reading between the lines, we realise that the December 1983 production forecasts were not fulfilled, so the predictions have to be changed after the event to conform with what was (perhaps) actually produced. Winston's job is 'rectification' (p. 42), a virtuous-sounding jargon word which in fact means the falsification of the official record of the historical past in line with the needs of the political present.

In 'Politics and the English Language' Orwell said that his concern was with language 'merely as an instrument for expressing and not for concealing or preventing thought' (*CEJL*, IV, p. 169, cf. above, p. 33). *Nineteen Eighty-Four* parodies certain varieties of political and managerial language, encouraged by the rulers of Oceania, criticising them on the grounds that— through jargon, euphemism, prefabrication, dead metaphors, stock phrases and the like—they dissociate thought and language, turning the speaker into an unconscious machine that is not expressing thought, and indeed, through the deadness and the purely symbolic character of his language, is prevented from thinking. The skills of doublethink, and the power of Inner Party status, bestow upon O'Brien and on the anonymous source of Winston's instructions a further dimension of language, a manipulative authority which can cause subordinates to assist in the concealment of material reality. So far in these processes, Newspeak figures as an élite jargon symbolising privilege and orthodoxy. But the rulers of the totalitarian society intend Newspeak to have an even more powerful role. It will not simply cloud the truth on the occasions when it is used. When, by 2050, it becomes the sole medium known by members of the Inner and Outer Parties, it will totally shape what they can say and therefore what they can think.

Orwell puts into the minds of the regime an extreme version of the theory which is known in modern linguistics as *linguistic determinism*.[19] Let me say at once that the extreme version, not only as expressed in Newspeak but in any context, is discountenanced by any sensible person and is in any case neither provable nor disprovable; and the extreme version is not proposed by the American anthropological linguists who first discussed the arguments about language determining thought. The theory is usually credited to Edward Sapir and Benjamin Lee Whorf, and is more popularly expressed in the writings of the latter. Whorf, a student of native American ('Indian') languages, which seem to be strikingly different from the European tongues, believed that languages could differ radically in their basic structures, and that these differences could have the effect of 'packaging' reality differently for speakers. Thus, for example, speakers of languages which have different tense systems might possess different mental pictures of the way time is organised. Whorf's arguments are provocatively phrased—he was an amateur enthusiast for language rather than an academic whose way of expressing claims would have to be more formal and cautious. His evidence is anecdotal, and he paraphrases his examples from indigenous American languages to make the point accessible to English readers. The fact that he can translate the exotic, other-reality, material shows that the different world-views are not accessible only to the speakers of the languages concerned. If an English speaker can, through translation, understand the concepts of time encoded in Hopi, and presumably vice-versa, then thought or world-view is not absolutely constrained by the language one speaks. The likelihood is—and this is supported by modern cognitive psychology—that different forms of linguistic organisation (for example different styles or vocabularies) will *dispose* a language user to chop up experience differently, will encourage a *tendency* to see the world in a specifically-slanted way. There is no suggestion that a deliberate organisation of language, like Newspeak, can produce a diminished, fixed and inescapable world-view in its speakers. However, the Newspeak proposal, though extreme and certainly unachievable, is quite closely related to the more plausible claim that language *encourages* a certain view of the world; closely enough to produce a bit of a chill even in readers who see through Newspeak: One has to think twice, and suppress a gut reaction that there is something plausible about Newspeak. This double-take reaction is the effect of the deadpan style of the Newspeak Appendix; the technique resembles the satirical strategy of Swift, whom Orwell much admired (he first read *Gulliver's Travels* at the age of eight).

The reader of *Nineteen Eighty-Four* can know a good deal about Newspeak even before encountering the Appendix, through the examples of its vocabulary which occur in the text and through the enthusiastic description given in Part 1, Chapter 5 by Syme, a Newspeak expert working on the Dictionary. Newspeak is a reduced version of English with a small, carefully controlled vocabulary including a number of invented compound words such as 'Minitrue', 'Minipax', 'Newspeak' itself, 'doublethink', 'unperson'; similar compounds in the novel appear to be Newspeak but in the Appendix are not: 'thoughtcrime' appears in the text but is replaced by 'crimethink' in the Appendix. At any rate, the habit of compounding appears to be a structural preference of this variety of English. Neither Duckspeak nor cablese is actually to be equated with Newspeak, though the Duckspeak *effect* is provided for in the Newspeak programme; in the novel Duckspeak is built on the ordinary political jargons which Orwell criticised in his essays, but in the future it will ideally be produced by polysyllabic Newspeak words. It is important to grasp that no 'pure' example of Newspeak is given in the text of the novel: this absence is covered by the admission that the language will not be completed until 2050, no one speaks it and so far it is used solely for *Times* editorials. The official varieties of English used by bureaucrats and politicians in 1984 are far indeed from Newspeak, though their language is peppered with bits of the vocabulary, even the odd term producing a very alienating effect. The point being made is surely that Newspeak is a long way short of completion.

Syme's account of Newspeak gives an informative succinct account of Newspeak: he stresses the central principle of reduction of vocabulary, the production by compounding of systems of related terms based on the same root—'good', 'ungood', 'plusgood' and 'doubleplusgood' in his example— and the central function of Newspeak, to control thought:

> 'Don't you see that the whole aim of Newspeak is to narrow the range of thought? In the end we shall make thoughtcrime literally impossible, because there will be no words to express it. Every concept that can ever be needed, will be expressed by exactly *one* word, with its meaning rigidly defined and all its subsidiary meanings rubbed out and forgotten ... the Revolution will be complete when the language is perfect.' (*Nineteen Eighty–Four*, pp. 48–9)

The Appendix's way of putting this is quoted below, pp. 223–4.

Although the general idea of Newspeak can be gleaned from the text of the novel (with also an indication of its essential absurdity, as we shall see), it is only through the Appendix that we fully realise, that Newspeak is designed to be a self-contained linguistic system replacing, not grafted on, the English language. It is organised into three vocabulary categories: the 'A vocabulary' which consists of ordinary words such as 'hit', 'run', 'dog'; the 'B vocabulary' which comprises the political compounds which have already been illustrated from the text; and the 'C vocabulary' which is a supplementary list of scientific terms. The language has its own simplified grammar, its rules for inflection, compounding and suffixing (pp. 259–60). When set out in a 'grammar' in the Appendix, Newspeak has much more the appearance of a complete constructed system than that of a variety of English. It would have been clear to contemporary educated readers with linguistic interests that Orwell's model was the system of *Basic English* proposed by C. K. Ogden in 1930, which drew a lot of attention in the 1930s and 1940s.[20] Basic ('British American Scientific International Commercial') English was designed as an easy-to-learn international English, its simplicity achieved by reduction of vocabulary to an amazing 850 words which, Ogden claimed, could serve to render most meanings communicated normally in the full vocabulary. Like Newspeak, the Basic vocabulary is classified into three categories, two of them with two subcategories. The classification systems do not of course coincide. Orwell seems to have been well informed about Basic, and to have favoured its chance of becoming an international language higher than the artificial languages such as Esperanto and Interglossa. He attributed to it nothing of the negative ideological role which characterises Newspeak, quite the reverse: in one approving comment he suggests that translation into Basic could deflate 'the oratory of statesmen and publicists', 'high-sounding phrases' (*CEJL*, III, p. 244; see also pp. 107–8). So Orwell is not attacking Basic through Newspeak; Basic is used rather as an analogy, an aid to readers to imagine what kind of a linguistic system Newspeak might be.

Note that there is one further major difference between Basic and Newspeak. Basic was designed as a supplementary language existing alongside natural English and with specific in functions; Newspeak is intended to *replace* English as the sole language of Party members, the complete resource they could draw on for all communicative functions. The absurdity of carrying out all our discourse in a very restricted language is palpable.

Orwell almost certainly had in mind a famous parallel absurdity in *Gulliver's Travels*.[21] In Chapter 5 of Part 3, Gulliver visits the Academy of Lagado, the capital of Balnibarbi. The city and its inhabitants are, like London and the proles in *Nineteen Eighty-Four*, in a sorry state:

> The next Morning after my Arrival he took me in his Chariot to see the Town, which is about half the Bigness of *London*; but the Houses very strangely built, and most of them out of Repair. The People in the Streets walked fast, looked wild, their eyes fixed, and were generally in Rags. (*Gulliver's Travels*, p. 149)

The buildings and agriculture are ruinous because they are awaiting improved methods of construction and farming to be devised by members of the Academy (a satirical portrait of the Royal Society). The examples of the projects of the academicians which are presented to Gulliver are without exception preposterous and unworkable, such as could be devised only by an intellectual élite out of touch with commonsense reality (cf. the Party in our novel): extracting sunbeams from cucumbers, building houses from the roof down, dyeing cobwebs by feeding coloured flies to spiders, etc., etc. Two of the projects are linguistic:

> The first project was to shorten Discourse by cutting Polysyllables into one, and leaving out Verbs and Participles; because in Reality all things imaginable are but Nouns.
>
> The other, was a Scheme for entirely abolishing all Words whatsoever ... [S]ince Words are only Names for *Things*, it would be more convenient for all Men to carry about them, such *Things* as were necessary to express the particular Business they are to discourse on. And this Invention would certainly have taken place, to the great Ease as well as Health of the Subject, if the Women in Conjunction with the Vulgar and Illiterate had not threatened to raise a Rebellion, unless they might be allowed the Liberty to speak with their Tongues, after the Manner of their Forefathers: Such constant irreconcileable Enemies to Science are the common People. However, many of the most Learned and Wise adhere to the new Scheme of expressing themselves by *Things*; which hath only this Inconvenience attending it; that if a Man's Business be very great and of various Kinds, he must be obliged in Proportion to carry a greater *Bundle of Things* upon his Back, unless he can afford one or two strong Servants to attend him. (*Gulliver's Travels*, p. 158)

The reduction of language in the first scheme has some resemblance to the 'clipping' which I pointed out in the style of the 'hybrid jargon' of the Ministry of Truth, and to the merger of parts of speech in Newspeak. The uselessness of the second scheme has a closer relationship to Newspeak. Notice that, like Newspeak, this project is framed in a class distinction: only the 'most Learned and Wise', communicate through 'Things' carried on the back, as the Party members are to use Newspeak; the Lagado equivalent of the proles continue to use their tongues, as the proles retain Oldspeak. It is implied that the élite academicians, anticipating their Ingsoc descendants, are far from 'learned and wise', they are in fact utterly foolish to employ such an unworkable system of communication. Now the real inconveniences of Newspeak, as illuminated by this analogy, are the limitations of a finite system, and the lack of provision for flexibility of meaning. You can only carry so many 'Things' on, your back and in your pockets, and these are bound to be far less than the topics you will want to talk about: real human language is infinitely creative and cannot be replaced by a restricted set of

signs. Equally, meanings in natural language are flexible and abstract, quite
unlike the fixity and precision of the academicians' 'Things' or the fixed
concepts of Newspeak.[22]

These are just two of the fundamental problems which have not been
examined by the inventors of Newspeak. If we do not read the bland
academic prose of the Appendix too quickly, we will fetch up against other
assumptions which have not been thought through properly. Here is the
opening of the Appendix, quoted at length to give a reasonable flavour of its
style, with tendentious statements about narrowing the language and
thought which parallel the account by Syme quoted above:

> Newspeak was the official language of Oceania and had been
> devised to meet the ideological needs of Ingsoc, or English
> socialism. In the year 1984 there was not as yet anyone who used
> Newspeak as his sole means of communication, either in speech
> or writing. The leading articles in *The Times* were written in it,
> but this was a *tour de force* which could only be carried out by a
> specialist. It was expected that Newspeak would have finally
> superseded Oldspeak (or Standard English, as we should call it)
> by about the year 2050. Meanwhile it gained ground steadily, all
> Party members tending to use Newspeak words and grammatical
> constructions more and more in their everyday speech. The
> version in use in 1984, and embodied in the Ninth and Tenth
> editions of the Newspeak Dictionary, was a provisional one, and
> contained many superfluous words and archaic formations, which
> were due to be suppressed later. It is with the final, perfected
> version, as embodied in the Eleventh Edition of the Dictionary,
> that we are concerned here.
>
> The purpose of Newspeak was not only to provide a medium
> of expression for the world-view and mental habits proper to the
> devotees of Ingsoc, but to make all other modes of thought
> impossible. It was intended that when Newspeak had been
> adopted once and for all and Oldspeak forgotten, a heretical
> thought—that is, a thought diverging from the principles of
> Ingsoc—should be literally unthinkable, at least so far as thought
> is dependent on words. The vocabulary was so constructed as to
> give an exact and often very subtle expression to every meaning
> that a Party member could properly wish to express, while
> excluding all other meanings and also the possibility of arriving at
> them by indirect methods. This was done partly by the invention
> of new words, but chiefly by eliminating undesirable words and

by stripping such words as remained of unorthodox meanings. (*Nineteen Eighty-Four*, pp. 258–9)

This kind of plain expository language is not found anywhere else in the novel, though it bears some resemblance to the style of 'the book' passed by O'Brien to Winston, though that is much more authoritarian and argumentative. This style has no affinity to the more excitable and fragmentary thoughts and speech of the main focaliser Winston, nor to the demotic rhetoric of Orwell himself, as found in his passionately critical essays. The Newspeak Appendix could not be written in the familiar Orwellian voice, for that voice could not refrain from crying that the Newspeak proposal is cynical self-delusion, humbug, swindle and perversion. And this is not an official version issuing from the Party, since it is written in Oldspeak.

Orwell seems to have created a viewpoint which is both distinct from his own persona, and quite outside the world of the fiction. To say that this is the voice of 'the narrator' would be a cop-out, for we have seen that there is no distinguishable narrator in *Nineteen Eighty-Four*, and the novel is certainly not narrated in the manner in which the Appendix is phrased. The voice of the Appendix may plausibly be attributed to a new, distinct and anonymous figure with Gulliver-like characteristics: a traveller, or in modern terms an anthropologist or a linguist, who studies a foreign society and its products and reports with apparent objectivity what he sees and hears. Cues to this role include the pronoun 'we' used twice in the first paragraph. The first 'we' (line six) refers to the writer and his readership: Oldspeak is explained in terms of what it would be called in the 'home' culture, somewhat as Gulliver makes Lagado more comprehensible by comparing it to London. This is a minimal cue, but 'we' is a demanding word, encouraging the reader to participate by preferring Newspeak to the English of the 'real' culture. The second 'we', at the end of the paragraph, has a different meaning: it is the impersonal 'we' of science, suppressing an 'I' which might seem to flag personal intervention inappropriately.

There is no 'I' in the text; contrast the writings in the mode of Orwell's persona, which use it liberally. Overt modality, or judgement from the point of view of the writer, is minimal. It would have been entirely inappropriate to the style for the sentence at the end of the above extract to speak of '*ruthlessly* stripping' words of unorthodox meanings, though that is just the sort of thing Orwell would have said if he had been writing in his own personal voice. Such modal judgements as do occur, for example 'superfluous words and archaic formations' and 'perfected' at the end of the first paragraph, or 'proper' in the first sentence of the second paragraph, or 'And rightly so' on p. 264 referring to euphony taking precedence over grammatical regularity, are to be attributed to the sources the Appendix is reporting, and are to be read ironically.

The 'objective' style of science or factual reporting is also suggested, unobtrusively, by a high proportion of passive verbs and by some nominal forms replacing full verbs; both move personal involvement into the background: 'had been devised', 'were written', 'be carried out', 'embodied', 'to be suppressed', etc., and 'communication', 'medium of expression', 'invention'. The nominal style is not taken to extremes, and there is none of the polysyllabic, Greek- and Latin-derived technical terminology which typifies the style of science: the genre of the Appendix seems to be 'objective report' rather than 'science'.

Orwell follows Swift, then, in using a non-judgmental, matter-of-fact style to report a project which to him was not only absurd (displayed in Newspeak 'examples' which are so self-evidently barbarous, fatuous and trivial that illustration is hardly necessary), but worse, philosophically and morally ill-grounded. Showing through the plain style are unanswered and unqualified questions of the most fundamental kind. Philosophically, the proponents of Newspeak take an extreme nominalist position, believing that meanings derive from words, not the other way around. They add to this an extreme determinism—that is, they believe that thoughts are controlled by words. We saw in Chapter 3 that Orwell, like Winston, held the opposite point of view: a fundamental faith in solid objects and in individual thought, and a passionate conviction that language should be used in such a way as to communicate without deception these elemental priorities. Of course, 'realist' and 'individualist' arguments do not get a look-in in the Newspeak proposal, but we would expect that gap; what does come through as irresponsible is the total failure to examine any of the sweeping nominalist and deterministic assumptions that are trotted out in the text, for example, the beginning of the second paragraph.

It is worth adding, briefly, that because the Newspeak project is theoretically ill-founded, it is inherently impracticable. We are bound to wonder how it is proposed to abolish words, how you prevent the remaining words having illicit meanings, how even a regime as powerful as that of Oceania can stop the normal processes of invention, semantic enrichment and natural change. Language is indeed a powerful weapon in the hands of the rulers of an unequal society.[23] However, as Orwell believed and as Winston wanted to believe, it is also an effective instrument of challenge, developing naturally and largely outside the reach of governmental and artificial control. That is why restrictive and prescriptive official bodies such as the French Academy have always experienced an uphill struggle, and why, fortunately, no deliberately contrived artificial language has ever been successfully established as a natural form of speech acquired spontaneously by the next generation. Planned forms of language like Basic English never catch on; unofficial developments such as the codes of CB radio[24] may be short-lived, but have their period of intense significance as yet another challenge to the official monologism of our culture. Winston need not have been so pessimistic.

I think it is characteristic of Orwell's fundamental traditionalism and romanticism that, in the Newspeak Appendix, he lets literature have the last laugh on Newspeak. The natural creativity and the semantic openness, richness and suggestivity of a real language like English are exploited to the full in literary texts. These properties, as we have seen, are quite alien to Newspeak, whose basic drive is towards closure and explicitness. Every centralised nationalist regime needs a Literature to express its ideological essence; but in 1984, the National Literature part of the project looked set to defeat Newspeak:

> Considerations of prestige made it desirable to preserve the memory of certain historical figures, while at the same time bringing their achievements into line with the philosophy of Ingsoc. Various writers, such as Shakespeare, Milton, Swift, Byron, Dickens, and some others were therefore in the process of translation ... These translations were a slow and difficult business, and it was not expected that they would be finished before the first decade of the twenty-first century ... It was chiefly in order to allow time for the preliminary work of translation that the final adoption of Newspeak had been fixed for so late a date as 2050.

NOTES

17. Usually cited in this connection is Eugene Lyons, *Assignment in Utopia* (New York: Harcourt Brace, 1937), which Orwell reviewed in 1938 (*CEJL*, I, pp. 368–71). Lyons was a correspondent in Russia for the United Press Agency 1928–34. His book gives an example of cablese, p. 338; samples are printed in Steinhoff, *Orwell and the Origins of 'Nineteen Eighty-Four'* p. 169, and Crick, ed. p. 430. To confirm the influence of *Assignment in Utopia* on *Nineteen Eighty-Four*, note that Lyons quotes and discusses the formula '2 + 2 = 5' used by the Soviets to sloganise 'The Five-Year Plan in Four Years': see Crick, ed. *Orwell: Nineteen Eighty Four* p. 440 and, for more detail and a quotation from *Assignment*, Steinhoff, *Origins of Nineteen Eighty Four*, pp. 172–3.

18. On the peculiar and reality-changing features of news discourse, see A. Bell, *The Language of News Media* (Oxford: Blackwell, 1991); R. Fowler, *Language in the News* (London: Routledge, 1991).

19. See B. L. Whorf, *Language, Thought and Reality* ed. by J. B. Carroll (Cambridge, Mass.: MIT Press, 1956); R. Brown, *Words and Things* (New York: Free Press, 1958); H. H. Clark and E. V. Clark, *Psychology and Language* (New York: Harcourt Brace Jovanovich, 1977), chs. 13 and 14; R. Fowler, *Language in the News*, ch. 3.

20. A handy synopsis of Basic, together with a reproduction of the original 850-word vocabulary, is contained in D. Crystal, *The Cambridge Encyclopedia of Language* (Cambridge: Cambridge University Press, 1987) p. 356.

21. Jonathan Swift, *Gulliver's Travels* ed. by Robert A. Greenberg (New York: W. W. Norton, 1961).

22. Beyond these three comparisons of class-division, lack of creativity, and fixity of 'meaning', the analogy breaks down, of course, and it would be misleading to pursue it.

23. See R. Fowler, R. Hodge, G. Kress and T. Trew, *Language and Control* (London: Routledge & Kegan Paul, 1979); N. Fairclough, *Language and Power* (London: Longman, 1989).

24. On the jargon of CB radio as 'antilanguage,' see M. Montgomery, *An Introduction to Language and Society* (London: Routledge, 1986) pp. 93–101.

MALCOLM PITTOCK

The Hell of Nineteen Eighty-Four

Did Orwell realise quite what he had done in *Nineteen Eighty-Four*? His post-publication glosses on its meaning reveal either blankness or bad faith even about its contemporary political implications. He insisted, for example, that his 'recent novel [was] NOT intended as an attack on Socialism or on the British Labour Party (of which I am a supporter)'.[1] He may well not have intended it but that is what it can reasonably be taken to be. Warburg saw this immediately after he had read the manuscript, and predicted that *Nineteen Eighty-Four* '[was] worth a cool million votes to the Conservative Party';[2] the literary editor of the *Evening Standard* 'sarcastically prescribed it as "required reading" for Labour Party M.P.s',[3] and, in the US, the Washington branch of the John Birch Society 'adopted "1984" as the last four digits of its telephone number'.[4] Moreover, Churchill had made the 'inseparably interwoven' relation between socialism and totalitarianism a plank in his 1945 election campaign[5] (and was not the protagonist of *Nineteen Eighty-Four* called Winston?). If, ten years earlier, an Orwell had written a futuristic fantasy in which Big Brother had had Hitler's features rather than Stalin's, would not the Left, whatever the writer's proclaimed political sympathies, have welcomed it as showing how capitalism, by its very nature, led to totalitarian fascism?

From *Essays in Criticism* Vol. 47, No. 2 (April 1997). © 1997 by Oxford University Press.

With *Nineteen Eighty-Four*, it is particularly necessary to trust the tale and not the teller, but even this has its pitfalls. Interpretations of the novel already exist which blatantly ignore the intentions of the author by reinterpreting its manifest content without any obvious justification. But all existing interpretations of *Nineteen Eighty-Four* are unsatisfactory in one regard or another. For many years *Nineteen Eighty-Four* 'served as a sort of an ideological super-weapon in the Cold War',[6] was used along with *Animal Farm* as propaganda in the Western occupied zones of Germany, which it was 'feared ... might be invaded by Soviet troops',[7] and was later also made use of by West Germany as 'warning ... about what a future under Stalin might be like'.[8] There is much in the novel, of course, which allowed it to be interpreted as an attack on Soviet Communism and its allegedly aggressive intentions. Nonetheless, such an interpretation does not quite fit: Ingsoc has been established in Oceania by internal revolution and not by military invasion or external pressure. The model is Trotsky rather than Stalin.

With the slackening of the Cold War, there were attempts, notably by Orwell's first biographer, Bernard Crick, to claim that *Nineteen Eighty-Four* was directed as much at the West as at the East.[9] But whatever minor swipes at the West *Nineteen Eighty-Four* could be said to be taking (the regime's encouragement of pornography and gambling among the working-class for example), such an interpretation, at any rate on a literal level, is perverse—a perverseness exemplified by Crick's extraordinary claim that in the terrible last paragraph of the novel the 'two gin-scented tears' which trickled down the sides of Winston's nose represents 'comic distancing'.[10]

Beside these divergent political interpretations, there were others which sought to interpret *Nineteen Eighty-Four* non-politically as either a study of the mental illness of the protagonist or a psychological document revealing the obsessions of the author. The mental illness reading logically involves the reinterpretation of what seem to be objective characteristics of a totalitarian society as items in a subjective phantasmagoria. Nobody takes this the whole way, but in arguing in these pages that Winston is 'a text-book schizophrenic', Robert Currie has shown the extreme lengths to which critics of this persuasion are prepared to go.[11]

Those who interpret *Nineteen Eighty-Four* as the product of the author's own neuroses, as in Anthony West's celebrated claim that Oceania was merely Orwell's prep school St. Cyprian's writ large,[12] are on firmer ground in that such a view does not involve standing the novel on its head. Even so, it does not explain why the novel has been so enduringly successful and why 'dissident intellectuals' (in Eastern Europe) were '"amazed" that the writer who never lived in Russia should understand the system so well'.[13] To those who knew nothing of St. Cyprian's and the details of his life, it seemed that Orwell was writing about a real and familiar world, not about himself.

The work has received such divergent and apparently contradictory interpretations that something more than a simple determination to trust the tale is required. Any fresh interpretation must not only be able to account in principle for the existence of such divergent readings but offer to transcend them. In *Nineteen Eighty-Four* Orwell depicts a society which, strictly speaking, can never exist because its rulers have the kind of powers traditionally attributed to demons: the closed immobility of the society depends, that is, on its rulers having access to resources which human beings, however wicked and however ordinarily powerful, cannot command. Some subliminal awareness of this is behind the claims both of those who read it politically and those who read it psychologically. For the first, who do not allow themselves to realise that a line has been crossed, that awareness is precipitated as exaggeration of the possible, and *Nineteen Eighty-Four* interpreted as a satire.[14] For the second, who sense that impossibilities are involved, it is registered as a need to see the book as really about the delusions and phobias of the unbalanced, whether character or author, for phobias frequently embrace the impossible.

Nineteen Eighty-Four has successfully recreated the idea of hell and endowed it with an immediacy and significance which Milton and Dante (whose *Divine Comedy* Orwell was reading in the last year of his life) can no longer command. Though for us, unlike Dante and Milton, hell and its demons are a fable, *Nineteen Eighty-Four*, by transcending the limitations of the cultural and political context of its immediate origin, provides an objective correlative of this century's 'return to what our nineteenth-century ancestors would have called the standards of barbarism'.[15] Millions of human beings have been the trapped and helpless victims of the pitiless, relentless and yet frequently insouciant cruelty of their fellows: on the ground or from the air. Fiends could scarcely have had more immediate power or behaved worse.

In *Nineteen Eighty-Four* variations of the same inhuman civilization are represented as global (though their ideological bases are not necessarily the same) and the cruelty manifested by O'Brien has historical precedent. His resemblance to an Inquisitor has been frequently remarked (though his electrical assaults on Winston's brain are those of modern psychiatry) and the torture in Room 101 stretches from Imperial China to the late twentieth century where torture victims can be 'exposed to the gnawing of rats through a tube inserted up the anus or vagina'.[16]

That in *Nineteen Eighty-Four* the regime is in some sense Satanic has, of course, been widely perceived. O'Brien has been compared to

Mephistopheles the celebrant in his flat of a kind of Black Mass with wine, wafer and ritual. However, such parallels are clearly regarded as metaphorical. Alone among the interpreters of *Nineteen Eighty-Four*, the millennial fundamentalists have realised that actual demonic powers are involved.[17] For them *Nineteen Eighty-Four* is a depiction of the reign of Antichrist foretold in the First and Second Epistle of Peter and in Revelation, 13.

I am not claiming that Orwell consciously set out to give the regime demonic powers: indeed, part of the effect of the novel may well depend on neither author nor reader allowing themselves to be explicitly aware of it. Orwell may have been in unconscious collusion with the details of his own fiction as readers of the torture scenes have sometimes uneasily suspected. Anthony West's approach to the novel reminds us how much of Orwell went into it: not only St. Cyprian's, but his sadism, his imperial guilt, his sexual encounters (some of them clearly sordid), his fear of atomic war, his Cold War hysteria,[18] and his experience of Communist tactics in Spain and of censorship at the BBC; his revulsion at rats;[19] his previous support for non-democratic socialist revolution;[20] his war-time suppression of his own previous anti-war position;[21] his support for the bombing of German cities,[22] his terminal illness, his pastoral nostalgia—the list could be extended. And yet, by transformation, transference, and substitution all these disparate experiences not only help to form a coherent whole but give to the novel a complex resonance unique both in Orwell's own fiction and in Utopian or Distopian literature generally.

Such complexity of origin, particularly if it involves elements of emotional collusion, does not make for clear awareness of exactly what one is doing. Orwell may have believed the novel's official position, that what the regime knows about Winston and Julia is merely the result of a combination of an extraordinarily effective system of surveillance and matching technology. Since, however, the whole of the action of *Nineteen Eighty-Four* is focalised through Winston Smith even this lacks final endorsement by an impartial narrator.

> He knew that ... the Thought Police had watched him like a beetle under a magnifying glass. There was no physical act, no word spoken aloud, that they had not noticed, no train of thought that they had not been able to infer. (p. 289)

The use of 'infer' keeps this within the limits of the humanly possible: the regime '"can't get inside you"' (p. 174). But when Julia and Winston made love in the clearing, they had specifically noted that the surrounding ash saplings were not 'big enough to hide a mike in' (p. 125). How then did the regime know what they said and did there? Because the aptly named Thought Police *can* 'get inside you'. They can know what you are thinking—and dreaming; they have telepathic powers including the power of suggestion, and they can know the future. With such powers at their command no one can stand against them and no one ever does ('Nobody ever escaped detection, and nobody ever failed to confess', p. 107). Individually, the rulers may die but the regime's immortality is symbolised by the mysterious figure of Big Brother (who provides the frisson of the diabolically numinous). '"Of course not"' (p. 272) is O'Brien's answer to Winston's question as to whether Big Brother would ever die. *Nineteen Eighty-Four* is a hell without a countervailing heaven: the reign of Antichrist for ever, not as a preliminary to the New Jerusalem. There are no angels, only devils.

That the regime is Satanic emerges in O'Brien's revelation of its objectives. They are not what Winston expected: 'He knew in advance what O'Brien would say. That the Party did not seek power for its own ends, but only for the good of the majority' (p. 274). But O'Brien does not say this at all: the explicit aim of the regime is to have power to cause pain and suffering for their own sake. '"If you want a picture of the future, imagine a boot stamping on a human face—for ever"' (p. 280). That has the authentic Satanic ring: 'Evil be thou my Good'.[23] Winston's expectations were nevertheless reasonable. All merely human regimes, however ruthless and wicked, always claim that their goal is some collective good. That was as true of Hitler as it was of Stalin. Significantly, the brainwashed Winston during his course of 're-education', writes on his slate: 'GOD IS POWER' (p. 290), the only strictly theological proposition in the novel. Antichrist indeed!

There are two crucial pieces of evidence that the regime commands the power to match its aims. The first exhibits its powers of telepathic suggestion. In the torture sequence, O'Brien tells Winston, '"For seven years I have watched over you"' (p. 256). Seven years before[24] Winston 'had dreamed that he was walking through a pitch-dark room. And someone sitting to one side of him had said as he passed 'We shall meet in the place where there is no darkness'.... It was O'Brien who had spoken to him out of the dark' (p. 27). When at O'Brien's flat Winston refers to the words of the prophecy, O'Brien behaves 'as though he had recognised the allusion' (p. 185)—the prophecy being a typical example of the way, as Macbeth complains, 'these juggling fiends ... palter with us in a double sense'. For Winston 'The place where there is no darkness was the imagined future, which one would never see, but which, by foreknowledge, one could mystically share in' (p. 107); what O'Brien is really referring to is the perpetually illuminated cells of the Ministry of Love. O'Brien's ultimate power, the power to break Winston, depends on his direct access to levels of Winston's mind which he himself cannot reach. Winston has a recurring nightmare: 'It was always very much the same. He was standing in front of a wall of darkness, and on the other side of it there was something unendurable, something too dreadful to be faced.... He always woke up without discovering what it was' (p. 151). O'Brien not only knows about Winston's dream, but also knows what Winston is repressing.

> 'Do you remember,' said O'Brien, 'the moment of panic that used to occur in your dreams? ... There was something terrible on the other side of the wall. You knew that you knew what it was, but you dared not drag it into the open. It was the rats that were on the other side of the wall.' (p. 297)

It is this knowledge that he uses to destroy Winston in Room 101. Julia has apparently succumbed in the same way:

> 'Sometimes', she said, 'they threaten you with something— something you can't stand up to, can't even think about. And then you say, "Don't do it to me, do it to somebody else, do it to so-and-so" ...' (p. 305)

The regime clearly has ultimate power over everyone because of its direct knowledge of inner weakness.

Once it has been conceded that the regime is shown as commanding special powers, the landscape of *Nineteen Eighty-Four* significantly alters and the clichés of conventional exposition need considerable revision. Take, for example, the well-known motif of the paperweight as expounded in a handbook on the novel aimed at Open University students: 'It is the paperweight, especially old and beautiful, that symbolises not just the past but the difference of the past, and by implication a past that was not only different but better and inviolable'.[25] This reading fails to account for the significance of the fact that Winston lights upon the paperweight in Mr. Charrington's shop, that it is Mr. Charrington who talks it up—'"It is a beautiful thing ... But there's not many that'd say so nowadays"' (p. 99)—and that it is Mr. Charrington who offers to sell it. Charrington turns out to be a member of the Thought Police, and there hangs about him the suggestion of a shape-shifting demon, who changes from the vaguely affable and bumbling old man of sixty-three to one who

... was not the same person any longer. His body had straightened, and seemed to have grown bigger. His face had undergone only tiny changes that had nevertheless worked a complete transformation. The black eyebrows were less bushy, the wrinkles were gone, the whole lines of the face seemed to have altered; even the nose seemed shorter. It was the alert cold face of a man of about five-and-thirty. (pp. 233–234)

The text may try to convey the impression that there is nothing here which is beyond the normal process of disguise but some details call this into question: 'His body ... seemed to have grown bigger ... the nose seemed shorter'.

What commentators never seem to take into account is the evidence that Charrington knew that Winston was coming before Winston himself did. Winston buys the 'peculiarly beautiful book' with 'the smooth creamy paper', which is to serve as his diary, from what he thinks is 'a frowzy little junk-shop in a slummy quarter of the town'. Having seen it 'lying in the window', he had been 'stricken immediately by an overwhelming desire to possess it' (p. 8). This clearly implies that the secret police had already set up and stocked the fake junkshop knowing that Winston would visit it, and would see its obviously carefully chosen wares as embodying a reality and values rooted in the past which he would regard as inimical to the very regime which established it to have exactly that appeal to him. The paperweight, the engraving of St. Clement Danes (behind which there lurks a telescreen), the bric-à-brac of the shop, and the persona of the shopkeeper himself, 'another extinct animal', have all been carefully chosen in advance. It is Mr. Charrington who introduces Winston to 'Oranges and Lemons' (though he pretends to remember only the first line and part of the second) which stimulates Winston to imagine the bells of a lost London: 'From one ghostly steeple after another he seemed to hear them pealing forth' (p. 103). In O'Brien's flat, Winston associates the 'dark-red liquid' which is to be used in the Black Mass with 'the glass paperweight of Mr. Charrington's half-remembered rhyme' as belonging 'to a vanished, romantic past' (p. 178). Moreover, O'Brien can quote the whole of the nursery rhyme stanza (p. 186).

Most significantly of all, at the very time when Winston believes Julia to be an enemy, a room has already been prepared for their liaison, with its mahogany double bed, its gate-leg table, its old-fashioned twelve hour clock (which is to help to betray Winston and Julia) and its concealed telescreen. It is Mr. Charrington who draws the room to Winston's attention ('"There's another room upstairs"', p. 100).

Although the regime can command supernatural powers, there is still a measure of uncertainty as to how far at any other stage Winston and Julia are being manipulated. It is this very uncertainty which gives the novel some of its terrible power. I am never quite sure how far Winston has any freedom at all (and this is, I think, felt even by those readers who do not allow themselves to be conscious that diabolic powers are involved). The Golden Country motif, for instance, is not so clear a case as Mr. Charrington's shop, but there are certain features which point to the collusion of the regime in its creation.

Winston has another dream of a landscape that 'recurred so often ... that he was never fully certain whether or not he had seen it in the real world' (pp. 32–33), but after he becomes aware of Julia for the first time it has a new element:

> The girl with dark hair was coming towards him across the field. With what seemed a single movement she tore off her clothes and flung them disdainfully aside.... With its grace and carelessness it seemed to annihilate a whole culture, a whole system of thought, as though Big Brother and the Party and the Thought Police could all be swept into nothingness by a single splendid movement of the arm. (p. 33)

This dream of Julia in the Golden Country occurs at a time when Winston believes that she is an ultra-orthodox party member who is probably spying on him to betray him to the very regime which her dream image appeared with a gesture to annihilate. This discrepancy, though improbable, is not psychologically impossible since Winston's underlying awareness of Julia's attitude to him and the Party could be different from the conclusions of his conscious mind. The most significant thing about Winston's dream, however, is that it is predictive: at his first and only open air tryst with Julia, Winston experiences 'a curious, slow shock of recognition' when he sees the spot to which Julia had taken him. 'He knew it by sight' (p. 129). Moreover, he correctly predicts that close by would be a stream with green pools where dace were swimming. As Winston says: 'It's the Golden Country—almost'. And Julia behaves 'almost' as in his dream: 'She flung [her clothes] aside ... with the same magnificent gesture by which a whole civilisation seemed to be annihilated' (p. 131).

The repetition of 'almost' might be regarded as an attempt to claim that there is nothing here but the workings of the (very) long arm of coincidence, but the most likely explanation is that the dream of the Golden Country is sent by the regime itself. Not only do they know in advance of

Winston's affair with Julia, but they know where it is to receive its first consummation and the challenge to the regime it will represent for him. But it is this very regime which again has provided Winston with the illusion of an effective alternative reality and an alternative value system to itself, so that the discovery that there are none will be all the more terrible. The two 'almosts' are, moreover, significant signs of the demonic, for fiends could not predict the future with absolute accuracy.

Significantly, the Golden Country motif only recurs after Winston is in the Ministry of Love and it, or landscapes associated with it, now include representatives of the regime ('He was in the Golden Country, or he was sitting among enormous, glorious, sunlit ruins, with his mother, with Julia, with O'Brien', p. 288), or are contained within an enormously expanded Ministry of Love ('He was rolling down a mighty corridor, a kilometre wide, full of glorious golden light,' p. 255). But at one point the Golden Country recurs almost in its original form:

> He was not any longer in the narrow white corridors of the Ministry of Love, he was in the enormous sunlit passage, a kilometre wide, down which he had seemed to walk in the delirium induced by drugs. He was in the Golden Country, following the foot-track across the old rabbit-cropped pasture. He could feel the short springy turf under his feet and the gentle sunshine on his face. At the edge of the field were the elm trees, faintly stirring, and somewhere beyond that was the stream where the dace lay in the green pools under the willows.
> Suddenly he started up with a shock of horror. The sweat broke out on his backbone. He had heard himself cry aloud:
> 'Julia! Julia! Julia, my love! Julia!'
> For a moment he had had an overwhelming hallucination of her presence. She had seemed to be not merely with him, but inside him. It was as though she had got onto the texture of his skin. In that moment he had loved her far more than he had ever done when they were together and free. Also he knew that somewhere or other she was still alive and needed his help. (pp. 292–293)

Winston's calling out gives O'Brien the opportunity to take him into Room 101. His is not, I think, a spontaneous dream and reaction (one may notice 'the enormous sunlit passage a kilometre wide', which is clearly associated with the Ministry of Love, and his horror at calling out). The regime wanted Winston to have the illusion of complete union with the beloved which is the supreme goal of romantic love in order that he may be made to destroy it.

Ambiguities in her presentation suggest that, though subjectively Julia is committed to Winston, yet objectively she is an agent of entrapment, a means by which Winston may be encouraged to glimpse the possibility of a different more human world so that it can be sadistically snatched away from him and lead to his destruction. So marked are these ambiguities that they have prompted Robert Currie to maintain that Julia really *could* be an agent of the Thought Police[26] (and, certainly, a first-time reader might well suspect up to the end of Part 2, that she is going to be unmasked as one). At first, Winston suspects her, but her 'I love you' note rightly convinces him otherwise. Nonetheless, O'Brien accosts Winston and gives him his address 'almost at the spot where Julia has slipped the note into his hand' (p. 164), while she frightens Winston by her inexplicable appearance in the vicinity of Charrington's shop (p. 104). Moreover, if Charrington supplies the first one-and-a-half lines of 'Oranges and Lemons' and O'Brien finally completes the stanza, it is Julia who provides the ending: 'Here comes a candle to light you to bed, here comes a chopper to chop off your head' (p. 153) which Charrington, in his true identity of Thought Policeman, mockingly repeats (p. 231). Winston's second intimate meeting with Julia is also associated with the nursery rhyme, being in 'the belfry of a ruinous church' (p. 134). And it is Julia who tries to give Winston the information about the behaviour of rats (p. 151) which O'Brien is to threaten him with in Room 101.

Even more suggestive of the probability that the regime is using her for its own purposes is the way she appears to bear a charmed life. Though 'The unforgivable crime was promiscuity between Party members' (p. 68) she has been indulging in such unforgivable conduct since she was sixteen, and it is obviously inconceivable that this would not have been known to the regime. What to Winston was 'the Golden Country almost' appears to have been a customary rendezvous for her ('"I've been here before"' p. 125). Julia appears to have no trouble in obtaining Party luxuries—real chocolate, real coffee, real sugar, real tea, as well as a loaf of bread and a pot of jam—which minister to Winston's sense of nostalgia. And, equally mysteriously, she manages to obtain cosmetics, scent, a frock, silk stockings, and high-heeled shoes.

More problematic is the extent to which Winston is programmed to believe that the Proles represent a hope for the future. It is certainly the burden of the book, and, though Winston does not have the opportunity to read so far, 'he knew that that must be Goldstein's final message. The future belonged to the proles' (p. 229). O'Brien, who has actually written the book, knows that Winston '"foresaw ... what it would say"' (p. 274). (Naturally, he has direct knowledge of how much Winston had actually read.) O'Brien has thus set a trap for Winston, for as he says, '"The proletarians will never revolt, not in a thousand years or a million ... The Rule of the Party is for ever"' (p. 274). In view of the demonic powers available to the Party he must be right. The point about hell is that it is 'for ever'.

There is also evidence of a more direct interference. The proletarian woman hanging out the washed diapers becomes for Winston a symbol of the future:

> The mystical reverence that he felt for her was somehow mixed up with the aspect of the pale, cloudless sky, stretching away behind the chimney pots into interminable distances.... And the people under the sky were also very much the same—everywhere, all over the world, hundreds of thousands of millions of people, just like this, people ignorant of one another's existence, held apart by walls of hatred and lies, and yet almost exactly the same—people who had never learned to think but who were storing up in their hearts and bellies and muscles the power that would one day overturn the world. (p. 229)

That there is something false and illusory about such euphoria is due not only to its general vagueness but to Winston's gross overestimate of the population of the world, 'hundreds of thousands of millions of people', and to the fact that the 'pale cloudless sky' is not as he thinks the sky of evening but that of morning (an inversion of the usual symbolism). Even more to the point, however, the woman is singing in the yard behind Charrington's shop, the very yard in which the thugs of the regime are to plant their ladders, and the song she sings is mechanically produced prolefeed. Almost immediately after this 'vision' the regime strikes, having ensured that Winston and Julia will oversleep and will misjudge the time because they have been provided with a twelve-hour clock (such are the uses of nostalgia). As before, Winston is lifted up so that he may be thrown down the harder.

But depicting the regime as having demonic powers is not enough: a demonic mode of consciousness has also to be created which can make credible O'Brien's statement of its nihilistic aims. This Orwell succeeds in doing through the concept of doublethink: 'the power of holding two contradictory beliefs in one's mind simultaneously, and accepting both of them' (p. 223). This is a key feature of Oceanic society but the sort practised by O'Brien and the Inner Party is so different in degree as to involve a difference in kind. Outside the Inner party doublethink is merely an extreme form of the phenomenon known to psychologists as cognitive dissonance.

The Victorian murderer, Dr. Pritchard, who wrote in his diary 'Died here at 1 a.m. Mary Jane, my own beloved wife'[27] a few hours after poisoning her, shows to what lengths cognitive dissonance can be taken even in a domestic context. Nor is it uncommon in the public and political world. 'Peace is our Profession', the legend inscribed over the entrances of US bomber bases in Britain in the Fifties and Sixties, is unnervingly close to *Nineteen Eighty-Four*'s 'War is Peace', while 'Freedom is Slavery' could be a sardonic summing up of the contradictory beliefs of a Simon Legree who venerated the Declaration of Independence while simultaneously believing that it was right to treat black citizens as chattels.

Outside the Inner Party, doublethink is not even consistent. If one has no serious interest in politics, which is true not only of the Proles but of a member of the Outer Party like Julia, then one does not live at the level at which doublethink really operates. Julia's public life is, indeed, one long pretence and 'during the two minutes Hate her great difficulty was to avoid bursting out laughing' (p. 160). But even an apparently cheerfully orthodox nullity like Parsons can't control his deeper awareness and is arrested for saying 'Down with Big Brother' (p. 245) in his sleep. Similarly, if all the members of the Outer Party had really believed that Oceania had always been at war with Eastasia, would they have spontaneously returned to their desks at the Ministry of Truth (p. 184)? They knew that an enormous job of falsification lay ahead.

With O'Brien it is, however, different. With him Orwell has to convince us of the existence of a state of mind which in human terms is inconceivable since it involves not only logical contradiction but the potentiality of infinite regress. As the book demonstrates, O'Brien has the ability to analyse how the regime functions, including the place in it of perpetual warfare and doublethink, in a way that is objectively true O'Brien indeed admits that 'Goldstein's' account is true '"as a description"' (p. 246)—while at the same time believing that what he has shown to be true is false, even though the true account had shown not only the falsity of the false account but its social function. That this involves the potentiality of infinite regress can be shown by reducing the particulars of what is involved to abstract variables:

(a) O'Brien, the Inner Party member, knows that x is not y, but knowing that x is not y, he believes all the more certainly that x is y (O'Brien knows).

(b) 'Goldstein' (i.e. O'Brien) knows that O'Brien, the Inner Party member, knows that x is not y, but knowing that x is not y, he believes all the more certainly that x is y (O'Brien knows that O'Brien knows).

This is Orwell at his most brilliant. O'Brien's position is thus compatible with the traditional idea of Satan as both supremely intelligent (Winston is in awe of O'Brien's superior intellect and believes that his mind contains his own, p. 268), and completely alienated both from the good and from truth and reality, which, since he can appear as an angel of light, he can nonetheless comprehend. The self-consciously lucid and regressive contradictions of diabolic consciousness are impossible for ordinary human beings to combat, as Winston finds. Nonetheless, the novel makes such a diabolic consciousness credible by relating it to the historically familiar. The Inquisition, evoked in the torture and interrogation scenes, believed in effect that the truth could be defined socially—as being what a human organisation said it was, and so confused received opinion with fact. When this was carried to the point, as with Galileo, that correct fact was treated as false opinion which had to be 'corrected' by adherence to an incorrect fact which was itself merely a false opinion, one is getting reasonably close to O'Brien. Indeed when the latter says, '"The earth is the centre of the universe. The sun and the stars go round it"' (p. 278), we are surely meant to be reminded of the trial of Galileo. O'Brien's claim that nothing exists outside the human mind can be related to the extreme idealism characteristic of Berkeley's position, 'that only minds and mental events can exist',[28] while for philosophers like Quine and Rorty who challenge the distinction between synthetic and analytic propositions, two and two is not necessarily four. Perhaps the more telling parallel occurs when O'Brien claims that he '"could float off this floor like a soap bubble if [he] wished to"' (p. 277)—a kind of demonic inversion (going up) of Christ's refusal to cast himself down from the pinnacle of the temple (going down).

The inescapable logic of the novel is that it would be impossible for anyone to escape the clutches of the regime with life and integrity intact. For anyone even to preserve himself morally he would have to be perfect. Although in actual societies there are always amazing human beings whose inner integrity nothing seems to be able to break down, in Oceania martyrdom is impossible. Moreover, leaving aside the special powers available to the regime, any would-be rebel is disabled from the start. Formed by an inhuman society, he will already be infected by it because he is serving its purposes. Winston grasps the significance of the systematic falsification of the past by the regime, but he is not only actively engaged in it but actually enjoys it ('Winston's greatest pleasure in life was his work' p. 46). And in his loving creation of the nonexistent Comrade Ogilvy, he not only falsities the past himself but furthers the perverse values of the regime, praising Ogilvy's betrayal of his family ('At eleven he had denounced his uncle to the Thought Police' p. 49). The would-be rebel has no access to any normative moral ideas and is habituated to callousness by public hangings and by the depiction and celebration of atrocities. Winston regrets not having murdered his wife ('"On the whole I'm sorry I didn't"', p. 141), a regret Julia shares ('"Why didn't you give her a good shove? I would have"' p. 141). He kicks a hand severed at the wrist into the gutter (pp. 87–8). She thinks it was '"a good job"' (p. 137) that her first lover committed suicide.

Because Winston reached adolescence before Ingsoc had come to power, he has, through memory, some conception of older values beyond the power of the regime to originate. For Winston 'the enveloping, protecting gesture of [his mother's] arm' is a sign of disinterested love, 'a kind of nobility, a kind of purity, simply because the standards that she obeyed were private ones' (p. 171)—though it is characteristic of the darkness of the novel that the possibility that his mother has become the alcoholic wreck who vomits copiously on the floor of the cell in the Ministry of Love is left open (p. 239). He believes these standards are still to be found among the Proles. He has a very early memory of the 'grief ... genuine and unbearable' of an old gin-sodden man, perhaps for the loss of his granddaughter (p. 35).[29] It was a proletarian woman, too, who had protested in the cinema against the gloating depiction of an atrocity involving a woman and child. His callous comment—'typical prole reaction' (p. 11) is made before he had been sensitised by recovered memories of his mother.

Julia, however, 'had grown up in the world of the Revolution, knowing nothing else' (p. 138) and, as a result, has no interest in truth and value at all. Her dismissive comment on Winston's affecting story of his childhood betrayal of his mother and sister—'"I expect you were a beastly little swine in those days"' (p. 171)—shows an insensitive incomprehension of the human meaning Winston had been trying to convey. She is, as Winston says, '"only a rebel from the waist downwards"' (p. 163), though such a rebellion (which, as I have suggested, is actually permitted by the Party) at least ensures that since her sexuality is not repressed, she is detached from the sexually based hysteria promoted by the Party, and is consequently immune from the hatred that it fuels.

Winston's relationship with Julia enabled him to recover buried memories of his mother and to register his own progress ('he remembered ... how a few weeks ago he had seen a severed hand lying on the pavement and had kicked it into the gutter as though it had been a cabbage stalk' p. 172). However, because his memories are also of betrayal, they serve the purposes of the regime by making future betrayals more likely as they constitute a consciousness of inner weakness. The regime plays on this by ensuring that the little room over Mr. Charrington's shop is associated with the dark bedroom where his mother spent her days, through the association of both with 'the glass paperweight and the steel engraving in a rosewood frame' (p. 186). The regime also mockingly ensures that Winston's only recollection of a happy family occasion should occur after his capitulation, when he identifies it as a 'false memory' (p. 309).

The basis of the regime's power in the perverse sublimation of repressed sexuality—'sexual privation induces hysteria, which was desirable because it could be transformed into war-fever and leader-worship' (p. 139)—is a major factor in perverting Winston's rebellion. Since in Winston's case the sublimation is imperfect, the distorted sexuality becomes unstable in its effects. When he inaugurates his rebellion by writing his diary, the deteriorating handwriting and the breakdown in punctuation and capitalisation indicate that what he records is beyond his conscious control: 'while he sat helplessly musing he had been writing as though by automatic action' (p. 20). Through the frigidity of his wife, Winston had already experienced on a personal level the socially induced sexual repression which has led to squalid visits to prostitutes (pp. 70ff) and a proneness to fantasies of sadistic lust (p. 17) as when he first noticed Julia and believed her to be unobtainable. Later he actually thinks of smashing her skull with the paperweight (p. 103)—so much for that sentimentalised symbol. That his feeling for Julia begins in this way means that their relationship, whatever genuine value it may embody, is shadowed by it. Julia is associated with the prostitute through the cheap violet scent which they both wear and, at their first tryst, Winston is thrilled by the idea of Julia's promiscuity. He wants her to have been a veritable Messalina—'scores of times she had done it; he wished it had been hundreds—thousands' (p. 131). That his emotions never escape from their beginnings is shown by the way in which, after projecting into him a hallucination of romantic identity with Julia, the regime makes sure that his early feelings return: '"Do it to Julia! Not me!"', he shouts in Room 101, '"Tear her face off, ... strip her to the bones"' (p. 300), a clear reprise of the sadistic erotic fantasy with which the relationship had begun.

The instability of Winston's sublimation means that his feelings about Big Brother are unstable too: 'at such moments his heart went out to the lonely, derided heretic on the screen.... And yet the very next instant ... his secret loathing of Big Brother changed into adoration' (p. 17). He transfers the feelings he is supposed to have for Big Brother (and ends up really having) to O'Brien: 'A wave of admiration, almost of worship, flowed out from Winston towards O'Brien' (p. 182); 'it was impossible to believe that he could be defeated' (p. 183). This feeling survives the experience of O'Brien as torturer ('He was the tormentor, he was the protector, he was the inquisitor, he was the friend' (p. 256). Not only masochism, but repressed homosexuality is involved here.

The corrupt elements in Winston's motivation lead him, despite his new-found moral awareness, and unprompted by torture, overt pressure or telepathic suggestion, to put himself in the moral pocket of the regime. The title of the phantom opposition group, the Brotherhood, which he thinks he is joining, significantly echoes Big Brother, and to further its cause he allows himself to be tricked into promising 'to lie, to steal, to forge, to murder, to encourage drug-taking and prostitution, to disseminate venereal diseases, to throw vitriol in a child's face' (p. 283). As that last horrible promise shows, the destructive power of the regime is greater than the human creativity he had learned from his mother, and his surrender to it is of his own free will. It is the regime's greatest triumph over him, prefigured perhaps in the locket containing 'a strand of long-dead baby's hair' (p. 158) which Mr. Charrington had thoughtfully provided among the bric-à-brac of his bogus shop. Earlier in the 'Golden Country—almost' he had not needed O'Brien's prompting to utter his own proleptic version of the regime's nihilistic credo: '"I hate purity. I hate goodness. I don't want virtue to exist anywhere. I want everyone to be corrupt to the bones"' (p. 132).

He has already sunk to the hellish level of that which he is opposing.

NOTES

1. 'Letter to Francis A. Henson' [extract]. *The Collected Essays; Journalism, and Letters of George Orwell*, ed. Sonia Orwell and Ian Angus (Harmondsworth, 1970), Vol. 4, p. 564.

2. Quoted in Bernard Crick, *George Orwell: A Life*, New ed. (Harmondsworth, 1992), p. 567.

3. See John Rodden, *The Politics of Literary Reputation. The Making and Claiming of 'St. George' Orwell* (Oxford, 1989), p. 26.

4. Ibid., p. 27.

5. See Alan Sked and Chris Cook, *Post-War Britain, A Political History*, 2nd ed. (Harmondsworth, 1984), pp. 20–21.

6. See '"1984"—The Mysticism of Cruelty' in Isaac Deutscher, *Heretics and Renegades, and Other Essays* (1955), p. 35.

7. John Rodden, *The Politics of Literary Reputation*, op. cit., p. 289.

8. Ibid., p. 292. The United States can be seen as the true driving force. See the title of Dean Acheson's State Department memorandum, 'Participation of Books in Department's Fight against Communism', ibid., p. 434.

9. George Orwell, *1984*, with a critical introduction and annotations (Oxford, 1984), passim. W. J. West in *The Larger Evils. Nineteen Eighty-Four: the Truth behind the Satire* (Edinburgh, 1992), argues that the novel is a kind of coded expose of Orwell's own experience of wartime Britain (and particularly of the BBC). It is of course true that Orwell did make use of many features of life in Britain during and after the war—flying bombs, war damage, shortages and rationing, for example—but these are not at the core of the novel.

10. Ibid., p. 55. Conor Cruise O'Brien took Crick severely to task in 'When re-reading "1984" has to stop', *Observer*, 25 March 1984, p. 7.

11. 'The "Big Truth" in *Nineteen Eighty-Four*', *Essays in Criticism*, XXXIV, 1 (1984), 56–69, p. 57; p. 61. See also Richard I. Smyer, *Primal Dream and Primal Crime: Orwell's Development as a Psychological Novelist* (University of Missouri, 1979), p. 143 'the Party itself is part of Winston's own psyche'.

12. See *The Politics of Literary Reputation*, op. cit., p. 114.

13. Ibid., p. 211.

14. For this they had Orwell's authority (see Crick, *George Orwell*, op. cit., p. 569). If *Nineteen Eighty-Four* is a satire, then *King Lear* is a comedy.

15. Eric Hobsbawm, *Age of Extremes: The Short Twentieth Century 1914–1921* (1994), p. 13. The period 1914–1990 is 'the most murderous era so far recorded in history' with 187 million killed. See also Norman Geras, 'Human Nature and Progress', *New Left Review*, 213, Sept/Oct 1995, 151–160, p. 152, quoting an article by Hobsbawm.

16. Norman Geras, 'Human Nature and Human Progress', *NLR*, op. cit., p. 152.

17. See *The Politics of Literary Reputation*, op. cit., pp. 259–260. One of their telling points is the regime's 'capacity to "get inside you" as only Satan and the Thought Police can'.

18. See Crick, *George Orwell*, op. cit., p. 556, for his McCarthyite list of Communist subversives. See also Warburg's press release, ibid., pp. 565–566, based on Orwell's statements to him, which expressed fears of what can only be described as a Communist takeover of the Labour Party.

19. 'If there is one thing I hate more than another it is a rat running over me in the darkness', *Homage to Catalonia* (Harmondsworth, 1966), p. 81.

20. See *Homage to Catalonia* passim and 'The Lion and the Unicorn', *Collected Essays*, etc., Vol. 2, 74–134, p. 126.

21. See Raymond Williams, *Politics and Letters*, Interviews with *New Left Review* (1979), p. 392.

22. See 'As I Please', *Collected Essays*, Vol. 3, 213–214.

23. In his war-time diary Orwell writes as follows: 'War is simply a reversal of civilized life; its motto is "Evil be thou my good"'. *Collected Essays*, Vol. 2, p. 396.

24. Seven is a significant number in symbolic numerology and is particularly prominent in theological contexts. There are seven deadly sins, seven sacraments, seven penitential psalms, and in Revelations sevens come thick and fast: thus in chapter one alone there are references to the seven churches, the seven spirits, the seven golden candlesticks, the seven stars.

25. Jenni Calder, *Animal Farm and Nineteen Eighty-Four* (Open University Press, 1987), p. 60.

26. 'The "Big Truth" in *Nineteen Eighty-Four*', *E in C*, loc. cit., p. 66.

27. See W. L. Burn, *The Age of Equipoise* (1964), pp. 43–4.

28. Bertrand Russell, *History of Western Philosophy* (1961), p. 632.

29. This incident—a sign of how closely the novel is worked—resonates with the famous last paragraph. Both Winston and the old man are gin-sodden; both weep. But the old man's tears are a sign of his humanity, Winston's of the loss of his.

STEVEN CARTER

The Masks of Passion

Present, I freeze; absent, my desire is hot.
—*Petrarch*

For you I would build a whole new universe but you obviously find it cheaper to rent one. Eurydice did too. She went back to hell unsure of what kind of other house Orpheus would build. "I call it death-in-life and life-in-death." Shot
In the back by an arrow, President Kennedy seemed to stiffen for a moment before he assumed his place in history. Eros
Do that.
I gave you my imaginary hand and you give me your imaginary hand and we walk together (in imagination) over the earthly ground.
—*Jack Spicer*

Being in love casts out love.
—*James Liddy*

I

Julia, Orwell's sexually active female protagonist in *Nineteen Eighty-Four*, is a member of the Anti-Sex League, an organization that requires its adherents

From *A Do-It-Yourself Dystopia: The Americanization of Big Brother*. © 2000 by University Press of America, Inc.

to wear scarlet sashes around their waists. Julia, a realist and a pragmatist, has few illusions about the hidden agendas of the Anti-Sex League:

> "When you make love you're using up energy; and afterwards you feel happy and don't give a damn for anything. They can't bear you to feel like that. They want you to be bursting with energy all the time. All this marching up and down and cheering and waving flags is simply sex gone sour." (89)

Winston agrees:

> That was very true, he thought. There was a direct, intimate connection between chastity and political orthodoxy. For how could the fear, the hatred, and the lunatic credulity which the Party needed in its members be kept at the right pitch except by bottling down some powerful instinct and using it as a driving force? (89)

Later in the novel, the inner Party member O'Brien informs Winston that Big Brother's neurosurgeons are busy at work abolishing the human orgasm, thus cutting out altogether the middleman of "marching up and down and cheering and waving flags."

In *Brave New World*, Aldous Huxley presents an alternative view of dystopian sexuality—free love for all. In his Preface to the 1946 edition of his best-known novel, Huxley comments:

> ... Nor does the sexual promiscuity of *Brave New World* seem so very distant. There are already certain American cities in which the number of divorces is equal to the number of marriages.... As political and economic freedom diminishes, sexual freedom tends compensatingly to increase. And the dictator (unless he needs cannon fodder and families with which to colonize empty or conquered territories) will do well to encourage that freedom. (xviii–xix)

Everyone agrees that as cultural commentators, George Orwell and Aldous Huxley share an abiding concern for the sovereignty of the individual, a sovereignty that both satirists saw as being threatened during their lifetimes as never before in the history of the West. *How* they delineate this concern in *Nineteen Eighty-Four* and in *Brave New World* is another question.

What critics of both novels often overlook is that the individuals who inhabit these fictional realms *ultimately* have at least a modicum of free choice, no matter what conditioning they are exposed to or what terrible constraints are put upon them. This may sound both odd and obvious at the same time, especially in connection with *Nineteen Eighty-Four*. Yes, nothing is against the law in Oceania because there are no laws. Indeed, for Big Brother and his minions, the notion of crime itself is arbitrary—one might almost say non-existent. In a *legal* sense, everything is permitted. For their part, of course, the Thought Police can arrest persons at any time of the day or night on the flimsiest of pretexts, haul them off to a labor camp, torture them—or simply shoot them in the back of the head.

But execution doesn't mean depriving one of one's *will*. The Party fully understands this; hence O'Brien tells Winston at one point that they *will not* shoot him as long as he hates Big Brother. Only when Winston learns to love Big Brother will the Party dispense with him: "When finally you surrender to us, it must be of your own free will," O'Brien insists (169). This learning process involves terrible tortures, needless to say, but the distinction between "fill[ing] you with ourselves" as O'Brien puts it and turning Winston into a mindless robot is crucial (170). In Orwell's Oceania, if turning the victim into a *thing* were Big Brother's ultimate aim, mind-altering drugs would do the job much more efficiently than torture and/or the threat of death.

In any case, Winston and Julia aren't the only "rebels" in the novel who wriggle free, at least temporarily, from the iron grip of Big Brother. According to Julia, who should know, rebellion against the sexual norm (i.e., the principles of the Anti-Sex League) isn't unusual at all in Oceania, especially among members of the inner Party, many of whom are less than holy, as she puts it, when it comes to erotic activity. And of course the proles are left to their own devices.

In like manner, in the World State of *Brave New World* the ubiquitous operant conditioning of human beings doesn't equate with the absence of free will. Rather, conditioning *shapes* free will, so that, as Ivy Lee, the godfather of Public Relations in the United States, once put it, "People will be led where they want to go." Advertising, of course, conditions them to "want" to buy this or that product. Obviously, there are worlds of difference between Lee's philosophy of advertising and the behavioral techniques of Huxley's Central London Hatchery and Conditioning Centre, but the difference is one of degree, not of kind. Even Lenina's addiction to *soma* is less physiological than it is psychological. At one point during a bloody primitive ritual on the Reservation, she sobs, "Too awful ... Too awful! That blood ... Oh, I wish I had my *soma*" (135). But then, on learning that the Savage "*wanted* to be hit with the whip," her incipient free will also kicks in:

"Astonishment made Lenina forget the deprivation of *soma*" (137). In both Orwell's Oceania and Huxley's World State, then, the power of government to control the feelings and the behavior of its citizens is limited, albeit in radically different ways.

As for the world beyond the novels—our world—Ernest van den Haag is correct in pointing out that

> Though society limits the ability of individuals to choose, and stresses some decisions as more desirable than others, it does not deprive us of choice altogether. It could not be otherwise, for culture is seldom transmitted in a uniform and unchanged way, nor does it consist of a homogeneous mass. (167)

Indeed, George Orwell's depiction of a futuristic London, so much grimmer than that of Aldous Huxley, may actually be said to understate the case. When, in *Nineteen Eighty-Four*, the gung-ho party member Parsons cries out, "Down with Big Brother" in his sleep, we're meant to understand that Big Brother can't gain access to the unconscious mind (155).

In everyday experience, in contrast, the unconscious may be used by the will as a weapon of repression. The classic bad dream, wherein the dreamer suddenly finds him- or herself unclothed in public, feels instant embarrassment and remorse, and wakes up bathed in cold sweat and racked by palpitations, is one example of this epiphenomenon. It's perfectly true, of course, that social institutions like church, school, family, and government may be blamed for the repression of sexual behavior; they may even be blamed for allowing sexual behavior to flourish *ex officio*, as during the sexual revolution of the permissive nineteen-sixties. But in sexual matters above all others, the individual almost always has the last word. As Karl Menninger has written,

> In contemporary civilization, as in primitive civilizations, the inhibitions in the erotic life of most men and women arise within and are related to religion only formally and nominally. This applies to people who do not have any conscious interest in religion, as well as to those who do. The primitive taboos have been incorporated into all religious faiths *as well as into social customs*. [italics added] (282)

Nonetheless, Menninger concludes, "To blame sexual inhibitions on institutions is ... to put the cart before the horse" (282). The feminist writer Ingrid Bengis puts the matter in an even clearer light:

Personal hatred and personal fear destroy our capacities for loving more thoroughly than any social system possibly could.... What we do not say is that love brings us face-to-face with the barest skeletons of our being. What we do not say is that we are all, every lest one of us, scared of love's power to create and destroy. (168)

On this subject the ancient Greeks also had much to say. Eros, the problem child of Aphrodite, was as cruel as he was charming. Aiming his poison-tipped arrows at gods and men alike, Eros wreaked so much havoc that his exasperated mother (herself an occasional target of his vicious tricks) had to clip his wings and confiscate his quiver on occasion. Before his relationship with her enjoyed an eventual happy ending in a wedding on Mt. Olympus, Eros drove his lover Psyche to attempt suicide by drowning. But Eros was his mother's son: Aphrodite herself was the cause of great pain in mortals. In her Roman incarnation, Charles Baudelaire brings her back to life in a famous prose poem entitled "Venus and the Motley Fool":

... At the feet of a colossal Venus, all of a heap against the pedestal, one of those so-called fools, those voluntary buffoons who, with cap and bells and tricked out in a ridiculous and gaudy costume, are called upon to make kings laugh when they are beset by Boredom or Remorse, raises his tear-filled eyes toward the immortal Goddess.

And his eyes say: 'I am the least and loneliest of men, deprived of love and friendship, wherein I am inferior even to the lowest animals. Yet I, too, am made to understand and to feel immortal Beauty! Ah! Goddess! take pity on my fever and my pain!'

But the implacable Goddess with her marble eyes continues to gaze into the distance, at I know not what. (10)

Above all, it's worth recalling that during the Judgment of Paris, when Aphrodite found herself in a beauty contest with Hera and Athena, all she had to do was take off her clothes. Hera, who promised Paris all of Asia, and Athena, who guaranteed him victory in battle, never had a chance.

II

When I teach the literature of romantic love in the university—*The Romance of Tristan and Iseult*, say, or *Romeo and Juliet*—I ask my students to perform a *gedanken*, or thought experiment. Suppose we take a field trip to the corner of California Avenue and Stockdale Highway, take off our clothes, and simply stand there, naked. What would happen? We'd all be arrested, comes the amused reply. Then begins a series of whys. The first one—*why would the police arrest everyone?*—draws an equally predictable reply: Indecent exposure is against the law. But then things get more interesting. *Why* is indecent exposure against the law? Here a volley of answers is often forthcoming: Because other people are offended; because children might be in the vicinity; because the unclothed human body is, well, *indecent*. *Why* is the unclothed body indecent?, I ask. At this point, the class usually divides into two groups and an argument ensues, one group arguing for, the other against, the intrinsic beauty or the intrinsic ugliness of the body. *If you want to take off your clothes in public*, one student comments, *go to a nudist colony*.

In a brilliant essay, "Summer in Algiers," Albert Camus talks about the youths of that sun-drenched city who swim naked in the sparkling summer Mediterranean Sea, and who

> [haven't] read the boring sermons of the nudists, those Protestants of the flesh (there is a theory of the body quite as tiresome as that of the mind). But they are simply 'comfortable in the sunlight.' The importance of this custom for our epoch can never be overestimated. For the first time in two thousand years the body has appeared naked on beaches. For twenty centuries men have striven to give decency to Greek insolence and naiveté, to diminish the flesh under delicate dress. Today, despite that history, young men running on Mediterranean beaches repeat the gestures of the athletes of Delos.

"[L]iving thus among bodies and through one's body," Camus adds, "one becomes aware that it has its connotations, its life, and ... a psychology of its own" (143).

In *Brave New World*, Mustapha Mond tells the incredulous Savage,

> Chastity means passion, chastity means neurasthenia. And passion and neurasthenia mean instability. And instability means the end of civilization. You can't have a lasting civilization without plenty of pleasant vices. (284)

Passion is also a form of anarchy in *Nineteen Eighty-Four*. Here O'Brien and his opposite number, Mustapha Mond, are in complete agreement. In Huxley's World State, the chief pleasant vice is, of course, unbridled sex. In Orwell's Oceania, this vice is sublimated in the form of marching up and down and cheering and waving flags—what O'Brien would doubtless call a pleasant virtue. Semantics aside, both attitudes toward passion represent opposite sides of the same coin. The coin, of course, is the psychology of the body. Keeping in mind once again that the underlying issue in both texts is free will, *not* wholesale erotic oppression from without, where do we as citizens of a democracy part company with the dystopian satiric scenarios of *Brave New World* and *Nineteen Eighty-Four*?

As a point of departure, let's consider the universal social custom of dancing. Dancing, as John Updike once observed, is a socially acceptable parable of sexual relations. But as an instrument of social control, dancing is a Huxleyan pleasant *vice* and an Orwellian pleasant *virtue*—a safety valve for the passions. The same is true of illegal activities like pornography and prostitution, both of which could be effectively abolished overnight if authorities were willing to enforce the letter of the law to its fullest extent. *Our society will countenance no such thing for two contradictory reasons.* On the one hand, there's the ever-present danger that the passions, if too severely repressed, will be sublimated into undesirable social action. This happened during Prohibition, when the pent-up bacchanalian passions of millions of people threatened to turn much of American society into an instant replay of Euripedean tragedy.[1] And this is exactly the opposite of what takes place in *Nineteen Eighty-Four*. On the other hand, there's also the danger that licentious behavior will result in social anarchy. This occurred during the Age of Aquarius, when the children of the Woodstock Nation helped to shatter the sexual status quo of American culture, perhaps forever. And this is exactly the opposite of what happens in *Brave New World*.

Here, then, we see the most fundamental difference between the societal visions of Orwell and Huxley and our own situation(s). In the do-it-yourself dystopia of the new American millennium, we appear to be caught up in an impossible paradox of our own making. This paradox didn't happen overnight, nor is it a strictly American phenomenon; it may be traced back to the beginnings of *donnoi*, or courtly love, in Western Europe.

From the famous "Judgement of the Countess of Champagne" in 1174 comes the statement:

> We declare and affirm ... that love cannot extend its rights over two married persons. For indeed lovers grant one another all things mutually and freely, without being impelled by any motive of necessity, whereas husband and wife are held by their duty to submit their wills to each other and refuse each other nothing.[2]

This is the pure stuff of myth; as we'll see in a moment, the Judgement could serve as a Cliff's Notes plot outline for *The Romance of Tristan and Iseult*. It's true that free will played little or no part in many arranged marriages among the nobility in the tenth, eleventh, and twelfth centuries; the cult of courtly love arose in part as a rebellion against the abuses of the rights of women who were often treated by fathers as chattel to be bartered off to the highest bidder. Today, of course, the situation is vastly different—and yet the myth persists. When the Italian film director Vittorio de Sica was asked why he made so many films about adultery, he replied, "But if you take adultery out of the lives of the bourgeoisie, there's nothing left." As Denis de Rougemont has written, however, marriage wasn't the *only* target of courtly fealty:

> The *Romance* [*of Tristan and Iseult*] misses no opportunity of disparaging the social institution of marriage and of humiliating husbands—e.g., the king with horse's ears who is always being so easily deceived—as well as of glorifying the virtue of men and women who love outside, and despite of, marriage. This courtly loyalty, however, displays one curious feature. *It is opposed to the 'satisfaction' of love as much as to marriage.* [italics added] (34)

De Rougemont interprets the mythic relationship of Tristan and Iseult as one that depends upon *absence*; as long as the lovers are parted, their passion burns with the proverbial hard, gem-like flame. On the other hand, when they meet, they have little to say to each other, and Tristan doesn't hesitate to return Iseult to her husband King Mark, not because he is obeying *suzerain* fealty but because he is obeying *courtly* fealty which demands that they love at long distance, lest they become—husband and wife.

Even today, when marriage is a matter of individual choice, the myth continues to haunt us. De Rougemont adds,

> The woman in my arms I must imagine as other than she is. I give her another guise, I cause her to recede in my dreams, I strive to disturb the emotional tie that is gradually being formed thanks to the smoothness and serenity of our lives. For I must devise fresh obstructions if I am to go on desiring, and if I am to magnify my desire to the dimensions of a conscious and intense passion that shall be infinitely thrilling.... Instead of the knight's sword, it is the sly dream of the husband that comes between him and the wife he can only continue to desire by imagining that she is his mistress. (284)

The notorious 50 percent divorce rate in America (57 percent as of 1998) bears ample witness that the myth incorporates a psychology of the body that is still very much part of our lives. Of course, ordinary men and women make peace with the paradox of passion in different ways. We've learned to speak the culture-language of friendship between husband and wife (Shakespeare's Juliet calls Romeo her "love-lord, ay, husband-friend" [106]). And many successful marriages continue to be based upon this happy premise. Nonetheless, at the heart of the matter of passion is—in a word—*suffering*. As de Rougemont says, assuming the *persona* of Tristan, "[O]nly suffering can make me aware of passion; and that is why I like to suffer and to cause to suffer" (284). And as the Kinsey surveys of the fifties and the Masters and Johnson interviews of the seventies revealed to a stunned American public, this condition is still very much a part of the hidden lives of our shadow-selves. This is why it's in the unavowed interest of society to make us afraid and ashamed of our own bodies, and why we eagerly acquiesce in that fear and shame.

NOTES

1. I refer, of course, to Euripides's *The Bacchae*.
2. This famous medieval document may be found in Claude Fauriel's classic *Histoire de la poesie provençale* (Paris, 1846).

WORKS CITED

Baudelaire, Charles. *Paris Spleen*. Trans. Louise Varese. New York: New Directions, 1970.

Bengis, Ingrid. *Combat in the Erogenous Zone*. New York: Bantam Books, 1972.

Camus, Albert. "Summer in Algiers." *The Myth of Sisyphus and Other Essays*. Trans. Justin O'Brien. New York: Alfred A. Knopf, 1967. 141–154.

de Rougemont, Denis. *Love in the Western World*. Revised and augmented edition. Trans. Montgomery Belgion. New York: Pantheon, 1956.

Huxley, Aldous. *Brave New World*. New York: Harper and Row, 1946.

Menninger, Karl. *Love Against Hate*. New York: Harcourt, Brace and Company, 1942.

Orwell, George. *Orwell's Nineteen Eighty-Four: Text, Sources, Criticism*. Ed. Irving Howe. 2nd ed. New York: Harcourt Brace Jovanovich, 1982.

Rilke, Rainer Maria. "The Difficult Work of Love." *The Essential Prose*. Ed. Dorothy Van Ghent and Willard Maas. New York: The Bobbs-Merrill Company, Inc., 1966. 150–154.

Shakespeare, William. *Romeo and Juliet*. Ed. John E. Hankins. New York: Penguin Books, 1970.

van den Haag, Ernest. *Passion and Social Constraint*. New York: Dell, 1963.

ANTHONY STEWART

The Heresy of Common Sense: The Prohibition of Decency in Nineteen Eighty-Four

In the end the Party would announce that two and two made five, and you would have to believe it. It was inevitable that they should make that claim sooner or later: the logic of their position demanded it. Not merely the validity of experience, but the very existence of external reality, was tacitly denied by their philosophy. The heresy of heresies was common sense. And what was terrifying was not that they would kill you for thinking otherwise, but that they might be right. For, after all, how do we know that two and two make four? Or that the force of gravity works? Or that the past is unchangeable? If both the past and the external world exist only in the mind, and if the mind itself is controllable—what then?

—Orwell, *Nineteen Eighty-Four*

At the level of the individual, John Flory and Gordon Comstock demonstrate the pitfalls of a perspective that is too narrow, too focused on one's own interests to the exclusion of the concerns and points of view of others. On a more systemic and portentous level, Napoleon highlights the impact of the same basic failing but with the crucial difference that Napoleon holds enough power to insist that others see the world exactly as he does. As a result of this lack of a broader perspective—a lack of a sensibility that I have been calling "doubled"—these characters are incapable of behaving decently towards others. Instead of a doubled perspective, each is exposed to the reader, through judgments implied by the narrator, as being guilty of duplicity—saying one

From *George Orwell, Doubleness, and the Value of Decency*. © 2003 by Taylor & Francis Books, Inc.

thing while meaning another—in order to forward his own selfish agenda. Dr. Veraswami, Rosemary Waterlow, and Boxer are all instrumental in revealing the protagonists' duplicities, and represent by contrast the positive contribution that decency can make within a political or social field. That each of these three decent characters is oppressed in some way (Veraswami by race, Elizabeth by gender, Boxer by his limited intelligence) suggests further that this potential to contribute positively to one's surroundings is not beyond the average, or even the disempowered, individual.

An emphasis on the political potential of everyday people is characteristic of Orwell's fiction. As John Rossi states, Orwell "never lost his faith in the rugged good sense of the English people and their simple patriotism. They, and not the upper classes of the hopelessly degenerated intelligentsia, would save England" (98). Flory, Gordon, and Napoleon distinguish themselves from the other characters in their stories because of their intellects. Flory is the only Englishman in Kyauktada with any interest in books; Gordon is a poet; Napoleon is the leader of the species on Manor Farm that separates itself after the rebellion by learning to read and write. Unfortunately, these same mental abilities lead them to see themselves as superior to others. Yet all are found wanting by the narrators of their stories, who judge them negatively, making clear that the capacity for decency is not the exclusive preserve of the élite within Orwell's writing, but a salutary capability within the grasp of all.

The fate of Boxer marks the first instance in Orwell's work when a decent character encounters directly a force that not only rejects the value of decency but also has the power to impose an excessively narrow view on others. Napoleon, in addition to being incapable of decency, actively prohibits this basic value from emerging in others. First, he exiles Snowball, who represents the potential for a leadership based on the decent treatment of the led. With Snowball gone, Napoleon is able to install a cult of personality with himself as the only permissible focus of the other animals' attention. With this as his sole priority, then, Napoleon has no compunctions at all in sending the increasingly problematic Boxer to the knacker's and then having Squealer lie to the other animals about the carthorse's subsequent death. The example of Boxer's admirably selfless nature could not be allowed to persist within Napoleon's domain. Since he is revered by the other animals for his tireless work on behalf of the farm, Boxer represents a potential threat to the narrow focus developing around Napoleon.

But Boxer's fate only hints at what we ultimately encounter in the story of Winston Smith in *Nineteen Eighty-Four*. Winston embodies both all that is potentially beneficial and all that is most costly in the posture of the decent individual that Orwell presents. Whereas in the first three novels examined here, the protagonist has been an example of a lack of decency (if we accept Napoleon as the protagonist of *Animal Farm*), Winston is at the same time the protagonist of *Nineteen Eighty-Four* and the principal representative of the value of decency in the novel.

There are remnants of Flory and Gordon in Winston. Like the two earlier protagonists, Winston betrays an admiration for the thing he claims to hate most. This internal tension is seen most clearly if we bear in mind Flory's grudging acknowledgment of the other men's sincerity in comparison to his own hypocrisy and Gordon's loathsome behavior once he receives some money when we examine Winston's conflicted relationships with rituals like the Two Minutes Hate, with O'Brien, and with his job as a rewriter of history in the Ministry of Truth. Winston also contains an important remnant of Boxer, since he, too, is overwhelmed by the power of a relentlessly indecent state, a state whose indecency manifests itself most extremely in its seemingly limitless capacity for cruelty.

Richard Rorty's reading of *Nineteen Eighty-Four* helps illuminate the significance of this capacity for cruelty. Rorty also provides a point of departure from which to draw some conclusions about the value of decency as represented in these four novels. His notion of "final vocabulary" makes clear what is at stake in the confrontation between the single-minded perspective of the Inner Party—the privileged and largely invisible cadre that runs Oceania—and the doubled sensibility that Winston Smith, as a member of the Outer Party, desperately tries to preserve for himself and as a future possibility for the citizens of Oceania, a possibility he sees as latent in the proles. The expression "final vocabulary" also encapsulates the vulnerability of the decent individual within a power structure where some can reject decency and then ruthlessly enforce that rejection on others. The vulnerability we have seen in Veraswami, Rosemary, and then Boxer, takes on its most extreme and disturbing form in Winston.

Winston Smith's harrowing experience in the Ministry of Love signals how the important relationship between decency and indecency becomes even more intense than it is in *Animal Farm*. There, Boxer was unable to think through the implications of the pigs' imposition of an exclusive point of view on the other animals. As a result, he is at first an unwitting instrument in Napoleon's consolidation of power because of his prodigious physical strength while working on the windmill (both times), and then, because he can't read the side of the knacker's wagon, he is easily disposed of when he loses his strength. Winston, on the other hand, is completely conscious of the evil perpetrated on the citizens by the state and attempts actively, although futilely, to understand and undermine it.

He writes in his diary, "*I understand HOW: I do not understand WHY*" (83). The important question "why" the Party oppresses its citizens so absolutely opens the possibility for various alternative interpretations of the Party and of life in Oceania in general to emerge. Such a variety of perspectives would undermine the Party's control over the people and so must be thwarted at all costs. Winston's desire to understand "why" makes him unlike the earlier protagonists in a highly significant way. Whether right or wrong, Flory and Gordon are already certain they understand why the systems they rail against are as they are and feel they need no further explanation. Napoleon makes Manor Farm into a reflection of himself, rendering the question of "why" moot. Winston's ability to ask "why" also differentiates him from the decent characters in the earlier books. Veraswami and Elizabeth have little choice but to accept the systems of oppression that subordinate them. If they ask "why" they do so silently. And for all of his admirable decency, the intricacies of such interpretive questions are simply beyond Boxer's intellectual capacity.

The confrontation between Winston's consciousness and the elaborate ideological mechanisms in place in Oceania to overcome the decent dissident marks *Nineteen Eighty-Four* as the logical summation of the idea of decency as Orwell presents it. While Boxer adopts his mottos of compliance, "I will work harder" and "Napoleon is always right," and is simply removed from the farm and killed, Winston must be re-educated. As O'Brien explains the Party's rationale to Winston while torturing him, "We do not destroy the heretic because he resists us: so long as he resists us we never destroy him. We convert him, we capture his inner mind, we reshape him. We burn all evil and all illusion out of him; we bring him over to our side, not in appearance, but genuinely, heart and soul. We make him one of ourselves before we kill him" (267). This is the last word on the distinction between the singular point of view and the doubled. The Party does not even consider any real exchange of ideas with an alternative perspective. Instead, it transforms—by force when necessary—the points of view of its citizens *into* that of the Party. No alternatives at all can lawfully or, according to the Party, even logically exist. Orwell's fear of the effects of totalitarianism on the individual manifests itself most memorably in his creation of a nightmare world in which simple human decency is not only lacking, but is actively and violently prohibited.

Winston Smith is completely overmatched and yet he is depicted not as foolhardy but as one to be admired. Up until he finally utters the words, "Do it to Julia," wishing upon her a horror he cannot face himself, he holds fast to his beliefs in the "spirit of Man" (282) and the revolutionary potential embodied in the human decency of the proles. The fact that we can still admire him demonstrates again Orwell's view that decency is always worthwhile as a good in itself, like the doctor who works to save the life of the dying patient. Winston searches continually for ways to maintain his belief in decency and humanity instead of capitulating as we see others in the novel do. Read in the context of doubleness and decency, Winston Smith is an optimistic characterization, who represents the value of decency at its best and demonstrates Orwell's belief that even in the cruelest place imaginable, the decent character will always emerge, even if he does not prevail.

This point about optimism, what I've been calling Orwell's mitigated optimism, is evident at the end of *Nineteen Eighty-Four* as it was at the end of *Animal Farm*. This optimism is intimated in four different but related ways, which combine to express one last time the potential latent in the doubled sensibility and suggest the possibility that decency might emerge even from within Oceania, despite the Party's elaborate efforts to outlaw this simple value. The fact that the appendix is written in the past tense demonstrates that the regime of indecency is eventually overthrown, as the pigs on the newly renamed Manor Farm will inevitably be. Also, the tensions within Newspeak itself threaten to rend the regime apart from within. And finally, both the physical and mental states of Winston Smith as he sits in the Chestnut Tree Café at the novel's conclusion suggest in two different ways the Inner Party's failure to extinguish the desire for decency in its principal target. He still maintains enough doubleness to conceive of hating Big Brother even as he thinks he loves him. As long as this desire to see the world in more than one way persists—to see it in ways the Party would deem heretical but cannot control—then the Party has failed to, in O'Brien's words, convert, capture the inner mind, and reshape the heretic. This failure means that the possibility for the emergence of decency still persists. As in *Animal Farm*, so here: for Orwell, a sense of decency need not translate into "victory" as such. It is to be pursued for its own sake, with the understanding that decency, along with the doubled perspective that helps to foster it, will always be beneficial. Even at the end of *Nineteen Eighty-Four*, it appears that a sense of decency will win out.

WINSTON SMITH AND THE DESIRE FOR DECENCY

Singularity of vision is imprinted upon the now-famous landscape of Oceania right from the beginning of the novel. The four "Ministry" buildings—the Ministries of Truth, Peace, Plenty, and Love—so dwarf everything else in 1984 London that from the roof of the Victory Mansions, where Winston lives, "you could see all four of them simultaneously" (6). Such architectural dominance of the landscape emphasizes that nothing else in the citizens' field of vision should be as important as the Party. The ubiquitous posters of Big

Brother, "so contrived that the eyes follow you about when you move" (3), stress further the importance of seeing in the prescribed way. And, of course, the memorable slogan of surveillance—"BIG BROTHER IS WATCHING YOU"— asserts yet again the priority of vision of a very specific and strictly enforced type within this society of surveillance.

Winston knows that keeping a diary could get him vaporized, or at least sent to a forced labor camp if it's discovered, because a diary indicates a priority other than the Party, a desire for "*ownlife*," the Newspeak word "meaning individualism and eccentricity" (85). Yet he keeps the diary anyway. It is this willingness to stand as a "minority of one" (83) in the face of an enormous machinery intended to foil such individualism that makes Winston admirable. He pursues, and is willing to die for, an alternative point of view, another way of looking at things, while living within a state in which any such doubled vision is forbidden. But this desire to view the present both as it is and as it might otherwise be is the only way to stay human, and possibly influence the future, as Winston sees things. Only by questioning the dictates of the Party can he make a connection with another person, as he eventually does, if briefly, with Julia.

In order to elaborate the significance of decency in *Nineteen Eighty-Four*, it is necessary to recognize the profoundly dehumanizing effects that living under such a regime have had on Winston Smith, an intelligent man who wants to remember how life was before the revolution that brought the Party to power. Winston is "a member of the last group of citizens to remember life without the Party, the last group that could use that connection to the past as a motive for rebellion" (Phelan 102). He looks simultaneously at a half-remembered past he suspects was different from the accounts he reads (and helps rewrite) and an all-too-real present from which the Party can always change the past. As such, his desires are diametrically opposed to the Party's objective of absolute power.

While Winston wishes to remember the past and see the present as complexly as possible in order to affect the future, the Party wants simply to imprint its version of the past, present, and future into the minds of its citizens and then to erase the fact of this imprinting. The essence of the Party's version of reality comprises the "sacred principles of Ingsoc [English Socialism]. Newspeak, doublethink, the mutability of the past" (28). Overarching these sacred principles is the requirement that the citizens love Big Brother unquestioningly and exclusively, and that this love appear spontaneous, as though it emerges naturally from the heart as well as the mind. The logic underlying this elaborate process is explained in its briefest form by the Party slogan, "Who controls the past ... controls the future: who controls the present controls the past" (37). The enforcement of thought on another is the ultimate indecency. Once this is possible, any atrocity may be committed against any who don't think as those in power do.

The mechanisms required to install the willful ignorance demanded of the citizens of Oceania are described in the famous definition of doublethink:

> To know and not to know, to be conscious of complete truthfulness while telling carefully-constructed lies, to hold simultaneously two opinions which cancelled out, knowing them to be contradictory and believing in both of them; to use logic against logic, to repudiate morality while laying claim to it, to believe that democracy was impossible and that the Party was the guardian of democracy; to forget whatever it was necessary to forget, then to draw it back into memory again at the moment when it was needed, *and then promptly to forget it again*; and above all, to apply the same process to the process itself. *That was the ultimate subtlety: consciously to induce unconsciousness, and then, once again, to become unconscious of the act of hypnosis you had just performed. Even to understand the word "doublethink" involved the use of doublethink.* (37–38, emphasis added)

Doublethink, then, imposes a constant internal battle upon the mind while at the same time requiring that the same mind forget that this battle is taking place at all. It also enables the Party to impose its singular will without responsibility to the citizens who must constantly undertake this mental exercise, since, according to the tenets of doublethink, there is nothing for the Party to justify. Instead of having to deal with many individuals, the Party only has to control one collective mind, thanks to the principle of doublethink.

The irony of this imposed collective single-mindedness, however, is that it cannot help but cause dualities to arise within its intended subjects. As Patricia Rae has put it: "The problem with Smith, however, is that he hasn't yet mastered the mental discipline known as 'double-think': He can't entirely forget what he has altered, or that he has altered it" (200). But Winston's problem goes beyond being *unable* to master doublethink; he does not *want* to master doublethink because of its requirement that he forget the disjunction between the way things are and the way they might otherwise be, and that he forget that the past might have been different from the ever-changing official versions of it. Even as he is being reprogrammed in Part III of the novel, even after he has supposedly "accepted everything" (290), Winston still experiences divisions within his own mind, which keeps wandering into unorthodox directions, as he first examines and then consciously dismisses the fallacies he recognizes in the prevailing logic of the Party. "The mind should develop a blind spot whenever a dangerous thought presented itself. The process should be automatic, instinctive. *Crimestop*, they called it in Newspeak" (291). He knows implicitly the importance of the singular perspective, but it is still more important to him to reject it.

The intellectual requirements necessary to keep this system of self-censorship functioning invisibly are summarized by the sort of implicit value judgment that Orwell's narrators have expressed in the other novels: "It needed also a sort of athleticism of mind, an ability at one moment to make the most delicate use of logic and at the next to be unconscious of the crudest logical errors. Stupidity was as necessary as intelligence, and as difficult to attain" (291–92). The necessity of stupidity for an unproblematic life in Oceania makes clear that the process is being recognized within the novel for what it is—a perversion of and an assault on human intelligence.

The overbearing pressures exerted on him leave Winston in conflict with himself whenever his vigilance flags even for a moment, allowing him to reflect too closely upon the hidden meanings which he sees everywhere in the world around him, but which he is required to pretend do not exist. To do otherwise is to risk being rendered an *unperson*—turned into someone who did not exist, who had never existed (48). As he participates in the Two Minutes Hate at the beginning of the novel, he experiences a sort of dissociation as he observes his own public conduct as if watching someone else:

> In a lucid moment Winston found that he was shouting with the others and kicking his heel violently against the rung of his chair. The horrible thing about the Two Minutes Hate was not that one was obliged to act a part, but that it was impossible to avoid joining in. Within thirty seconds any pretence was always unnecessary. A hideous ecstasy of fear and vindictiveness, a desire to kill, to torture, to smash faces in with a sledgehammer, seemed to flow through the whole group of people like an electric current, turning one even against one's will into a grimacing, screaming lunatic. (16)

Ironically, the Party is actually designed to banish this sort of occasional "lucid moment." As Winston's will is overtaken by the ambient insanity of the Two Minutes Hate, he becomes another example of what Orwell describes so memorably in his 1936 essay, "Shooting an Elephant": Winston wears the mask of the Hate and his face grows to fit it. That such lucid moments still occur at all demonstrates how difficult it is for Winston to maintain the necessary façade as well as the difficulty of the Party's task of legislating and enforcing opacity of consciousness.

The mania of the Two Minutes Hate causes such thoroughgoing confusion within Winston that he is unable to control his impulses or emotions for any length of time at all:

> And yet the rage that one felt was an abstract, undirected emotion which could be switched from one object to another like the flame of a blowlamp. Thus, at one moment Winston's hatred was not turned against Goldstein at all, but, on the contrary, against Big Brother, the Party and the Thought Police; and at such moments his heart went out to the lonely, derided heretic on the screen, sole guardian of truth and sanity in a world of lies. And yet the very next instant he was at one with the people about him, and all that was said of Goldstein seemed to him to be true. At those moments his secret loathing of Big Brother changed into adoration, and Big Brother seemed to tower up, an invincible, fearless protector, standing like a rock against the hordes of Asia, and Goldstein, in spite of his isolation, his helplessness and the doubt that hung about his very existence, seemed like some sinister enchanter, capable by the mere power of his voice of wrecking the structure of civilization. (16–17)

The repetition of "And yet" and the movement from one kind of "moment" to its opposite demonstrates the internal back-and-forth Winston experiences as he hates Big Brother one minute and then loves him the next, supports Goldstein and then decries him with the rest of the crazed mob. He is unable to control the abstract, undirected emotion of the Hate; it controls him, always moving him against his will back into line with the unified mood of the collective. Even as he sees that it is possible "at moments, to switch one's hatred this way or that by a voluntary act" (17), enabling him to indulge momentarily in violent fantasies about Julia—whom he has not yet met—as the hate rises to its climax, he again experiences internal conflict, at one moment sharing in the "general delirium" (19) of the frenzied mob as Big Brother's face appears on the screen and yet almost simultaneously feeling a sense of horror as the crowd rhythmically chants "B-B! ... B-B!" (18), in homage to their mythical leader.

In spite of this feeling of horror, "he chanted with the rest: it was impossible to do otherwise" (19). To breach the group's expectations in such a public way as refusing to chant along with them would be disastrous. And even though the pull of the crowd's will is irresistible, Winston's recurrent lucidity allows him to recognize yet another horror, prefigured by the crowd's irresistibility, "To dissemble your feelings, to control your face, to do what everyone else was doing, was an instinctive reaction. But there was a space of a couple of seconds during which the expression in his eyes might conceivably have betrayed him" (19). Winston always feels the pull towards doubleness at the same time that he tries to maintain unity with the perspective enforced on the rest of the population by the Party. Such is the disorienting effect on the individual who tries to maintain a doubled perspective—one that participates in the ritual while simultaneously attempting to critique that ritual as well as one's participation in it—while living under an indecent regime in which only one perspective—unconscious participation—is permitted. Winston can never be completely sure that he is being orthodox enough, and will only know that he has failed to meet the required standard of subjugation when he is taken away by the Thought Police. This early scene at the Two Minutes Hate spares no effort in representing just how complicated the Party's effects on the individual are.

We have encountered internal conflicts in earlier Orwell protagonists, of course. Even though he hates them, Flory finds himself wanting in comparison to the other Englishmen in the Club, as he thinks to himself: "All those fools at the Club, those dull louts to whom you are so pleased to think yourself superior—they are all better than you, every man of them. At least they are men in their oafish way. Not cowards, not liars. Not half-dead and rotting. But you—" (62). He grudgingly acknowledges the willingness the other men show to stand up for their convictions, reprehensible though they are to him. And, though Gordon has declared war on money, he never behaves worse than when he finds himself in possession of more money than usual, a bit of good fortune which ironically enables him to act in the same self-satisfied and obnoxious manner he decries when he encounters it (or thinks he is encountering it) in others. Both men indulge vicariously in the narrow and exclusive behaviors they claim to despise most.

But these minor inconsistencies do not cost these two men anything more than some additional self-doubt (Flory) or a hangover and the loss of a bad job (Gordon). Neither is in mortal danger as a result of the moments in which his duplicity is exposed. Winston, in stark contrast to the other two, realizes that even a momentary inattention to his facial expressions could cost him his life. The internal division effected by the relentless stress of surveillance and self-surveillance is encapsulated in Winston's own thoughts: "Your worst enemy, he reflected, was your own nervous system" (67). As he thinks this, he remembers a man he recently saw on the street, whose face was "suddenly contorted by a sort of spasm. It happened again just as they were passing one another: it was only a twitch, a quiver, rapid as the clicking of a camera shutter, but obviously habitual. He remembered thinking at the time: That poor devil is done for. And what was frightening was that the action was quite possibly unconscious" (67). The Party's demand for unanimity, ironically, cannot help but produce division, which in turn produces external symptoms of division, whether facial tics or the keeping of a diary.

The pressure to love Big Brother unquestioningly in public while hating him completely in private makes Winston Smith a complicated and endlessly fascinating character who highlights dramatically how an inhumane regime can dehumanize a man whose primary motivation is to stay human, to stay decent. Even as he rejects the Party's leadership, unconsciously and incautiously writing "DOWN WITH BIG BROTHER" (20) over and over again in the diary he secretly keeps, he nevertheless loves his job, which is a key instrument in the Party's control of the past, present, and future. He is one of the numerous functionaries in the Ministry of Truth who perpetually revise documents from the past so that they always accord in one coherent national narrative, as told by Big Brother: "Winston's greatest pleasure in life was in his work. Most of it was a tedious routine, but included in it there were also jobs so difficult and intricate that you could lose yourself in them as in the depths of a mathematical problem—delicate pieces of forgery in which you had nothing to guide you except your knowledge of the principles of Ingsoc and your estimate of what the Party wanted you to say. Winston was good at this kind of thing" (46).[1] It would be one thing for Winston to be making the best of a horrible situation, deriving what little pleasure afforded him in the London of 1984 by losing himself in his work; it is quite another, however, for him to enjoy his work as enthusiastically as he obviously does. His pleasure in this type of intricate occupation reiterates the kind of intelligent sensibility Winston possesses, a sensibility that highlights the demands of the Party more explicitly than would be the case were he less intellectually acute, were he more like Boxer, in other words. And yet, this type of sensibility is invaluable to the elaborate system of forgery on which the Party's power relies, just as Boxer's physical strength is crucial to the development of the farm and then the consolidation of Napoleon's power.

Winston's diary reveals his conflicted nature in another way. As he writes his first entry, which quickly descends into an unpunctuated stream-of-consciousness, he comments casually on the propaganda "flicks" he watched the previous evening: "*One very good one of a ship full of refugees being bombed somewhere in the Mediterranean. Audience much amused by shots of a great huge fat man trying to swim away with a helicopter after him. First you saw him wallowing along in the water like a porpoise, then you saw him through the helicopters gunsights, then he was full of holes and the sea round him turned pink and he sank as suddenly as though the holes had let in the water"* (10). As he catalogues one horror after another, he evinces a similar common cause with the mob that he conveys and simultaneously critiques at the Two Minutes Hate. When he is writing in his diary, though, he is not displaying his reactions for the approval of the Party or the rest of the mob; he is alone. His callous account of this evening at the flicks reveals how Party indoctrination—as could only have been expected—has infiltrated his innermost private thoughts in addition to dictating his public conduct. His unfeeling and jaded attitude continues in the same passage from the diary when he recounts the reaction of a woman *"down in the prole part of the house"* (11) who protests the depictions on the screen. As the woman shouts that *"they didnt oughter of showed it not in front of kids they didnt it aint right not in front of kids"* (11) and is then taken away by the police, Winston callously dismisses her compassion as mere prole ignorance: *"nobody cares what the proles say typical prole reaction"* (11).

Winston's rejection of the prole woman's point of view is especially notable because of the symbolic importance the proles play in his growing desire for decency as the novel progresses. Later, while walking alone through one of the prole areas, Winston absentmindedly kicks a severed human hand into a gutter along the street. It is significant that he commits this unthinking act in one of the prole quarters because it is the proles, "those swarming disregarded masses, 85 per cent of the population of Oceania" (72), who come to exemplify for him the decency he feels Party members— himself included—have lost. The affinity he develops for the proles becomes central to his quest to recover his own sense of decency and their ability to care about one another instead of only for Big Brother becomes a talisman of decency for Winston.

During the same trip through the prole sector during which he kicks the severed hand into the gutter, Winston seizes upon an old man "who must be eighty at the least" and so "had already been middle-aged when the Revolution happened" (90). So, immediately after kicking the hand, Winston is pursuing the other half of his nature. He desperately wants to learn from the old man what things were like before the Revolution. However, he gets no useable information from the man because history has been revised so many times as to make it impossible for anyone to remember anything accurately. (Of course, given his job, Winston should have anticipated this outcome.) Nevertheless, Winston's motto—"if there was any hope, it lay in the proles" (89)—announces his determined reliance on the decency of these "swarming, disregarded masses," even if this one prole disappoints his expectations.

Winston's dawning recognition of the proles' importance to his own alternative perspective eventually causes him to compare himself to them and find himself wanting. That a member of the Outer Party, a relatively privileged group, all things considered, can learn from the marginalized mass suggests the potential benefits to be gained from a doubled perspective. The proles, Winston realizes, have much to teach members of his own class. As he thinks about the proles, he even retrospectively disapproves of his own earlier conduct:

> They were governed by private loyalties which they did not question. What mattered were individual relationships, and a completely helpless gesture, an embrace, a tear, a word spoken to a dying man, *could have value in itself*. The proles, it suddenly occurred to him, had remained in this condition. They were not loyal to a party or a country or an idea, they were loyal to one another. For the first time in his life he did not despise the proles or think of them merely as an inert force which would one day spring to life and regenerate the world. The proles had stayed human. They had not become hardened inside. They had held on to the primitive emotions which he himself had to re-learn by conscious effort. And in thinking this he remembered, without apparent relevance, how a few weeks ago he had seen a severed hand lying on the pavement and had kicked it into the gutter as though it had been a cabbage-stalk. (172, emphasis added)

This moment of self-criticism is extremely important for understanding Winston and the notion of decency that Orwell presents in his fiction. The completely helpless gesture can, like decency, have value in itself. This is a sustaining thought for Winston. What befalls him in Part III, after he is captured by the Thought Police and turned over to O'Brien, does not negate the worth of the helpless gesture. The above passage also shows that not only is Winston able to adopt a doubled perspective while examining the world he lives in, he is able to adopt a similarly broadened point of view towards his own earlier opinions. As he realizes that he no longer despises the proles but in fact admires their resiliency even in the face of a dehumanizing regime, a regime which has hardened him on the inside, he shows his growing appreciation for the importance of human interaction that is not mediated through the interests of the Party.

Winston's ability to see his concerns in relation to those of others and his desire to treat others with decency even as the Party prohibits decency reaches its highest point immediately before he and Julia are discovered in the room above Charrington's shop. He looks at a prole woman hanging laundry out to dry: "As he looked at the woman in her characteristic attitude, her thick arms reaching up for the line, her powerful mare-like buttocks protruded, it struck him for the first time that she was beautiful" (228). The exchange he and Julia have regarding the woman's appearance emphasizes the completion of his transformation just in time for him to be captured and re-educated:

> 'She's beautiful, ' he murmured.
> 'She's a metre across the hips, easily,' said Julia.
> 'That is her style of beauty,' said Winston. (228)

His observation and defense of the prole woman's "style of beauty" recalls Flory in his best moments, as he defends to Elizabeth the Chinese custom of foot-binding, saying it's no queerer than bustles or crinolines. Winston's appreciation of the prole woman's style is a similar mark of decency, but it surpasses Flory's since Winston's carries none of Flory's ulterior motives. In fact, he and Julia know that their private meetings cannot last much longer. Both risk their very lives as they look at the prole woman out the window. The hope Winston sees in the proles has nothing to do with his own happiness, as opposed to Flory's desire to find a bride, except for the revolution he imagines will rehumanize Oceania in some future he knows he will not see.

Winston's revelations regarding the proles also emphasize the sense of optimism to be derived from *Nineteen Eighty-Four*. Even in the extreme world Orwell creates, a world in which indecency is an easy, safe, and sanctioned default position to which to descend, he still features one man— even if he is the last "dissident intellectual" (Reilly, "Insufficient Self" 129)— who is willing to see himself in relation to others, and if need be, see his own conduct as lacking in comparison to the example set by even the most disenfranchised population in his society. Winston is willing and able to learn, in other words, that his are not necessarily the only ways, or even the best ways. Moreover, he is willing to risk his life in order to preserve this newly germinating sense of decency. As a member of the Party, he must be more judicious in his actions and unorthodox thoughts than a prole would be. He is intelligent in a world in which stupidity is a goal to be striven for. He is also one of the last generations of people who might have any recollection at all of London before the Revolution.

These are all attributes which Orwell need not have included in Winston Smith, bringing to mind, by way of contrast, the complete capitulation of D-503, the narrator of Yevgeny Zamyatin's *We*, a French edition of which Orwell read in 1946, before beginning *Nineteen Eighty-Four*. Zamyatin's narrator informs on his compatriots whose coup has been suppressed by the state, and then sits quietly at a table next to the Benefactor (the perpetual ruler of OneState, the Oceania-like setting of the novel) as I-330, the leader of the revolutionaries (and whom D-503 had ostensibly been in love with) is tortured hideously in a glass bell of compressed air. I-330, a secondary character, is actually the admirable figure since she refuses to capitulate in spite of her torture. As D-503 dispassionately describes the event:

> Then they put her under the Bell. Her face got very white, and since she had eyes that were dark and big, this was very beautiful. When they started pumping the air out of the Bell, she threw her head back, and half closed her eyes and pressed her lips together, and this reminded me of something. She was looking at me, holding on tight to the arms of the chair, until her eyes closed completely. Then they pulled her out, quickly brought her to with the help of electrodes, and put her back under the Bell. This happened three times, and she still didn't say a word. (225)

As this is the last scene of the novel, we cannot help but admire I-330, especially in comparison to D-503. Her courage makes him appear callous and small by contrast. Winston comes to admire the proles because they have maintained a sense of decency in their relationships with others, a decency that he can only relearn consciously and at great personal risk. Unlike D-503, though, he is willing to take the risk.

Julia and the Citizens of Oceania

The other characters who move across the bleak landscape of Oceania add further texture to our understanding of the effects of indecency, and, by contrast, the extent of Winston's attempt to cling to his own growing sense of decency. An arresting contrast is set up between the mundane and the extreme effects of the regime on its citizens when some of the other characters are examined. One case of the mundane is Syme, one of Winston's friends, although "'friend' was not exactly the right word. You did not have friends nowadays, you had comrades" (51). Syme works on the supposedly definitive eleventh edition of the Newspeak dictionary. While queuing for lunch early on in the novel, he asks Winston if he attended a recent hanging of prisoners. When Winston says he could not make it, Syme casually fills him in on what he missed:

> 'It was a good hanging,' said Syme reminiscently. 'I think it spoils it when they tie their feet together. I like to see them kicking. And above all, at the end, the tongue sticking right out, and blue—a quite bright blue. That's the detail that appeals to me.' (52)

Syme's offhand recollection of the hanging displays what living under the Party has done to him. He has been hardened inside in the way Winston feels all Party members have become. Syme still possesses an aesthetic sense and a keen interest in the intricacies of the language coming into being, and in the dictionary that is intended to codify it. But his sense of beauty has been corrupted so that he sees destruction and violence as beautiful: "It's a beautiful thing, the destruction of words" (54), he says reflectively while explaining to Winston the purpose of the Newspeak dictionary. Syme's nonchalant enjoyment of death and destruction is reminiscent of Winston's perverse pleasure in the murders shown in the propaganda flicks, which he describes in his first diary entry.

Importantly, Syme introduces to the story the fact that "Newspeak is the only language in the world whose vocabulary gets smaller every year" (55). This shrinking vocabulary, when distilled to its final form, is supposed to render decency impossible, although such implications are invisible or merely irrelevant to Syme. Winston recognizes in his comrade—as he recognizes in the involuntary facial tic of the man he passes on the street—that Syme will soon be vaporized: "He is too intelligent. He sees too clearly and speaks too plainly. The Party does not like such people" (56). If stupidity is an asset, then intelligence is obviously a liability.

After Syme is in fact rendered an *unperson*, he makes one final ghostly appearance in the novel, on the occasion of O'Brien's and Winston's first conversation, when O'Brien casually mentions having recently spoken to "a friend" of Winston's "who is certainly an expert" on Newspeak (164). Winston knows instantly that the friend in question is Syme and that by referring to him, even obliquely, O'Brien has committed thoughtcrime. Unfortunately for him, Winston misinterprets O'Brien's transgression as a sign that he, like Winston, is willing to work towards the downfall of Big Brother.

Parsons, Winston's neighbor, represents another mundane expression of the indecent regime's effects on the citizenry. Parsons, "a tubby, middle-sized man with fair hair and a froglike face" (58), appears completely innocuous, exactly the sort of man the Party wants everyone to be. He also stands in for another of the effects of the exclusivity imposed by the Party and of a too-narrow perspective in general—xenophobia. Having transmitted his orthodox zeal to his children, Parsons brags at lunch about his daughter's latest exploits as a member of the Spies, the children's surveillance brigade that, as a matter of course, turns people in to the Thought Police at the slightest hint of thoughtcrime or mere difference. He tells a story of his daughter and another girl from the Spies following a "strange man" (60) around town for two hours and eventually handing him over to the patrols. When Winston asks why the girls did this, Parsons is triumphant in response: "My kid made sure he was some kind of enemy agent—might have been dropped by parachute, for instance. But here's the point, old boy. What do you think put her onto him in the first place? She spotted he was wearing a funny kind of shoes—said she's never seen anyone wearing shoes like that before. So the chances were he was a foreigner" (60). Of course, there is never any proof that the "strange" man was, in fact, an enemy agent or even a foreigner. Yes, the man "might have" been dropped by parachute, and "the chances are" he was a foreigner. But this is the great thing about xenophobia. The stranger is guilty by association. No proof is necessary. The lesson to the citizens is that anyone different, in even the most minor of ways, is to be turned in as a potential enemy. The lack of a doubled point of view results in vigilantism and necessitates that "others"—however they are to be designated—be persecuted. Moreover, this persecution is to be met with the kind of reaction we see in Parsons, with xenophobic pride. It is only fitting, then, that Parsons is one of the prisoners Winston encounters in the Ministry of Love before his torture begins. The same daughter who turned in the alleged foreigner turns in her own father for thoughtcrime.

Regarding the extremity of the Party's effects on the citizens of Oceania is the unnamed man with the "tormented, skull-like face" (247) who arrives in the Ministry of Love in the hours after Winston's capture. This man's brief appearance in the novel expresses all that is most terrible about living under an indecent regime as he completely abandons any semblance of dignity or nobility when confronted with the prospect of going to room 101. Somewhat predictably, he is willing to denounce others in the room in order to save himself. They are strangers, after all, and, given a choice, he'd much rather see them suffer in his place. But he offers up these strangers only after he has registered, in the starkest terms, his level of panic as well as the depths to which people in such circumstances are sometimes forced to sink:

You've been starving me for weeks. Finish it off and let me die. Shoot me. Hang me. Sentence me to twenty-five years. Is there

> somebody else you want me to give away? Just say who it is and I'll tell you anything you want. I don't care who it is or what you do to them. I've got a wife and three children. The biggest of them isn't six years old. You can take the whole lot of them and cut their throats in front of my eyes, and I'll stand by and watch it. But not room 101! (248–49)

It is easy to forget, even in this short passage, that the man is willing to be sentenced, shot, or hanged. The shock of watching a husband and father offer up his wife and three small children for torture in place of himself supplants whatever else he might have said.

The unnamed man's capitulation makes him look hateful and cowardly at first, and as Winston watches this spectacle, he wonders to himself, "If I could save Julia by doubling my own pain, would I do it?" (250). He initially answers his own question in the affirmative, but then, after subjecting his somewhat reflexive response to further scrutiny, he recognizes his answer as "an intellectual decision, taken because he knew that he ought to take it. He did not feel it" (250). Winston's silent reflections put his fellow prisoner's panic into context. The unnamed man's extreme reaction and Winston's consideration of it both foreshadow the crucial moment when Winston finds himself facing exactly the same choice regarding Julia that the man faces regarding his family. Winston's own moment of truth, as he finally offers up Julia to the rats only inches from his own face, is very similar to the unnamed man's in its extremity: "Do it to Julia! Do it to Julia! Not me! Julia! I don't care what you do to her. Tear her face off, strip her to the bones. Not me! Julia! Not me!" (300). Both men's reactions make clear the brutalizing effects of life under the Party.

Julia, like many of the women in Orwell's fiction, is more symbol than character. Once she and Winston are captured, Julia becomes an inspiring memory that Winston holds onto in order to find the strength to withstand O'Brien's torture. Beatrix Campbell argues that Julia appears to lack any intellectual curiosity: "She's not interested in politics as such, even though she'll lay down her life for her revolt. When Winston finally gets his hands on Goldstein's bible of dissidence, he tells her urgently that they must read the forbidden text together. What does she do? She tells him to read it to her. And when he does? She falls asleep" (71). But Julia is able to accomplish and understand things in a way that the intellectual Winston is not; she has "a practical cunning which Winston lacked" (133). After all, she is the one who contrives a way to establish their first contact; she arranges their meetings, and procures Inner Party coffee, tea, sugar, and chocolate through the black market.

Julia also appears more in command of her relationship with the rituals and requirements of the Party than Winston is. Whereas Winston is confused and carried along with the mob's emotions during the Two Minutes Hate, Julia understands implicitly how things work, and knows that she understands: "I'm good at games. I was a troop-leader in the Spies. I do voluntary work three evenings a week for the Junior Anti-Sex League. Hours and hours I've spent pasting their bloody rot all over London. I always carry one end of a banner in the processions. I always look cheerful and I never shirk anything. Always yell with the crowd, that's what I say. It's the only way to be safe" (128). Even though Winston sees her as merely "a rebel from the waist downwards" (163), it is clear that Julia has a practical grasp of life in Oceania which Winston lacks.

Of course, the subject of the Party's effects on the characters, whether extreme or mundane, culminates, as do most things in *Nineteen Eighty-Four*, when Winston and Julia are discovered in the room above Charrington's junk shop. Although Julia prides herself in her ability "at spotting people who don't belong" (128), as she explains to Winston her initial attraction to him, she is no more adroit than Winston in spotting the true motivations of O'Brien, the member of the Inner Party who pretends to belong to the underground Brotherhood that is purportedly working for the overthrow of Big Brother.

That Julia doesn't recognize O'Brien any more accurately than Winston does summarizes the enclosed nature of the world in which the characters live and the effects this world has on them. It is a world in which there is no room for alternatives, making the emergence of decency practically out of the question. In fact, the Party cynically contrives what appear to be alternatives, which are also under their strict control. The Party builds a culture industry like that described by Max Horkheimer and Theodor Adorno in *Dialectic of Enlightenment*. The culture industry they describe exists under monopoly, an unbalanced economic condition that makes their notion of the culture industry all the more applicable to Oceania under Big Brother:

All are in such close contact that the extreme concentration of mental forces allows demarcation lines between different firms and technical branches to be ignored. The ruthless unity in the culture industry is evidence of what will happen in politics. Marked differentiations such as those of A and B films, or of stories in magazines in different price ranges, *depend not so much on subject matter as on classifying, organizing, and labelling consumers.* Something is provided for all *so that none may escape*; the

distinctions are emphasized and extended. (123, emphasis
added)[2]

A "ruthless unity" of politics *and* culture describes the Party's oppressively
singular vision. The proles are provided with the lottery and pornography (to
which tapes of Julia and Winston's encounters above Charrington's junk shop
will contribute) to distract them. Party members watch the propaganda
flicks, as do the proles, although their seating is segregated. The Party
provides Winston and Julia with the room above Charrington's shop for their
clandestine meetings, since Charrington is actually a member of the
Thought Police. The two dissidents are even given hope, in the form of the
symbolic text of the incipient revolution against the Party. The text that
promises to overthrow Big Brother, *The Theory and Practice of Oligarchical
Collectivism*, ostensibly written by Emmanuel Goldstein, was, of course,
actually written in part by O'Brien. The enclosed nature of the culture
industry contrived by the Party is even hinted at lexically in the similarity of
the principal symbols of oppression and freedom—Big Brother and
Brotherhood, respectively—since both names lead back to the Party. The
state in all of its forms and productions works inexorably towards singularity
and the defeat of any type of doubleness.

O'Brien—Imposing the Party's Final Vocabulary

O'Brien is as integral to our understanding of Winston as Veraswami is to
Flory, Rosemary is to Gordon, and Boxer is to Napoleon. He is the Party's
attack dog, except there is no overpowering him, as Boxer was able to do with
Napoleon's enforcers. As has already been mentioned, in *Nineteen Eighty-
Four* the decent character is central to the narrative and the indecent one is
the contrasting figure, which is the reverse of the relationships in the first
three novels. By the time we reach *Nineteen Eighty-Four*, though, the
elaborate nature of the society in which the protagonist lives highlights the
lack of decency so completely that Winston becomes the character who wins
our approbation almost by default, because of the insurmountable odds he
faces. In Part III, O'Brien becomes a condensation of all that is arrayed
against Winston, and it is very easy for Winston to appear sympathetic next
to him.

Winston Smith believes early on that he and O'Brien actually share a
common hatred of the Party and a desire for its overthrow. During the Two
Minutes Hate, Winston is sure he intuits a moment of unspoken agreement
between himself and O'Brien, as their eyes briefly meet: "It was as though
their two minds had opened and the thoughts were flowing from one into the

other through their eyes. 'I am with you,' O'Brien seemed to be saying to him. 'I know precisely what you are feeling. I know all about your contempt, your hatred, your disgust. But don't worry, I am on your side!'" (19). Of course, it is true that O'Brien knows about Winston's contempt, hatred, and disgust for the Party, although he is hardly on Winston's side.

In *Contingency, Irony, and Solidarity*, Richard Rorty describes Part III of *Nineteen Eighty-Four* as "something different—something not topical, prospective rather than descriptive. After Winston and Julia go to O'Brien's apartment, 1984 becomes a book about O'Brien, not about twentieth-century totalitarian states" (171). While Rorty argues that Part III is different from the first two-thirds of the novel, I would argue that it is the logical conclusion to Winston's attempt throughout the narrative to discover, first in private, then in public (at least in O'Brien's presence), the importance of a doubled perspective and a capacity for decency.

While I disagree with his characterization of the separateness of Part III, Rorty's reading of *Nineteen Eighty-Four* establishes a framework for the argument that goes on between Winston and O'Brien in the Ministry of Love. Although at first it might not appear that my argument about the value of decency as Orwell presents it would have much in common with Rorty's antifoundationalism,[3] his chapter on *Nineteen Eighty-Four* is very helpful in understanding the portrayal of decency in this novel as well as the development of this subject throughout the four novels under examination here. While Rorty's arguments do not lend themselves to easy précis, concentrating on three crucial concepts of *Contingency, Irony, and Solidarity* enables the examination of the important relationship between Winston Smith and O'Brien, the ultimate representatives of decency and indecency in Orwell's work. The three concepts from Rorty's argument are "final vocabulary," "redescription," and "ironism."

Rorty defines "final vocabulary" as follows:

> All human beings carry about a set of words which they employ to justify their actions, their beliefs, and their lives. These are the words in which we formulate praise of our friends and contempt for our enemies, our long-term projects, our deepest self-doubts and our highest hopes. They are the words in which we tell, sometimes prospectively and sometimes retrospectively, the story of our lives. I shall call these words a person's 'final vocabulary.' (73)

To Rorty, Part III of *Nineteen Eighty-Four* is a speculation on what can happen when final vocabularies come into conflict and one vocabulary gets

redescribed in terms of another. The term "redescription" builds on the idea
of final vocabulary, since in redescribing we engage with our own final
vocabularies as well as with those of others. One potential that lies at the
heart of redescription is what happens to Winston when he finally
encounters the Thought Police:

> They broke his paperweight and punched Julia in the belly,
> thus initiating the process of making him describe himself in
> O'Brien's terms rather than his own. The redescribing
> ironist, by threatening one's final vocabulary, and thus one's
> ability to make sense of oneself in one's own terms rather than
> hers [the ironist's], suggests that one's self and one's world are
> futile, obsolete, *powerless*. Redescription often humiliates.
> (90)[4]

Redescription can create an environment of hostility, danger, suspicion, and
humiliation. Because of the importance of our final vocabularies in allowing
us to make sense of our worlds and our places in those worlds, redescription
brings with it the possibility that is represented in Part III of *Nineteen Eighty-
Four*, the possibility that two different final vocabularies may not be able to
coexist peacefully, with one rendering the other futile, obsolete, and
powerless.

This possibility of warring vocabularies makes the "ironist" very
important because this figure is not wedded to the idea of a definitively
"right" way of seeing the world. As such, the ironist need not be tempted into
bigotry or any otherwise narrow exclusion in order to justify the existence of
his or her own final vocabulary. The ironist's vocabulary can coexist with
those of others. The ironist fulfils three conditions:

> (1) She has radical and continuing doubts about the final
> vocabulary she currently uses, because she has been impressed by
> other vocabularies, vocabularies taken as final by people or books
> she has encountered; (2) she realizes that argument phrased in
> her present vocabulary can neither underwrite nor dissolve these
> doubts; (3) insofar as she philosophizes about her situation, she
> does not think that her vocabulary is closer to reality than others,
> that it is in touch with a power not herself. Ironists who are
> inclined to philosophize see the choice between vocabularies as
> made neither within a neutral and universal metavocabulary nor
> by an attempt to fight one's way past appearances to the real, but
> simply by playing the new off against the old. (73)

The ironist, then, is engaged in a process as opposed to simply trying to prove or, worse still, impose a "truth."

The notion of the ironist is important to my reading of decency in Orwell's fiction because it comprises the commitment to doubt one's final vocabulary as a response to the influence of others' final vocabularies. Without needing to accept the radical contingency that Rorty posits, the doubled perspective that I find advocated in Orwell's work does require the ironist's ability and willingness to doubt his or her own vocabulary. In fact, ironist doubt comprises the value of decency and its attendant willingness to accept the fact that just because what is most important to "me" (whoever "I" am) is not what is most important to "you" (whoever "you" are) does not negate the ability for us to teach and learn from one another.

While the notion of the ironist helps explain the significance of doubting one's vocabulary, it is nevertheless crucial to recognize that Winston, even though possessed of a doubled sensibility and profound doubts about the vocabulary with which he conceives of his world, is no ironist. He believes, to the point of an almost religious faith, in the "spirit of Man" (282), for instance, that the Party cannot help but be overthrown by some mystical life force within humanity. As he says to O'Brien, "I don't know—I don't care. Somehow you will fail. Something will defeat you. Life will defeat you" (282). He also believes in the power of love, a belief he holds onto desperately until O'Brien finally takes even that away from him.

It's useful to see Winston, again the doubled sensibility, as somewhere between an ironist and what Rorty calls a metaphysician: "The metaphysician is still attached to common sense, in that he does not question the platitudes which encapsulate the use of a given final vocabulary, and in particular the platitude which says there is a single permanent reality to be found behind the many temporary appearances" (74). Given what Winston faces at the hands of O'Brien, it is hardly surprising that he would want to cling to something, anything, he can conceive of as permanent, even if it is something as simple as "two plus two make four" (84). At the same time, when faced with the preponderance of ideological weight amassed against him, Winston cannot help but doubt his final vocabulary: "He wondered, as he had many times wondered before whether he himself was a lunatic. Perhaps a lunatic was simply a minority of one. At one time it had been a sign of madness to believe that the earth goes round the sun: today, to believe that the past is unalterable. He might be *alone* in holding that belief, and if alone, then a lunatic. But the thought of being a lunatic did not greatly trouble him: the horror was that he might also be wrong" (83). Winston's is the kind of doubt in which Rorty contends the metaphysician does not engage. Tellingly, the example chosen to prove a past indicator of lunacy is one that has long been accepted as scientific fact.[5] What was once lunacy has become truth, proving that there are times when the minority of one is neither insane nor wrong, even though the individual questions his or her vocabulary.

When Winston writes in his diary, "*I understand HOW: I do not understand WHY*" (83), he summarizes the potential role decency might eventually play in a revolutionized Oceania. The question "how" is easily answered by simple observation. Anyone in Oceania can see how the rules of Ingsoc are enforced—divergence from the rules results in vaporization or a sentence in the salt mines or a forced-labor camp. He knows how the historical record is perpetually updated, since he is part of the updating apparatus. There is little or no room for interpretation or difference of opinion in the question of "how"; the citizen's responsibility is simply to obey.

The question "why," though, necessitates interpretation and interpretation in turn will result invariably in multiple answers. Winston desires this multiplicity, which could render the Party's hold on the people less absolute. Since it could not prescribe every possible interpretation of even this simplest of questions—why—the alternative perspectives begin to look potentially infinite. Once the alternatives gain expression in the public forum, the man in the "funny" shoes need not be turned in as a spy, for instance, and a sense of decency may begin to emerge. But first, the question "why" must be permitted. The hope for this sense of decency is enough to sustain Winston in all but his worst moments of torture.

The worst moments bring Winston face to face with the most harrowing aspect of the novel as well as with "the worst thing in the world" (297). This is also the most direct instance in Orwell's fiction of the confrontation between the decent and the indecent. By pursuing *ownlife*—by keeping a diary, by having a relationship with Julia, by holding to a version of reality that incorporates his own desire for decency in addition to enduring the version of reality enforced by the Party—Winston has committed thoughtcrime, "the essential crime that contained all others in itself" (21). O'Brien marks more than merely the exposure of Winston's transgressions; he symbolizes and enacts in anatomical detail the punishment for his ostensible crimes.

This is what makes *Nineteen Eighty-Four* significantly different even from *Animal Farm*. Instead of merely seeing the prominent character who lacks the value of decency in contradistinction to the minor but decent character (as we have seen in the three earlier novels), *Nineteen Eighty-Four* allows us to watch *how* the indecent character overwhelms the decent one through the advantage of power. The extent of Winston's torture displays the magnitude of his sense of decency, as he argues against the Party's ability to torture even as he is being tortured. In addition, we are finally given the reason *why* the Party does what it does. But instead of opening up levels of interpretation, the explanation of "why"—"The object of persecution is persecution. The object of torture is torture. The object of power is power" (276)—is intended to foreclose permanently upon further interpretations. O'Brien's resorting to tautologies reveals his explanation as no answer at all.[6]

O'Brien is introduced as "a large, burly man with a thick neck and a coarse, humorous, brutal face. In spite of his formidable appearance he had a certain charm of manner. He had a trick of re-settling his spectacles on his nose which was curiously disarming—in some indefinable way, curiously civilised. It was a gesture which, if anyone had still thought in such terms, might have recalled an eighteenth-century nobleman offering his snuff-box" (12). O'Brien, like Winston, is an intelligent figure. But, unlike Winston, he has embraced completely the exclusive vision of the Party. A very telling description of the attitude O'Brien conveys adds a further layer of complexity to the villain's persona: "More even than of strength, he gave an impression of confidence and of an understanding tinged by irony. However much in earnest he might be, he had nothing of the single-mindedness that belongs to a fanatic" (182). O'Brien, while capable of conveying irony, is no more an ironist than is Winston. Whereas the ironist doubts his or her final vocabulary, O'Brien believes completely and uncompromisingly in his.[7] He is, however, a redescriber, in fact, the ultimate redescriber. It is his job to make Winston accept the Party's final vocabulary and only this one, without doubt or irony. O'Brien is, in fact, the worst kind of redescriber—one who can simply insist, through an almost unbelievable ruthlessness, on the ultimate rightness of his vocabulary to the exclusion of any other. While he is characterized as having nothing of the "single-mindedness" of the fanatic, his forcible imposition of the Party's vocabulary on Winston is motivated by the fanatical single-mindedness of the Party. The potential for redescription as humiliation is easily understood through O'Brien.

The tinge of irony in this character makes him an especially chilling figure as well as an ingenious creation. To make him a barbarian along the lines of the menacing Eastasian hordes (or Eurasian, it doesn't really matter which) who always lurk just beyond the frame of the story would be to distance his cruelty from the reality Orwell is trying to portray. O'Brien must be seen as friendly and courteous, in fact different "from the majority of Inner Party members" (164), whom we never see. His ostensible civility reminds us that just as anyone is capable of decency, anyone—irrespective of his or her outwardly "civilized" appearance—is also capable of indecency.

Rorty calls O'Brien "as terrifying a character as we are likely to meet in a book" (183), adding that "Orwell managed, by skilful reminders of, and extrapolations from, what happened to real people in real places—things that nowadays we know are still happening—to convince us that O'Brien is a plausible character-type of a possible future society, one in which the intellectuals had accepted the fact that liberal hopes had no chance of realization" (183). O'Brien, put another way, represents the very real possibility, and the very real fear, that the value of decency may simply be the enormous platitude that Orwell says readers sometimes find in Dickens, that if people behaved decently the world would be decent. But Rorty's reading of O'Brien adds more of an edge to the critique of decency as mere liberal platitude. The implicit conflict in Orwell's work between the sorts of people who see themselves as leaders or potential leaders (Flory, Gordon, and Napoleon) and the rest of society finds its ultimate expression in O'Brien, as Rorty stresses: "O'Brien is a curious, perceptive intellectual—much like us. Our sort of people don't do that sort of thing" (183). O'Brien's inclusion in the novel suggests that, under some circumstances—possibly under the totalitarianism Orwell always fears—our sort of people *can* do the sort of things depicted in Part III of *Nineteen Eighty-Four*. Both Orwell and Rorty, then, shed an unflattering light on—and prompt close scrutiny of—"our" sort of people. Both break ranks with their presumed peers in order to scrutinize their peers' motives. *Nineteen Eighty-Four* features two intelligent characters on opposite sides of a question. Two crucial details separate them: the willingness to treat others decently and the ability of one individual to impose his will on the other without acknowledging that other's concerns. Again, it is this lack of concern, this lack of decency, that makes horrors such as those depicted in Part III of *Nineteen Eighty-Four* possible.

That Winston's desire for decency runs afoul of the Party's drive to maintain a narrow and exclusive vision of the past, present, and future means that something must give. Because of the Party's capacity for cruelty it is only a matter of time before Winston is forced not only to relent but to reimagine his vocabulary entirely. The key to this profound transformation lies in humiliation. As is the case in *Animal Farm*, there are moments when the effects of propaganda must be supported by physical force. Napoleon has his dogs; the Party has O'Brien.

Rorty's description of the moment in the novel when Winston's final vocabulary is irreparably changed is the most arresting passage in his chapter on *Nineteen Eighty-Four*:

> 'Now that I have believed or desired *this*, I can never be what I hoped to be, what I thought I was. The story I have been telling myself about myself—my picture of myself as honest, or loyal, or devout—no longer makes sense. I no longer have a self to make

sense of. There is no world in which I can picture myself as living, because there is no vocabulary in which I can tell a coherent story about myself.' For Winston the sentence he could not utter sincerely and still be able to put himself back together was 'Do it to Julia!' and the worst thing in the world happened to be rats. But presumably each of us stands in the same relations to some sentence, and to some thing. (179)[8]

This description marks the irreparable rupture within Winston's final vocabulary. With the idea of the final vocabulary still in mind, we can also appreciate with new clarity the magnitude of the defeat suffered by the unnamed man with the "tormented, skull-like face" (247) whose capitulation prefigures Winston's. He, too, and presumably Syme and others, has been changed beyond repair as a result of having been forced to utter some sentence after which he will be unable to reconstitute himself as he was before.

Rorty's description of Winston's redescription by O'Brien sounds very much like O'Brien's account of the same process:

What happens to you here is for ever. Understand that in advance. We shall crush you down to the point *from which there is no coming back*. Things will happen to you from which you could not recover, if you lived a thousand years. Never again will you be capable of ordinary human feeling. Everything will be dead inside you. Never again will you be capable of love, or friendship, or joy of living, or laughter, or curiosity, or courage, or integrity. You will be hollow. We shall squeeze you empty, and then we shall fill you with ourselves. (268–69, emphasis added)

O'Brien essentially tells Winston that his desire for decency will no longer be a part of his final vocabulary once the Party has finished with him. O'Brien, a man as astute and sensitive in his observations of the world as Winston is, explains to Winston what his new final vocabulary will consist of. This new vocabulary will render forever impossible the decency to which Winston has been desperately clinging. The capacities for love, friendship, joy of living, laughter, curiosity, courage, and integrity are the sort of "human" qualities Winston so admires in the proles. O'Brien's speech redescribes Winston's vocabulary in the Party's terms. In fact, he presages the time when Winston will *become* the Party.

When Winston finally yells, "Do it to Julia," two things happen to him. In addition to a permanent change in his vocabulary, he is forced to abandon his desire for decency in favor of its polar opposite. In uttering these words in particular, he actively wishes the worst thing in the world upon another person. The prospect of being attacked by rats makes it impossible, at this moment, for him to see the value of treating another as befitting their status as a human being. He would rather she be torn apart by the rodents. Moreover, Julia is the one person in the world whom he claims to love. There is no reconstituting himself as the man he once was after this.

As Winston retains his lucidity during his debates with O'Brien, debates punctuated by excruciating electrical shocks, he is confronted by the sort of inescapable internal reflections that come with a doubled perspective: "What can you do, thought Winston, against the lunatic who is more intelligent than yourself, who gives your arguments a fair hearing and then simply persists in his lunacy?" (275). It is difficult for Winston to understand the singular extremity of O'Brien's motivation. How can he appear sane and yet act as he does? O'Brien's certainty cannot help but add to the doubt in Winston's own mind.

Nineteen Eighty-Four is the logical final expression of the implications regarding decency made in the earlier novels. But there is little sustained, direct conflict in those novels between the duplicities that the protagonists indulge in and some force attempting to expose them. Veraswami goes along with Flory's hollow condemnations of the Empire believing that Flory actually means them; Rosemary sticks by Gordon, even though she is certain that his proclamations against money hold little water. Even Boxer does not directly oppose the pigs for very long because of his lack of intellectual sophistication. There is no sustained debate in these stories; any judgments against the protagonists' duplicities are voiced largely by the narrators. O'Brien's ability to engage in dispute with Winston is hardly an indicator of his intelligence or his ability to give Winston's arguments a fair hearing. If either were the case, there would be no need for Winston to be connected to a machine that delivers painful shocks whenever O'Brien receives an answer he does not like. The argument is played out for the *reader's* consideration. The extremity of the Party's narrow vocabulary reveals itself as lunacy.

Another mark of the progression from the earlier novels occurs when O'Brien reads in Winston's mind the word that best describes the destructively narrow vision of the Party: "And yet he knew, he *knew*, that he was in the right. The belief that nothing exists outside your own mind—surely there must be some way of demonstrating that it was false? Had it not been exposed long ago as a fallacy? There was even a name for it, which he had forgotten" (278–79). Winston thinks this to himself but dares not utter it aloud. But the narrator makes sure that *we* know that Winston, for all he has suffered, still holds to his beliefs, still clings to his sense that human beings are more than subjects to be tortured and bent to the will of the powerful.

O'Brien delivers the metaphysical punchline in the scene, "The word you are trying to think of is solipsism," he says. But then he goes on to concede that the Party's worldview is in fact solipsistic: "This is not solipsism. Collective solipsism, if you like" (279). But a collective solipsism is still solipsism nonetheless. Here the joke is on O'Brien, since the narrator introduces the concept of solipsism through Winston's thoughts. As with the other novels, this is a moment in the story in which the narrator's account of events is intended to point out the flaw in the indecent character's argument. Winston cannot point out such a flaw aloud because to do so is to bring on still further abuse. But the narrator, from the safe distance of omniscience, can make this point for the reader's benefit. These moments of narrative judgment make it clear that O'Brien's narrow vision is presented as something to be feared and warned against.

OPTIMISM ... AFTER A FASHION

Nineteen Eighty-Four is the high point of Orwell's career of expressing the mitigated optimism he steadfastly maintains. The character of Winston Smith clearly symbolizes Orwell's belief that even from the direst of circumstances the desire for decency will emerge. For all of the overwhelming infrastructure in place in Oceania to enforce one viewpoint and one viewpoint only, *Nineteen Eighty-Four* still offers the hope that the capacity for doubleness, and therefore the hope of decency, will endure.

Four elements of *Nineteen Eighty-Four* combine to emphasize, finally, the novel's underlying mitigated optimism. All four elements show that the Party is unable to impose definitively its oppressively narrow point of view on its citizens. First, the appendix is written in the past tense and in Oldspeak, suggesting the passing of the Party into history by the time the appendix is written. Second, Newspeak itself reveals its own inner tensions, which threaten to destabilize it from within. Third, the physical condition of Winston Smith at the novel's end mocks the Party's lofty self-image. Lastly, and most importantly for the fate of decency in the novel, Winston's thoughts as he sits in the Chestnut Tree Café express his residual doubleness, left over even after all O'Brien has subjected him to. The four items listed accumulate to make a strong case for a mitigatedly optimistic reading of *Nineteen Eighty-Four*, a reading premised on the inability of the Party to impose—once and for all—a singular, exclusive perspective on its citizens that will outlaw the capacity for decency.

First, to the appendix: Roger Fowler argues that "the tone of the Newspeak Appendix—which I suspect is rarely read carefully, or not in the context of the other styles of the novel—is quite clearly satirical" (211).[9] The Party's ongoing project for complete linguistic control, according to Fowler, is central to Orwell's satire of the Party itself. The satire of the appendix also derives from the fact that it is written in the past tense, suggesting that the elaborate lengths to which the Party goes to ensure its longevity have, at the end of the day, failed. The joke of history is on them.

Frank Winter has been able to assemble a quite compelling case for the appendix "as an integral part of the narrative" (79). He argues that a literal reading of the appendix "pinpoints the end of Newspeak ... somewhere between the Eleventh Edition of the Newspeak Dictionary (shortly after *Nineteen Eighty-Four*) and the time set for the completion of the (in fact, unfinished) translations [of various classic authors into Newspeak, as set out in the appendix], i.e. before the first decade of the twenty-first century" (86). Likewise, Robert Paul Resch has noted the importance of "a utopian frame" around *Nineteen Eighty-Four*, which establishes the relationship of the appendix and the end of the Inner Party:

> The existence of a utopian frame is both a most interesting and frequently overlooked feature of *Nineteen Eighty-Four*. It exists as the post-totalitarian world of the 'author,' whose footnote, early in the first chapter, serves to inform us that we are reading a historical novel written sometime after the demise of Oceania, and whose appendix, 'The Principles of Newspeak,' takes the form of a scholarly monograph looking back on Oceania as an extinct and almost incomprehensible civilization. (158)

The retrospective attitude of the author of the appendix, combined with the obvious fact that the appendix is written in Oldspeak, encourages us to infer that by the time of the appendix's authorship something—be it the "spirit of Man" (282) for which Winston argues or what Judith Wilt calls a "quirky aliveness" of the proles' oral culture (254)—has rendered the Party a historical (and novelistic) footnote. The principles of Ingsoc and the absolute rule of the Party as intoned by O'Brien are again clearly the butt of the satire, just as the pigs, Gordon, and Flory all are.

If the "spirit of Man" does not undo the Party by itself, there is a second factor—related directly to the Party's desire for complete linguistic control—lying in wait to dismantle the regime of indecency described in *Nineteen Eighty-Four*, and that is the very logic of the language on which the regime is based. The logical inconsistencies that start to proliferate once

Newspeak is closely examined as a linguistic enterprise highlight the self-destructive tensions within the Party's structure itself. If Syme, the resident expert on Newspeak in the novel, is correct, and the "Revolution will be complete when the language is perfect" and that "Newspeak is Ingsoc and Ingsoc is Newspeak" (55), then the stakes of getting the basics of the burgeoning language exactly right are very high indeed.

And yet, Alan Kennedy is able to deconstruct Syme's explanation of the contradictory meanings for the Newspeak word "*duckspeak*," "one of those interesting words that have two contradictory meanings. Applied to an opponent, it is abuse; applied to someone you agree with, it is praise" (57). Kennedy's observation throws the validity of the word "duckspeak" as an orthodox Newspeak word into question, using the tenets of Newspeak as set out in the novel as the instrument of its own unraveling. Kennedy says, regarding Syme's explanation:

> Gone, it seems, is the rule of one word for one meaning. Are we meant to read this as an inconsistency on Orwell's part? Or are we meant to read it as Orwell's indication that Big Brother is a logical impossibility? And, if Big Brother is a logical impossibility, what are we to do with a novel in which the characters are so much living in fear of him? If the duckspeak principle is a qualification of the earlier 'one to one' position, then it means that one must tailor meanings to situations, which is of course what we always try to do with language. (81)[10]

The word "duckspeak," then, is an aporia, an undecidable double bind within a language established in order to render unorthodox thought impossible. This one example introduces the notion of interpretation into a language whose principal function is to render interpretation impossible, since interpretations are subjective and thus uncontrollable. So, as the Party attempts to enforce the singular at all costs, the doubled still manages to emerge, even from within the Party's own creation.

The third and fourth points regarding the mitigated optimism of *Nineteen Eighty-Four*—Winston's physical condition and his thoughts—are closely related. While I have portrayed Winston as the champion of doubleness and decency, who perseveres in his hopes despite overwhelming odds, the hollowed-out state to which he is reduced by the end of the novel works as much against the Party's ideals as it does Winston's own. Crick reads the novel's ending as "*Galgenhumor*, 'gallows humor'" ("Introduction" xiii), suggesting that the last paragraph is "broad satire all the way" ("Introduction" xiii). His point is this:

I read the passage as saying that the Party can break Winston Smith but that it cannot remake him in any heroic image, only as a miserable, beaten, frightened drunk, neither dedicated proletarian nor purified Aryan. And notice it is not 'the last passage,' as is so often sepulchrally said. After 'THE END' comes the 'Appendix.' I suspect that the capitalized 'THE END' is another little bit of *Galgenhumor*, for it appears in no other book by the same publisher in this period, but usually only appeared in popular novelettes and at the end of Hollywood B-movies—presumably in case the reader or viewer ran one into the next by mistake. ("Introduction" xiii)

Crick sees Winston's diminished physical state as mocking the Party's goals for singularity and control, what it sees as perfection. During his torture of Winston, O'Brien tells his victim, by way of perverse reassurance, "I shall save you, I shall make you perfect" (256). What he has produced in the Winston Smith who ends the novel may hardly be interpreted as perfection. Certainly Winston's fate may be a cautionary tale to other prospective dissidents in Oceania, but there is no way for the Party to control how every single citizen will view Winston's final status. His hollowed out state as he sits in the Chestnut Tree Café is a sort of martyrdom. He has, at least for now, survived. Once again, this inability to control interpretation lies at the heart of the Party's self-destruction at the hands of doubleness.[11]

Finally, following from the observation of Winston's physical state is the fourth element regarding the mitigated victory of doubleness and decency over narrowness. This fourth point concerns Winston's mental state. The condition of that precious "few cubic centimetres inside your skull" (29) which Winston desperately wants to keep as his own and which O'Brien works to change becomes crucial to the status of decency at the end of Orwell's last novel. As he sits in the Chestnut Tree Café after he is released from the Ministry of Love, Winston listens to news of the Party's latest victory and looks up at a portrait of Big Brother. This scene reprises his conflicted feelings at the Two Minutes Hate from the opening pages of the novel. At first he imagines himself running with the joyous crowds at the news of Oceania's victory over the Eurasian army: "Under the table Winston's feet made convulsive movements. He had not stirred from his seat, but in his mind he was running, swiftly running, he was with the crowds outside, cheering himself deaf" (310). He thinks to himself that with the news of victory, the "final, indispensable, healing change" has finally come to him. His ultimate acceptance of Big Brother had not occurred "until this moment" (311).

But, as is the case in the Two Minutes Hate, so here, as Winston immediately imagines himself back in the Ministry of Love: "He was not running or cheering any longer. He was back in the Ministry of Love, with everything forgiven, his soul white as snow. He was in the public dock, confessing everything, implicating everybody. He was walking down the white-tiled corridor, with the feeling of walking in sunlight, and an armed guard at his back. The long-hoped-for bullet was entering his brain" (311). The long-hoped-for bullet is the one that will actually set Winston free, as he thinks to himself earlier, while he is actually in the Ministry of Love, still trying desperately to resist O'Brien: "And almost in the same instant bang! would go the bullet, too late, or too early. They would have blown his brain to pieces before they could reclaim it. The heretical thought would be unpunished, unrepented, out of their reach for ever. They would have blown a hole in their own perfection. To die hating them, that was freedom" (294). So even as he thinks he has finally accepted Big Brother, he nevertheless continues to hope for that fleeting moment of freedom that he will attain if he can manage to hate the Party at the instant of his execution. As he thinks to himself, then, that everything is all right, "the struggle was finished" and that he loves Big Brother, as the novel ends, *we* know the more complicated subtext of this thought. We know that the struggle is not over and that Winston Smith can still fleetingly lay claim, almost in spite of himself, to the few cubic centimeters inside his skull. Just as he was at the Two Minutes Hate at the beginning of the novel—sympathetic to the Party one minute, hating it the next—so he is after being "cured" by O'Brien. The last laugh, in one sense, is Winston's. An uncontrollable doubleness still remains.[12] Winston's final conflict within himself, then, still represents hope.

Between the manner in which the appendix is written, the internal tension of Newspeak, and Winston's physical and, most importantly, his mental state at the novel's conclusion, the Party's project of an enforced and inescapable singularity is besieged by more forces than it could possibly anticipate or control. This is the nature of Orwell's particular brand of optimism. It is mitigated, it requires some work in order to be discovered, but, like the hope for decency it describes, this optimism exists to the last.

NOTES

1. Patricia Rae makes an important point that crystallizes the relationship between Winston's public and private motivations:

> Winston's interest in Charrington originates, of course, in his quest to retrieve some sense of the past, and with it the capacity for critical

comparisons between past and present—for discovering whether things were 'better than they are now, or ... worse' (*Nineteen Eighty-Four* 90). His junk-shop scavengings represent his effort to reverse the work he conducts every day at the Ministry of Truth, burning incriminating photographs and scraps of obsolete text. ("Just Junk" 75)

2. Lynette Hunter describes the enterprise of containment in terms very similar to Horkheimer and Adorno's:

> The rhetoric of the nation-state structures its ethos simultaneously to build a norm as an artificial construction and then to forget that it is artificial. Orwell talked about this extensively in his later work under the term doublethink, and began to understand the incredible stress it puts on the relatively empowered.... Technically doublethink works from the accepted common grounds of corporate agreement, and uses a representing medium in such a way as to repeat without variation, or with as little as possible. (205)

Repetition without variation creates the same sense of containment that results from the classification, organization, and arrangement of consumers to which Horkheimer and Adorno refer. Even Hunter's notion of the "relatively empowered" only partially describes Winston and Julia, since no individuals have any real power in Oceania.

3. While Rorty's reading of *Nineteen Eighty-Four* is very helpful in elucidating the value of decency in Orwell's work as a whole, it's worth clarifying an important distinction to be drawn between his underlying philosophy and Orwell's Fowler, in explaining the satirical nature of the appendix, makes the point that Orwell was a realist when it came to the relation between language and meaning, not a nominalist, as Rorty is. Orwell, according to Fowler, "did *not* suggest that language might mould reality in some specific way (the nominalist position), as some commentators—misconstruing the import of Newspeak in *Nineteen Eighty-Four*—have suggested. His simple realism—words fail the truth of facts, and thus corrupt thought—makes his presentation of Newspeak less ambiguous but no less dramatic: Newspeak is an absurdly projected nominalism, a false belief that language can be manipulated to channel thought absolutely" (33). With respect to the difference between realism and nominalism, Rorty forcibly characterizes his own position in a way that distinguishes clearly between himself and Orwell: "For reasons already given, I do not think there are any plain moral facts out there in the world, nor any truths independent of language, nor any neutral ground on which to stand and argue that either torture or kindness are preferable to the other" (173). In "Chaos versus Contingency Theory: Epistemological Issues in Orwell's *1984*," Alexander J. Argyros criticizes Rorty's position by saying that "Rorty's vision of history is one in which social regimes rise and fall for purely contingent, and purely unpredictable reasons" (110–11). He adds: "Rorty's reasoning implies that the criteria whereby O'Brien is interpreted as an evil person are as malleable as any others. It just happens that almost all contemporary readers of *1984* view O'Brien as a baneful human being. It is just as likely that another culture might read him as a chevalier in service to the good" (111). Orwell's opinions on the necessity of Indian independence and the immorality of Britain's empire, as well as his urgent sense that Britain had to fight against Germany even though he agreed with the pacifists' argument that war is evil are just two examples that demonstrate he believed quite strongly in plain moral facts and that people *could* intervene in the path of history. These beliefs argue directly against Rorty's suggestion that Orwell helps us see that "it may have

just happened that Europe began to prize benevolent sentiments and the idea of a common humanity, and that it may *just happen* that the world will wind up being ruled by people who lack any such sentiments and any such moralities" (185). Leaving aside the obvious point that this idea of a common humanity accommodated quite comfortably the colonialism Orwell vociferously criticized, it is important to say that he believed too strongly in the ability of ordinary people to effect social change to accept the radical contingency Rorty champions.

4. The broader implications of Rorty's notion of redescription are also suggestive in understanding the relationship between the powerful who redescribe and the disenfranchised who are redescribed according to others' vocabularies: "Something like that presumably happens to a primitive culture when it is conquered by a more advanced one. The same sort of thing sometimes happens to nonintellectuals in the presence of intellectuals" (90). The ability to humiliate attendant in redescription comes in various degrees but occurs in numerous fields of human interaction. Orwell's hostility towards the monopolizing of socialism by intellectuals is another reaction to the power of redescription, since the intellectuals impose their vocabulary upon the working class, whose vocabulary is ignored, even though they would be best served by a socialist revolution.

5. In "The Hell of *Nineteen Eighty-Four*," Malcolm Pittock makes the point:

> The Inquisition, evoked in the torture and interrogation scenes, believed in effect that the truth could be defined socially—as being what a human organization said it was, and so confused received opinion with fact. When this was carried to the point, as with Galileo, that correct fact was treated as false opinion which had to be 'corrected' by adherence to an incorrect fact which was itself merely a false opinion, one is getting reasonably close to O'Brien. Indeed when the latter says, 'The earth is the centre of the universe. The sun and the stars go round it' ... we are surely meant to be reminded of the trial of Galileo. (157)

He adds, on the subject of O'Brien's philosophical underpinnings: "O'Brien's claim that nothing exists outside the human mind can be related to the extreme idealism characteristic of Berkeley's position, 'that only minds and mental events can exist,' while for philosophers like Quine and Rorty who challenge the distinction between synthetic and analytic propositions, two and two is not necessarily four" (157–58). What Pittock identifies as idealism is called solipsism in the novel.

6. Adding to this same point about O'Brien being a target of the satire, John Newsinger writes,

> O'Brien's statement of the Party's intentions and objectives is not intended as a terrible vision of what humanity's future is going to be ("If you want a picture of the future, imagine a boot stamping on a human face—forever") but is rather a satire of totalitarianism, a stripping away of the rationalization of Fascist and Communist rule to reveal the reality. Smith, the Last Man, could be any one of millions of concentration camp victims swallowed up by the totalitarian regimes of the 1930s and 1940s. This was Orwell's intention rather than any prediction of the future. (80)

7. In fact, as Gorman Beauchamp would have it, not only does O'Brien impose the Party's will on Winston, but he represents the worst that the present-day academy has to

offer. Beauchamp's invocation of O'Brien indicates another twenty-first-century relevance for Orwell—the debate over academic language:

> Although transmogrified, the smelly little orthodoxies that Orwell despised so much are still very much with us, and their academic O'Briens are busily at work in their respective Ministries of Love demonstrating to bemused undergraduate Winstons that what they had taken to be truths are merely cultural constructions not to be counted on. (268)

Beauchamp describes the dire consequences of what he sees as the relativism of many academic postmodernists. While he deliberately misses out a couple of crucial mechanisms that would be necessary to lead inexorably, as he seems to suggest, from undergraduates' inability to state the years in which World War II began and ended to the sort of totalitarian state Orwell creates in *Nineteen Eighty-Four* (most obviously, the need for a secret police as well as—and perhaps this is the main stumbling block—an irresistible dictator), Beauchamp shows another use for Orwell's writing. Perhaps more importantly, though, his pressing into service of Orwell to make an anti-orthodoxy claim runs the risk of becoming itself another orthodoxy, a criticism to which Orwell has also been subjected. And if one orthodoxy starts to look very much like the next, then Beauchamp may actually find himself helping to prove the relativist arguments of the postmodernists he intends to oppose.

A useful contrast to Beauchamp may be found in "Orwell and the Bad Writing Controversy," by Eugene Goodheart. Goodheart, while also making a forcible case in favor of the vernacular over the increasing specialization and opacity of academic prose, is more convincing than Beauchamp because he does not seem to be grinding an axe but instead clearly and lucidly making an argument. He acknowledges, for instance, that the vernacular "may not always provide what is needed for new insight" (441), citing the advent of the word "hegemony" as an example. His brief and balanced discussion attempts to be fair to both sides of the argument. He also writes:

> The vernacular and plain sense are not synonymous. Neither a party nor a cause, it is subject to a variety of uses. It can accommodate counterintuitive, difficult, and complex thought. (Stanley Fish's writing, for example, is proof that poststructuralist thought can be lucidly exposed in the vernacular.) Those who disdain the vernacular reflect a disdain for poems, novels, and plays, which have the vernacular as their medium. (442)

He is not arguing against the entire poststructuralist project, which appears to be Beauchamp's objective, and instead identifies a clear point and makes it compellingly and concisely.

Another excellent rendition of the debate, which includes Orwell as part of the discussion, is James Miller's "Is Bad Writing Necessary?" Miller employs Theodor Adorno and Orwell as proponents for less prosaic transparency and more, respectively, and does so in an article that is a model of balance, thoroughness, and, as fate would have it, lucidity. His illumination of the backgrounds and biases of both Adorno and Orwell make it difficult to judge, from the essay alone, which "side" Miller is on, making his possibly the best vehicle for the reader's making up his or her own mind. He concludes by acknowledging how some things, including the debate pitting transparency against opacity, never change, and adds,

But the next time one of our latter-day critical theorists attacks the desire for plain talk as a Trojan horse for 'left conservatism,' I suggest a thought experiment. Imagine poor old Adorno rolling over in his grave, still waiting for a messiah who may never come. And then picture Orwell, the 'Maggot of the Month,' as the communists used to call him, doubled over in laughter and delighted to discover a brand-new oxymoron being deployed as a rhetorical weapon of perfectly Orwellian proportions. (44)

8. While not using Rorty's approach to the novel, Edward J. Brown notes the same point about Winston's experiencing the worst thing in the world: "The pathetic Winston Smith, Julia's love, failed to know that having the rats gnawing his eyes would have been a happy fate compared to the final degradation of that 'Do it to Julia'" (168).

9. By following the line of inquiry that imputes a great deal of importance to the Appendix's having been written in the past tense, I might be included in what Richard K. Sanderson calls a "small school of optimists who argue that the true purpose of the Appendix is to give a positive twist to the seemingly hopeless ending of the novel" (590). Sanderson chooses instead to leave open the question of the Appendix's importance: "Just as O'Brien plays upon Winston's desire for certain knowledge about Oceania's social and political structure, leading him on with the possibly spurious 'Goldstein' tract, so the story's narrator draws the truth-seeking reader into an Appendix whose truth value cannot be determined" (593). While Sanderson's perspective is not optimistic, in itself, it does accord with my central argument about the Party's inability—no matter its elaborate efforts—to impose definitively a singular perspective on its citizens.

10. Andrei Reznikov notes the same point that Kennedy does about the ambivalence built into Newspeak. Reznikov writes: "one cannot help noticing an important feature: an orthodox user of Newspeak has to decide for himself or herself what meaning to attach to this word [*duckspeak*] in a given situation!" (47). Reznikov, however, does not see this as flaw in the language, but as another example of the oppressiveness of its structure: "War is peace, freedom is slavery, ignorance is strength—all are represented by a pair of antonyms united in a contradictory equation. By claiming that they are the same, Newspeak eliminates their opposition, and war really *becomes* peace, freedom really *becomes* slavery, and ignorance really *becomes* strength" (48). The enforced equation of clear opposites stands as another example of indecency, as the Party simply demands that its citizens train themselves to ignore the obvious opposition of the words, or risk vaporization.

11. The Russian novelist Vladimir Voinovich, in his dystopia, *Moscow 2042*, describes the same inability of the oppressive state to control absolutely its citizens. His main character, Kartsev, says of *Nineteen Eighty-Four*:

Orwell wrote a parody of what already existed at the time. He described a totalitarian machine that worked perfectly well and could simply never exist in a real human society. Take the Soviet Union—its population only displays an outward obedience to the regime; in fact, people have nothing but contempt for slogans and catch phrases. They respond by working poorly, drinking heavily, and stealing left and right. Big Brother is the target of ridicule and the subject of endless jokes. (qtd. in Olshanskaya 428)

Again, interpretation falls outside the control of the Party.

12. James Phelan's observations add to the impression of uncontrollable doubleness still left at the end of *Nineteen Eighty-Four*:

> The world revealed through these scenes and incidents is a curious mixture of efficiency and inefficiency, a world with sophisticated technology and a poor standard of living. Telescreens can both transmit and receive, and individuals can be watched vigilantly by the Thought Police, but elevators frequently don't work and food is barely palatable. Winston can rewrite newspaper articles and the historical record can be swiftly altered, but the streets don't get cleaned, and decent medical care for such things as Winston's varicose ulcer seems to be nonexistent. (99–100)

Of course, Phelan's observations point to the simple equation of guns or butter. The priority on surveillance renders the satisfaction of consumer desires impossible, as well as irrelevant. Nevertheless, his is yet another example of the Party's inability to impose complete control over the world in which its citizens live.

BIBLIOGRAPHY

Althusser, Louis. "Ideology and Ideological State Apparatuses." *Lenin and Philosophy and Other Essays*. Trans. Ben Brewster. New York: Monthly Review Press, 1971. 127–86.

"Andre Gide." Crossman 175–95.

Argyros, Alexander J. "Chaos versus Contingency Theory: Epistemological Issues in Orwell's 1984." *Mosaic* 26.1 (Winter 1993): 109–20.

"Arthur Koestler." Crossman 15–75.

Averill, Roger. "Empathy, Externality, and Character in Biography: A Consideration of the Authorized Versions of George Orwell." *CLIO* 31.1 (Fall 2001): 1–31.

Baker, Houston A. *Modernism and the Harlem Renaissance*. Chicago: U of Chicago P, 1987.

Barber, Benjamin R. *Jihad vs. McWorld: How Globalism and Tribalism Are Reshaping the World*. New York: Ballantine, 1995.

Beauchamp, Gorman. "Orwell, the Lysenko Affair, and the Politics of Social Construction." *Partisan Review* 68.2 (Spring 2001): 266–78.

Benda, Julien. *The Betrayal of the Intellectuals*. Trans. Richard Aldington. Intro. Herbert Read. Boston: Beacon, 1928.

Boggs, Carl. *Intellectuals and the Crisis of Modernity*. Albany: State U of New York P, 1993.

Bourdieu, Pierre. *In Other Words: Essays Towards a Reflexive Sociology*. Trans. Matthew Adamson. Stanford: Stanford UP, 1990.

Breton, Rob. "Crisis? Whose Crisis? George Orwell and Liberal Guilt." *College Literature* 29.4 (Fall 2002): 47–66.

Brown, Edward J. "Zamyatin's *We* and *Nineteen Eighty-Four*." *On Nineteen Eighty-Four*. Ed. Peter Stansky. New York: W. H. Freeman, 1983. 159–69.

Bryant, Marsha. "Auden and the Homoerotics of the 1930s Documentary." *Mosaic* (June 1997) 30:2. 69–92.

Buitenhuis, Peter and Ira B. Nadel, eds. *George Orwell: A Reassessment*. New York: St. Martin's, 1988.

Campbell, Beatrix. "Orwell—Paterfamilias or Big Brother?" Holderness et al. 64–75

Carter, Stephen L. *Integrity*. New York: Basic, 1996.

Conquest, Robert. "In Celia's Office: Orwell and the Cold War." *TLS* (21 Aug. 1998): 4–5.

Cose, Ellis. *The Rage of a Privileged Class*. New York: HarperCollins, 1993.

Crick, Bernard. "Introduction: An Essay." *The Penguin Essays of George Orwell*. Harmondsworth: Penguin, 1994.

———. *George Orwell: A Life*. London: Penguin, 1992.

———. "Orwell and English Socialism." Buitenhuis, 3–19.

Crossman, Richard, ed. *The God That Failed: Six Studies in Communism*. New York: Harper, 1949.

Davison, Peter, *George Orwell: A Literary Life*. Literary Lives Series. Gen. Ed. Richard Dutton. New York: St. Martin's, 1996.

Diggins, John Patrick. "Gramsci and the Intellectuals." *Raritan* 9.2 (Fall 1989): 129–52.

DuBois, W. E. B. *The Souls of Black Folk*. Norton Critical Edition. Ed. Henry Louis Gates, Jr., and Terri Hume Oliver. New York: Norton, 1999.

Early, Gerald, ed. *Lure and Loathing: Essays on Race, Identity, and the Ambivalence of Assimilation*. New York: Penguin, 1993.

Ellison, Ralph. *Invisible Man*: New York: Vintage, 1995.

Felski, Rita. "Nothing to Declare: Identity, Shame, and the Lower Middle Class." *PMLA* 115 (January 2000): 33–45.

Fitzgerald, E Scott. "The Crack-Up." *The Crack-Up*. Ed. Edmund Wilson. New York: New Directions, 1945.

Forster. E. M. *A Passage to India*. Ed. Oliver Stallybrass. Harmondsworth: Penguin, 1979.

Fotheringham, John. "George Orwell and Ernst Toller: The Dilemma of the Politically Committed Writer." *Neophilologus* 84.1 (January 2000): 1–18.

Fowler, Roger. *The Language of George Orwell*. New York: St. Martin's, 1995.

Germino, Dante. *Antonio Gramsci: Architect of a New Politics*. Political Traditions in Foreign Policy Series. Ed. Kenneth W. Thompson. Baton Rouge: Louisiana State UP, 1990.

Goodheart, Eugene. "Orwell and the Bad Writing Controversy." *CLIO* 28.4 (Summer 1999): 439–43.

Gottlieb, Erika. "Room 101 Revisited: The Reconciliation of Political and Psychological Dimensions in Orwell's *Nineteen Eighty-Four*." *Buitenhuis* 51–76.

———. *The Orwell Conundrum: A Cry of Despair or Faith in the Spirit of Man?* Ottawa: Carleton UP, 1992.

Gramsci, Antonio. *Selections from the Prison Notebooks of Antonio Gramsci*. Ed. Quintin Hoare and Geoffrey Nowell Smith. New York: International Publishers, 1971.

Guha, Ranajit. "Not at Home in Empire." *Critical Inquiry*. 23:3. (Spring 1997): 482–93.

Hitchens, Christopher. *Why Orwell Matters*. New York: Basic, 2002.

Holderness, Graham, Bryan Loughrey, and Nahem Yousaf, eds. *George Orwell*. New Casebook Series. New York: St. Martin's, 1998.

Holy Bible. 1611 Edition. King James Edition.

hooks, bell. *Yearning: Race, Gender, and Cultural Politics*. Toronto: Behind the Lines, 1990.

Horkheimer, Max and Theodor W. Adorno. *Dialectic of Enlightenment*. Trans. John Cumming. New York: Herder and Herder, 1972.

Hunter, Lynette. "Blood and Marmalade: Negotiations between the State and the Domestic in George Orwell's Early Novels." *Rewriting the Thirties: Modernism and After*. Eds. Keith Williams and Steven Matthews. London: Longman, 1997. 202–16.

Ingle, Stephen. *George Orwell: A Political Life*. Lives of the Left Series. Gen. Ed. David Howell. Manchester: Manchester UP, 1993.

Jay, Martin. "Hierarchy and the Humanities: The Radical Implications of a Conservative Idea." *Telos Special Issue: Debates in Contemporary Culture* 62 (Winter 1984–85): 1.31–44.

Kearney, Anthony. "Orwell's *Animal Farm* and *1984*." *Explicator* 54.4 (Summer 1996): 238–40.

Kennedy, Alan. "The Inversion of Form: Deconstructing 1984." Holderness et al. 76–96.

Kerr, Douglas. "Colonial Habits: Orwell and Woolf in the Jungle." *English Studies* 78.12 (March 1997): 149–61.

———. "Orwell, Animals, and the East." *Essays in Criticism* 49.3. (July 1999): 234–55.

Koestler, Arthur. *The Yogi and the Commissar and Other Essays*. London: Cape, 1964.

Laskowski, William E., Jr. "George Orwell and the Tory-Radical Tradition." Rose 149–90.

Lassner, Phyllis. "A Bridge Too Close: Narrative Wars to End Fascism and Imperialism." *JNT: Journal of Narrative Theory* 31.2 (Summer 2001): 131–54.

"The Legacy of Orwell: A Discussion." Panel discussion—Graff, John Lukacs, Edward Said. *Salmagundi* 70–71 (Spring–Summer 1986): 121–28.

Letemendia, V. C. "Revolution on *Animal Farm*: Orwell's Neglected Commentary." Holderness et al. 15–30.

Levine, Lawrence. *Highbrow/Lowbrow: The Emergence of Cultural Hierarchy in America*. Cambridge. MA: Harvard UP, 1988.

Lynes, Russell. *The Tastemakers*. New York: Harper, 1954.

March, Thomas. "Orwell's 'Marrakech.'" *Explicator* 57.3 (Spring 1999): 163–64.

Marcus, Greil. *Lipstick Traces: A Secret History of the Twentieth Century*. Cambridge, MA: Harvard UP, 1989.

Marks, Peter. "Where He Wrote: Periodicals and the Essays of George Orwell." *Twentieth-Century Literature* 41.4 (Winter 1995): 266–83.

Marx, Karl and Friedrich Engels. "The Manifesto of the Communist Party." *The Marx-Engels Reader*. 2nd Edition. Ed. Robert C. Tucker. New York: Norton, 1978.

McCarthy, Thomas. "An Exchange on Truth, Freedom, and Politics. II: Ironist Theory as a Vocation: A Response to Rorty's Reply." *Critical Inquiry* 16 (Spring 1990): 643–55.

———. "Private Irony and Public Decency: Richard Rorty's New Pragmatism." *Critical Inquiry* 16 (Winter 1990): 355–70.

Meyers, Jeffrey, ed. *George Orwell: The Critical Heritage*. Gen. Ed. B. C. Southam. London: Routledge, 1975.

———. "How True to Life Is Biography?" *Partisan Review* 68:1 (Winter 2001): 11–20.

———. *Orwell: Wintry Conscience of a Generation*. New York: Norton, 2000.

Meyers, Valerie. *George Orwell*. Modern Novelists Series. Gen. Ed. Norman Page. New York: St. Martin's, 1991.

Miller, James. "Is Bad Writing Necessary? George Orwell, Theodor Adorno, and the Politics of Language." *Lingua Franca* 9:9 (December 2000): 33–44.

Mouffe, Chantal, ed. *Gramsci and Marxist Theory*. London: Routledge, 1979.

Newsinger, John. "*Nineteen Eighty-Four* since the Collapse of Communism." *Foundation* 56 (Autumn 1992): 75–84.

Olshanskaya, Natalia. "Anti-Utopian Carnival: Vladimir Voinovich Rewriting George Orwell." *Forum of Modern Language Studies* 36.4. (October 2000): 426–37.

Orwell, George. *The Complete Works of George Orwell*. 20 vols. Ed. Peter Davison. London: Secker & Warburg. 1998.

Patai, Daphne. *The Orwell Mystique: A Study in Male Ideology*. Amherst: U of Massachusetts P, 1984.

Pearce, Robert. "Orwell, Tolstoy, and *Animal Farm*." *Review of English Studies* 49.193 (Feb 1998): 64–69.

Phelan, James. "Character, Progression, and Thematism in 1984." Holderness et al. 97–115.

Pittock, Malcolm. "The Hell of *Nineteen Eighty-Four*." *Essays in Criticism* 47.2 (April 1997): 143–164.

Rae, Patricia. "'Just Junk': George Orwell's Real-Life Scavengings and *Nineteen Eighty-Four*." *English Language Notes* 38.1 (September 2000): 73–79.

———. "Mr. Charrington's Junk Shop: T. S. Eliot and Modernist Poetics in *Nineteen Eighty-Four*." *Twentieth-Century Literature* 43.2. (Summer 1997): 196–220.

———. "Orwell's *Heart of Darkness: The Road to Wigan Pier* as Modernist Anthropology." *Prose Studies* 22.2 (April 1999). 71–102.

Rees, Richard. *George Orwell: Fugitive from the Camp of Victory*. London: Secker & Warburg, 1961.

Reilly, Patrick. "*Nineteen Eighty-Four*: The Insufficient Self." Holderness et al. 116–38.

———. *George Orwell: The Age's Adversary*. London: Macmillan, 1986.

Resch, Robert Paul. "Utopia, Dystopia, and the Middle Class in George Orwell's *Nineteen Eighty-Four*. *boundary* 2 24.1 (Spring 1997): 137–76.

Reznikov, Andrei. *George Orwell's Theory of Language*. San Jose: Writers Club P, 2001.

Robbins, Bruce, ed. *Intellectuals: Aesthetics, Politics, Academics*. Social Text Collective. Cultural Politics 2. Minneapolis: U of Minnesota P, 1990.

Rodden, John. *The Politics of Literary Reputation: The Making and Claiming of 'St. George' Orwell*. New York: Oxford UP, 1989.

———. "On the Political Sociology of Intellectuals: George Orwell and the London Left Intelligentsia." Rose 207–33.

Rorty, Richard. *Contingency, Irony; and Solidarity*. Cambridge: Cambridge UP, 1989.

———. "Truth and Freedom: A Reply to Thomas McCarthy." *Critical Inquiry* 16:3 (Spring 1990): 633–43.

Rose, Jonathan, ed. *The Revised Orwell*. East Lansing: Michigan State UP, 1991.

Ross, Andrew. "Defenders of the Faith and the New Class." Robbins 101–32.

Ross, William T. "Pacifism vs. Patriotism. The Case of George Orwell." *Weber Studies* 12.2 (Spring/Summer 1995): 54–66.

Rossi, John. "Orwell and Patriotism." *Contemporary Review* 261.1519 (Aug 1992): 95–98.

Rushdie, Salman. "Outside the Whale." *Granta 11* (1984): 125–38.

Said, Edward W. *Representations of the Intellectual: The 1993 Reith Lectures*. New York: Pantheon, 1994.

Sanderson, Richard K. "The Two Narrators and Happy Ending of *Nineteen Eighty-Four*." *Modern Fiction Studies* 34.4 (Winter 1988): 587–595.

Schwartz, Stephen. "The Spanish Civil War: The Continuing Controversy: 2: Rewriting Orwell." *New Criterion* 20.1 (September 2001): 63–65.

Shelden, Michael. *Orwell: The Authorized Biography*. New York: Harper, 1991.

Showstack Sassoon, Anne. "The People, Intellectuals, and Specialized Knowledge." *boundary 2 Special Issue: The Legacy of Antonio Gramsci* 14.3 (Spring 1986) 137–68.

Siegel, Paul. "The Style of *The Communist Manifesto*." *Science and Society* 46 (Summer 1982) 222–229.

Slater, Ian. *Orwell: The Road to Airstrip One*. New York: Norton, 1985.

Smyer, Richard I. *Animal Farm: Pastoralism and Politics*. Twayne's Masterwork Studies. Gen. Ed. Robert Lecker. Boston: Twayne, 1988.

Stansky, Peter and William Abrahams. *The Unknown Orwell*. London: Constable, 1972.

Tirohl, Blu. "'We are the dead ... you are the dead.' An examination of sexuality as a weapon of revolt in Orwell's *Nineteen Eighty-Four*." *Journal of Gender Studies* 9.1 (March 2000): 55–61.

Total Information Office. 21 February 2003 <http://www.darpa.mil/iao/TIASystems.htm>.

Voorhees, Richard. J. *The Paradox of George Orwell*. Purdue University Studies Humanities Series. Purdue Research Foundation, 1961.

West, Cornel. *Race Matters*. New York: Vintage, 1993.

Williams, Keith. "'The Unpaid Agitator': Joyce's Influence on George Orwell and James Agee." *James Joyce Quarterly* 36.4. (Summer 1999): 729–63.

Williams, Raymond. *Culture and Society: 1780–1950*. London: Chatto & Windus, 1960.

———. *George Orwell*. Modern Masters Series. Ed. Frank Kermode. New York: Viking, 1971.

Wilt, Judith. "Behind the Door of *1984*: 'The Worst Thing in the World.'" *Modernism Reconsidered*. Harvard English Studies 11. Ed. Robert Kiely and John Hildebidle. Cambridge, MA: Harvard UP, 1983. 247–62.

Winter, Frank. "Was Orwell a Secret Optimist?" *Essays From Oceania and Eurasia: George Orwell and 1984*. Ed. Benoit Suykerbuyk and Clem Neutiens. Antwerp: Universitaire Instelling Antwerpen, 1984.

Woodcock, George. *The Crystal Spirit: A Study of George Orwell*. London: Minerva, 1966.

Young, Iris Marion. "Polity and Group Difference: A Critique of the Ideal of Universal Citizenship." *Throwing Like a Girl and Other Essays in Feminist Philosophy and Social Theory*. Bloomington: Indiana UP, 1990. 114–37.

Zamyatin, Yevgeny. *We*. Trans. Clarence Brown. New York: Penguin. 1993.

HOMI K. BHABHA

Doublespeak and the Minority of One

It is one of the curious comforts of our lives that we prefer those who are virtuous not to be virtuosos. It is unclear to me why "strength in goodness" should somehow seem oddly anomalous with the fluency and acclaim of genius. In the opinion of many literary critics and political essayists alike, George Orwell was a virtuous man, somewhat shy of genius. This description of Orwell as a virtuous man is central to Lionel Trilling's essay in *The Opposing Self.* Virtue makes Orwell no less significant than the great writers of his time; but his *not* being a "genius" is, in Trilling's opinion, what makes him a "figure."[1] Orwell looks "at things simply and directly, having in mind only our intention of finding out what [things] really are, not the prestige of our great intellectual act of looking at them.... [Orwell] tells us that we can understand our political and social life merely by looking around us," by checking the "tendency to abstraction and absoluteness."[2] His virtuosity lies in preserving the concrete integrity of language that ensures the authority of the "whole body" and enables a person to stand courageously in the place of "the minority of one":

> Orwell was using the imagination of a man whose hands and eyes and whole body were part of his thinking apparatus.... He told the

From *On Nineteen Eighty-Four: Orwell and Our Future,* edited by Abbott Gleason, Jack Goldsmith, and Martha C. Nussbaum. © 2005 by Princeton University Press.

truth and told it in an exemplary way, quietly, simply, with due warning to the reader that it was only one man's truth.[3]

How do we recognize such virtuousness in language? What strength and goodness must we exercise to protect ourselves from ideological indoctrination or the utopian indulgence of our imaginations?

The reform of language, Orwell suggests, is our best hedge against political hegemony and corruption of public virtue. In his essay "Politics and the English Language," Orwell insists on the importance of giving precedence to concrete objects and mental images in our construction of discourse.[4] Words must be held at bay: "it is better to put off using words for as long as possible and get one's meaning as clear as one can through pictures or sensations,"[5] he writes. This process of linguistic clarification keeps consciousness focused and makes it capable of sustaining "one man's truth." Concreteness of thought plays its part by ensuring that the intellectual apparatus—the whole body—is inoculated against ready-made abstractions, prefabricated phrases, and, above all, the epidemic of euphemism. Euphemisms, like "pacification" for the bombing of defenseless villages, or "rectification of frontiers"[6] for the sacking of populations or ethnic cleansing, are "euphonious,"[7] that numbing and dissembling quality of Newspeak that allows doublespeak to prosper. Euphony allows terms and phrases to slip off the tongue, or smoothly slide off the politician's TelePrompTer in a way that allows one to "name things without calling up mental pictures of them."[8]

If we look at the mental pictures projected by Orwell's own writings as he proposes a cure for the language of the body politic, we quickly realize that his underlying metaphors throw up images of some pretty nasty things done to the body of language in the effort to reform it. His own metaphors for the clarification and cure of a language made decadent by ten or fifteen years of European dictatorship are suffused with the imagination of totalitarian violence, even a kind of eugenicist enthusiasm. Let me quote Orwell:

> I said earlier that the decadence of our language is probably curable.... Silly words and expressions have often disappeared, not through any evolutionary process but owing to the *conscious action of a minority*.... There is a long list of flyblown metaphors which could similarly *be got rid of* if enough people interested themselves in the job ... to *reduce* the amount of Greek or Latin in the average sentence, *to drive out* foreign phrases and strayed

scientific words ... *scrapping ... every word or idiom which has outworn its usefulness*. (Emphasis added)[9]

"The conscious action of a minority," "[curing] the decadence of our language," "[driving out] foreign phrases," "the scrapping of every word or idiom which has outworn its usefulness"[10]—all this, proposed as a kind of provisional, if not a "final," solution for the English language, must have conjured up rather strange sensations and mental pictures in 1946, when Orwell wrote the essay.

Now before I am accused of "political correctness," metaphoric naïveté, or the failure to read parodic intention, let me say, at once, that I come not to bury Orwell but to praise him. I do not propose to condemn his imagination of violence but to try to understand his narrative identification with extreme states. In fact, I want to argue that it is precisely when he narrates the vicious that the virtuousness of Orwell turns into a kind of virtuosity. It is when the proselytizer tips over into the paranoiac in the service of the good cause that Orwell is at his most inventive and insightful. "This invasion of one's mind by ready-made phrases (*lay the foundations achieve a radical transformation*)," Orwell writes (as if to make my point), "can only be prevented if one is constantly on guard against them, and every such phrase anaesthetizes a portion of one's brain."[11] It is this constant vigilance that requires that we cure language by the *action of a minority*, killing *this*, getting rid of *that*, driving out the "other." The mental image that we form of the Orwellian figure—as a style of writing, and as a *genre* of man—is much more complex than the honest workman of words and things, the *homo faber*, that has been passed down to us as the virtuous one among the more devilish geniuses of our times—Joyce, Stein, Woolf, Lawrence, and Conrad, to name a few.

If *Nineteen Eighty-Four* is about the decline of the "good society," tracked in the decadence and deception of doublethink, leading to a kind of controlled paranoia among its characters and readers, then it is also written from a quasi-paranoiac position. I don't mean to say, as Raymond Williams does, that Orwell was himself so pessimistic and paranoiac that he evaded the responsibility of depicting the positive and productive affiliations between progressive individuals and classes.[12] I want to suggest that the project of reforming the practice of language by repeatedly and incessantly demonstrating the duplicitous and reductive structures of doublethink and Newspeak cannot help but induce a kind of paranoia in the *writer*, not the person, as he crafts a persona for himself in the narrative. This is supported by an essay written in 1940 called "New Words" in which Orwell suggests that "any attack on such a fundamental thing as language, an attack as it were on the very structure of our own minds, is blasphemy and therefore dangerous."[13] To attempt a reform of language, he continues, is practically an interference with the work of God, and it induces the kind of paranoiac and superstitious belief that children hold, "that the air is full of avenging demons waiting to punish presumption."[14] Incidentally, Freud's favorite paranoiac, Judge Schreber, presiding judge of the Saxon Supreme Court, shared both the presumption and the paranoia. His description of the "invention" of basic language (*Grundsprache*) is worth quoting as a precursor to the method-in-the-madness of doublethink. This is from Schreber's account of his illness written in 1903:

> The souls to be purified learned during purification the language spoken by God Himself, the so-called "basic language" ["Grundsprache"], a somewhat antiquated but nevertheless powerful German, characterized particularly by a wealth of euphemisms (for instance, reward in the reverse sense for punishment, poison for food, juice for venom, unholy for holy, etc.).[15]

What Orwell describes as a "deliberate exercise[] in *doublethink*" (178) induces recurrent bouts of a kind of "fictional" paranoia as Winston is relentlessly pursued for his particular thoughtcrime, his belief in the "minority of one." The destruction of Winston's "intellectual apparatus," the whole body, results in the manipulation of his thoughts or memories. Secrets are passed on from mind to mind; orders come from the "iron voice" in the wall or through the telescreen. Doublethink destroys the event of memory and the verifiability of history by arresting language and consciousness in an endless, "frozen" present: a "present" that is constituted through the act of holding two contradictory beliefs in one's mind simultaneously. At one moment, the Party intellectuals have to be *conscious of the contradiction* in order to manipulate reality with strategic precision and control the process of "doublethink"; at the very next moment, the use of the word "doublethink" suggests that reality has been tampered with, and one has to subject doublethink to *doublethink*, so that the knowledge of holding contradictory beliefs is erased. The effect, as Orwell describes it, is an infinite process "with the lie always one leap ahead of the truth. Ultimately it is by means of *doublethink* that the Party has been able ... to arrest the course of history" (177).

After that horrific scene of electrical torture when Winston feels that his backbone is about to break, and the torture machine registers 40 on a scale of 100, O'Brien begins the process of doublethink: He warns Winston against the liberal disease of believing in the virtue of the minority of one, or, as he puts it, the belief in *"Your truth"* (203). He charges Winston with having held the treacherous view that the Party had executed three members whose innocence had been established by a New York newspaper photograph. O'Brien produces a copy of the yellowing newsprint and tantalizingly holds it within Winston's angle of vision. Winston writhes, he yells, he forgets the torture dial and cries, triumphantly, "It exists!" (204).

O'Brien, then, burns the incriminating paper in the memory hole, reducing it to ashes, and denies that it ever existed.

> "But it did exist! It does exist! It exists in memory. I remember it. You remember it.
> "I do not remember it," said O'Brien.
> Winston's heart sank. *That was doublethink....* If he could have been certain that O'Brien was lying, it would not have seemed to matter. But it was perfectly possible that O'Brien had really forgotten the photograph. And if so, then already he would have forgotten his denial of remembering it, and forgotten the act of forgetting. How could one be sure that it was simply trickery? Perhaps that lunatic dislocation in the mind could really happen: that was the thought that defeated him. (204, emphasis added)

In this brief moment the process of doublethink is no longer a textbook program or a totalitarian theory; it is grasped in the living, writhing form of its performance as a *practice* of mental manipulation and torture. *That was doublethink!* Against all the odds, this horrific exchange allows the victim some faint inkling of "imagined" agency, a futurity that perhaps only fiction allows; or, perhaps not. Although Winston is sure that he has just been "doublethinked," he is still able to stand aside and reflect on the procedure which has not succeeded in erasing that movement of memory which allows him to construct an account of what has happened to him—*he has partially escaped the forgetting of the forgetting and is now strangely adjacent to the event.* This account of doublethink, unequal and terrifying though it is, reveals something that pushes Orwell beyond "the minority of one" (179), the figure who stands *by*, and stands *for*, "one man's truth." Winston's concern here is not, primarily, with the vicious circle of deceit that structures *doublethink as the discourse that keeps* "the lie always one leap ahead of the truth." As Winston admits, there is a strong possibility that O'Brien may have really forgotten the photograph so that *he* could not simply be lying. If he had "forgotten the forgetting," then, he may have repressed or disavowed the truth, and who knows, this side of an analyst's couch, what the symptoms of such repression might turn out to be, or where they may be acted out? The issue that concerns Winston is somewhat different from the "content" of lying and truthfulness, although it does *not* neglect that important aspect of the relationship of language to reality. Why does Winston so desperately hope that O'Brien was lying, *and that he was aware of it*? If that were true, it would establish that despite the "deliberate exercises in *doublethink*" (Orwell's phrase) a distinction between truth and falsehood was maintained, however skewed the line between them. If that were so, then there would be some grounds to continue the argument about the existence and significance of the exonerating documents.

There is, however, another intriguing possibility. If O'Brien had genuinely "forgotten the forgetting," then how would Winston—in the minority of one—ever be sure that *he, Winston*, remembered, and would continue remembering? *In this folie à deux, could the minority of one exist without the other*? This opens up an issue about the underlying conditions of social utterance or enunciation, now struggling to be recognized even when they are being hopelessly violated. Any transformation or dislocation of social reality articulated in/*as* social discourse—whether it is manipulative or mutually supportive—requires a dialogic relation or identification between persons. I mean this in the various senses suggested by the work of Bakhtin and Benveniste, and more recently proposed by Charles Taylor. Human existence and expression is crucially marked by its fundamentally dialogical character because, Taylor suggests, "people do not acquire the languages needed for self-definition on their own."[16] He suggests that we are continually in dialogue with, or in struggle against, the things significant others want to see in us—and we in them—and even when they disappear, we continue to be in conversation with them. Now what passes between O'Brien and Winston is hardly a mutual conversation, but it cannot be denied that they are, in Orwell's view, "significant others" to each other.

Breyten Breytenbach, the great South African writer, recognized something about the possibility of a demonic dialogism in conditions of coercion when he addressed his prison poems to his jailer, who was aware of the dire irony and wanted to be "recognized" in them. Language may have its referential realm—factual, concrete, rational—but it also has its dialogic "addressee" who may be an actual person, a virtual presence, an invocatory muse, a superego, a sprite, or a spirit. In each case the significance of the dialogical lies in introducing social discourse to the principle of difference and plurality—to be struggled for or against—in order to "authorize" a perspective or to "take up a position," or yield to someone else's. It is the dialogical process that O'Brien so desperately wants to stamp out; it is the dialogical principle that Winston equally desperately will not relinquish. He might experience himself in the struggle as being in a "minority of one," but there is also a realization that there have to be at least two parties to any struggle over the "truth"; and that within any one person there are likely to be inner dialogical tensions of the kind that W.E.B. Du Bois called "double consciousness."

One of the strange asymmetries of the human condition is our desire to relate to each other at the level of the unconscious, through projections, fantasies, defensive and compensatory strategies. The dialogical process signifies the quality of *alteritas*, that principle of "otherness" that Hannah Arendt once described as the "paradoxical plurality of unique beings."[17] We *want* access to ourselves and others at levels at which we are least accessible and most vulnerable. Our desire for sociality often arises out of an intimacy that is based on unintelligibility. And our need to affirm the simple human virtue of *affection*—to feel for another—and affiliation—to belong with another—demands that we sharpen our imaginations and instincts to "read" the opacity of others, to get under their signifying skins. Winston holds what he describes as a hope or a "secretly held belief" that O'Brien's political orthodoxy was not perfect: "Something in his face suggested it irresistibly" (13). We are irresistibly led to ask: Is this a belief about himself that Winston projects onto O'Brien? And why is it a secret belief? What is so irresistible in O'Brien's face that can't be described? Is Winston merely hoping against hope, as we are later to discover? Why are there no concrete, mental images to be found that will represent this sensation? When O'Brien tries to break Winston by convincing him that he is mentally deranged, he does so by attacking what Winston had earlier confessed to himself, as his private credo: "Being in a minority, even a minority of one, did not make you mad. There was truth and there was untruth, and if you clung to the truth even against the whole world, you were not mad" (179). Quite apart from our seeking to understand and respond to the intentions and objectives of the speech act, we have to throw ourselves into a form of intersubjective interpretation which works through those figurative, gestural signs of language that have to be interpreted as if there is a kind of "unconsciousness" at work within them. Is O'Brien mad *and* bad? Is he a trickster? Is he lying or is he playing a game? Winston has to ask these questions in order to ensure his own survival, but they are not simply matters of textual interpretation or the shrewd calculation of the other person's character and game plan. They are dialogical in a sense that is at once self-questioning and interlocutory: they ask us to confront our own "forgetting of the act of forgetting"; to try to "work through," however imperfectly and tentatively, our own repressions and projections in order to "read" the other person's mind, and the way in which they might hold, or hide, their beliefs *even from themselves*.

This is not an invasion of privacy. It is an acceptance of the complex, psychic negotiations that accompany our interactions and utterances. Such "unconscious determinations" may not always sit easily with reasonable or commonsensical explanations, but this does not mean that they cannot be representative of character or personhood in a public sense, or useful for the purposes of democratic dialogue. The very point of subsuming all other selves into the Ideal Ego of Big Brother is to end the struggle over meaning and being that is at the heart of the discourse of the dialogic condition. Orwell makes this very point in "The Principles of Newspeak," an appendix to *Nineteen Eighty-Four*: "Short, clipped words of unmistakable meaning" like Ingsoc, goodthink or prolefeed, were encouraged because they "roused the minimum of *echoes* in the speaker's mind.... The intention was to make speech, and especially speech on any subject not ideologically neutral, *as nearly as possible independent of consciousness*" (253, emphasis added). What I have described as Winston's attenuated, though unmistakable, desire for a dialogical relationship should be seen as an attempt to restore an ongoing struggle for "consciousness" to the process of speech. If this were achieved, it would be possible to undo the reductive verbal gagging of "the A vocabulary," which was imposed on ordinary people involved in the business of everyday life:

> All ambiguities and shades of meaning had been purged out....
> [so] a Newspeak word of this class was simply a staccato sound
> expressing one clearly understood concept. It would have been
> quite impossible to use the A vocabulary for literary purposes, or
> for political or philosophical discussion. (247)

The freedom that dialogic discourse envisions is at once fragile and compelling: it is a struggle over the quality and the equality of consciousness; it is evident in the revision and the representation of reality; it is signified in the uses of ambiguity and shades of meaning. A dialogical perspective suggests that there are capacities, capabilities, and qualities of the person— both conscious and unconscious—that should welcome the imaginative, futuristic logic of poetic justice because it puts us in touch with the "paradoxical plurality of unique beings." But what are these paradoxical forms of poetic justice?

Perhaps a story about pigs who are capable of playing the power games that political regimes consider the exclusive preserve of human intelligence—that would certainly turn pigs into unique beings, and human beings into paradoxical animals. Or perhaps poetic justice is to be found in an attempt to write the history of the future, *Nineteen Eighty-Four*, as if it had already happened in 1949, so that what was new was also old, and what we thought we knew was yet to come. In that time warp, History is shadowed by fantasy and Fiction is burdened with fact. They create, in between themselves, a "paradoxical plurality"—a kind of doublespeak that happily condemns fiction and history to a dialogue from which neither one can easily recover the uniqueness of its voice or the singularity of its vision.

NOTES

1. Lionel Trilling, *The Opposing Self: Nine Essays in Criticism* (New York and London: Harcourt Brace Jovanovich, 1955), 136.

2. Ibid., 139, 143.

3. Ibid., 144, 151.

4. George Orwell, "Politics and the English Language," in *Collected Essays* (London: Secker & Warburg, 1961), 344–45.

5. Ibid., 350.

6. Ibid., 347.

7. Ibid., 345.

8. Ibid., 347.

9. Ibid., 349–50.

10. Ibid., 349, 350.

11. Ibid., 349.

12. See Raymond Williams, *George Orwell* (New York: Columbia University Press, 1971).

13. George Orwell, "New Words," in *The Collected Essays, Journalism and Letters of George Orwell*, vol. 2, *My Country Right or Left, 1940–1943*, ed. Sonia Orwell and Ian Angus (New York and London: Harcourt Brace Jovanovich, 1968), 9.

14. Ibid., 8.

15. Daniel Paul Schreber, *Memoirs of My Nervous Illness*, trans. Ida Macalpine and Richard A. Hunter (London: W. H. Dawson and Sons, 1955), 50.

16. *Charles Taylor, Multiculturalism and "The Politics of Recognition"* (Princeton: Princeton University Press, 1992), 32.

17. Hannah Arendt, *The Human Condition* (Chicago and London: University of Chicago Press, 1958), 176.

Chronology

1903	Eric Arthur Blair (later to become George Orwell) is born June 25 in Bengal, India, to Richard Walmesley Blair and Ida Mabel Blair. The Blairs are a middle-class English family with connections to the British colonial administration in India and Burma.
1907	Moves to England with his mother and sister.
1911–1916	Schooled at St. Cyprian's.
1917–1921	Attends Eton on scholarship.
1922–1927	Serves with Indian Imperial Police in Burma.
1928–1929	In Paris; works as dishwasher and writer; his first articles are published in newspapers.
1930–1934	Lives mainly in London. Publishes articles and translations. *Down and Out in Paris and London* is published in 1933 under pen name George Orwell. In 1934, *Burmese Days* is published.
1935	*A Clergyman's Daughter* is published.
1936	*Keep the Aspidistra Flying* is published. Marries Eileen O'Shaughnessy. Leaves for Spain in December to join anti-Fascists in Barcelona. Serves four months on the Aragon Front.
1937	*The Road to Wigan Pier* is published. Wounded in the throat, returns to England.

1938	*Homage to Catalonia* is published. Spends several months in a sanatorium to treat his tuberculosis; then visits Morocco for winter.
1939	*Coming Up for Air* is published.
1940–1943	Publishes *"Inside the Whale" and Other Essays* in 1940. Medically unfit for service in World War II, joins Home Guard in London. Writes and broadcasts as wartime propagandist for the BBC. In 1941, publishes *The Lion and the Unicorn: Socialism and the English Genius*. In 1943, becomes literary editor of the *Tribune*.
1944	Adopts a child, whom he names Richard Horatio Blair.
1945	Serves as correspondent for *The Observer*. Wife Eileen O'Shaughnessy dies. *Animal Farm* is published.
1946	Publishes *Critical Essays: Dickens, Dali, and Others*. Rents house in Hebrides, Scottish islands.
1947–1948	Hospitalized for seven months, starting in December, for tuberculosis.
1949	Publishes *1984*. Marries Sonia Brownell; health continues to decline.
1950	Dies of tuberculosis on January 21. *"Shooting an Elephant" and Other Essays* is published.
1953	*"England, Your England" and Other Essays* is published.
1961	*Collected Essays* is published.

Contributors

HAROLD BLOOM is Sterling Professor of the Humanities at Yale University. He is the author of 30 books, including *Shelley's Mythmaking* (1959), *The Visionary Company* (1961), *Blake's Apocalypse* (1963), *Yeats* (1970), *A Map of Misreading* (1975), *Kabbalah and Criticism* (1975), *Agon: Toward a Theory of Revisionism* (1982), *The American Religion* (1992), *The Western Canon* (1994), and *Omens of Millennium: The Gnosis of Angels, Dreams, and Resurrection* (1996). *The Anxiety of Influence* (1973) sets forth Professor Bloom's provocative theory of the literary relationships between the great writers and their predecessors. His most recent books include *Shakespeare: The Invention of the Human* (1998), a 1998 National Book Award finalist, *How to Read and Why* (2000), *Genius: A Mosaic of One Hundred Exemplary Creative Minds* (2002), *Hamlet: Poem Unlimited* (2003), *Where Shall Wisdom Be Found?* (2004), and *Jesus and Yahweh: The Names Divine* (2005). In 1999, Professor Bloom received the prestigious American Academy of Arts and Letters Gold Medal for Criticism. He has also received the International Prize of Catalonia, the Alfonso Reyes Prize of Mexico, and the Hans Christian Andersen Bicentennial Prize of Denmark.

RAYMOND WILLIAMS, now deceased, was a professor at Jesus College, Cambridge. He wrote many nonfiction books, such as *Modern Tragedy*; *Marxism and Literature*; and *Writing, Culture and Politics*. He also wrote several novels.

SUE LONOFF is senior associate of the Derek Bok Center at Harvard University. She is the author of *Wilkie Collins and His Victorian Readers* and has edited and translated *Belgian Essays*, the work of Charlotte and Emily Brontë.

ERIKA GOTTLIEB has taught at various institutions, including Seneca College, McGill, and The Budapest University of the Elte. She is the author of *Dystopian Fiction East and West*.

LAURENCE LERNER is a professor at the University of Sussex, UK. His work includes *Baudelaire* and *Angels and Absences: Child Deaths in the Nineteenth Century*. He also has co-authored a title and writes poetry.

ROBERT PLANK, now deceased, authored *The Emotional Significance of Imaginary Beings; a Study of the Interaction between Psychopathology, Literature, and Reality in the Modern World*.

ROGER FOWLER has been professor of English and linguistics in the School of Modern Languages and European Studies, University of East Anglia. He published many books, among them *Linguistics and the Novel, A Dictionary of Modern Critical Terms*, and *Linguistic Criticism*.

MALCOLM PITTOCK has been a professor at Oxford. He has published *The Prioress's Tale [and] the Wife of Bath's Tale* and a book about the German playwright Ernst Toller.

STEVEN CARTER has taught at California State University, Bakersfield. Titles he has published include *Bearing Across: Studies in Literature and Science* and *Devotions to the Text*. He has also written a novel and book of essays.

ANTHONY STEWART teaches English at Dalhousie University, Halifax, NS. He has authored *Black Masque* and *What He Doesn't Know*.

HOMI K. BHABHA holds appointments in both the departments of English and of African and African American studies, has been on the board of trustees of the English Institute, and chairs the Program in History and Literature at Harvard University. He is also a distinguished visiting professor at University College London. He is the author of *The Location of Culture* and editor of *Nation and Narration*, a collection of essays.

Bibliography

Agathocleous, Tanya. *George Orwell: Battling Big Brother.* New York: Oxford University Press, 2000.

Berman, Ronald. *Modernity and Progress: Fitzgerald, Hemingway, Orwell.* Tuscaloosa: University of Alabama Press, 2005.

Bhat, Yashoda. *Aldous Huxley and George Orwell: A Comparative Study of Satire in Their Novels.* New Delhi: Sterling Publishers; New York: Distributed by Apt Books, 1991.

Bloom, Harold, ed. *George Orwell's 1984.* Philadelphia: Chelsea House Publishers, 2004.

Bluemel, Kristin. *George Orwell and the Radical Eccentrics: Intermodernism in Literary London.* New York: Palgrave Macmillan, 2004.

Bowker, Gordon. *Inside George Orwell.* New York: Palgrave Macmillan, 2003.

Brannigan, John. *Orwell to the Present: Literature in England, 1945–2000.* Houndmills, Basingstoke, Hampshire; New York: Palgrave Macmillan, 2003.

Breton, Rob. *Gospels and Grit: Work and Labour in Carlyle, Conrad and Orwell.* Toronto; Buffalo: University of Toronto Press, 2005.

Brunsdale, Mitzi. *Student Companion to George Orwell.* Westport, Conn.: Greenwood Press, 2000.

Carter, Steven. "The Rites of Memory: Orwell, Pynchon, DeLillo, and the American Millenium." *Prospero* 6 (1999): pp. 5–21.

Casement, William. "*Nineteen Eighty-Four* and Philosophical Realism," *Midwest Quarterly* 30, no. 2 (Winter 1989): pp. 215–228.

Connelly, Mark. *Orwell and Gissing.* New York: Peter Lang, 1997.

De Lange, Adriaan M. *The Influence of Political Bias in Selected Essays of George Orwell.* Lewiston: E. Mellen Press, 1992.

Fenwick, Gillian. *George Orwell: A Bibliography.* Winchester, UK: St. Paul's Bibliographies; New Castle, Del.: Oak Knoll Press, 1998.

Ford, Boris, ed. *From Orwell to Naipaul.* London: Penguin Books, 1995.

Fowler, Roger. *The Language of George Orwell.* New York: St. Martin's Press, 1995.

Gleason, Abbott, Jack Goldsmith, and Martha C. Nussbaum, eds. *On Nineteen Eighty-Four: Orwell and Our Future.* Princeton, N.J.: Princeton University Press, 2005.

Goldstein, Philip. *Communities of Cultural Value: Reception Study, Political Differences, and Literary History.* Lanham, Md.: Lexington Books, 2001.

Hammond, J. R. *A George Orwell Chronology.* Houndmills, Basingstoke, Hampshire; New York: Palgrave, 2000.

Hitchens, Christopher. *Orwell's Victory.* London; New York: Allen Lane/Penguin Press, 2002.

———. *Why Orwell Matters.* New York: Basic Books, 2002.

Holderness, Graham, Bryan Loughrey, and Nahem Yousaf, eds. *George Orwell.* New York: St. Martin's Press, 1998.

Huber, Peter W. *Orwell's Revenge: The 1984 Palimpsest.* New York: Free Press; Toronto: Maxwell Macmillan Canada; New York: Maxwell Macmillan International, 1994.

Ingersoll, Earl G. "The Decentering of Tragic Narrative in George Orwell's *Nineteen Eighty-Four.*" *Studies in the Humanities* 16, no. 2 (December 1989): pp. 69–83.

Kerr, Douglas. *George Orwell.* Tavistock, Devon, U.K.: Northcote House in association with the British Council, 2003.

Matthew, Kenneth. "'Guardian of the Human Spirit': The Moral Foundation of *Nineteen Eighy-Four.*" *Christianity and Literature* 40, no. 2 (Winter 1991): pp. 157–67.

Meyers, Jeffrey, ed. *George Orwell: The Critical Heritage.* London; New York: Routledge, 1997, 1975.

———. *Orwell: Wintry Conscience of a Generation.* New York: W.W. Norton & Co., 2000.

Meyers, Valerie. *George Orwell.* New York: St. Martin's Press, 1991.

Newsinger, John. *Orwell's Politics.* New York: St. Martin's Press, 1999.

Plank, Robert. *George Orwell's Guide Through Hell: A Psychological Study of 1984*. San Bernardino, Calif.: Borgo Press, 1994.

Resch, Robert Paul. "Utopia, Dystopia, and the Middle Class in George Orwell's *Nineteen Eighty-Four*." *Boundary 2* 24, no. 1 (Spring 1997): pp. 137–76.

Rodden, John. *George Orwell: The Politics of Literary Reputation*. New Brunswick, N.J.: Transaction Publishers, 2002.

———. *Scenes from an Afterlife: The Legacy of George Orwell*. Wilmington, Del.: ISI Books, 2003.

Rodden, John, ed. *Irving Howe and the Critics: Celebrations and Attacks*. Lincoln: University of Nebraska Press, 2005.

Todorov, Tzvetan. "Politics, Morality, and the Writer's Life: Notes on George Orwell." *Stanford French Review* 16, no. 1 (1992): pp. 136–42.

Varricchio, Mario. "Power of Images/Images of Power in *Brave New World* and *Nineteen Eighty-Four*." *Utopian Studies* 10, no. 1 (1999): pp. 98–114.

Waterman, David F. *Disordered Bodies and Disrupted Borders: Representations of Resistance in Modern British Literature*. Lanham, Md.: University Press of America, 1999.

West, W. J. *The Larger Evils:* Nineteen Eighty-Four: *The Truth Behind the Satire*. Edinburgh: Canongate Press, 1992.

Young, John Wesley. *Totalitarian Language: Orwell's Newspeak and Its Nazi and Communist Antecedents*. Charlottesville: University Press of Virginia, 1991.

Acknowledgments

"Afterword: *Nineteen Eighty-Four* in 1984" by Raymond Williams. From *Orwell*: 95–126. © 1991 by Raymond Williams. Reprinted by permission.

"Composing *Nineteen Eighty-Four*: The Art of Nightmare" by Sue Lonoff. From *The Revised Orwell*, edited by Jonathan Rose: 25–45. © 1991 by Jonathan Rose. Reprinted by permission.

"The Demonic World of Oceania: The Mystical Adulation of the 'Sacred' Leader" by Erika Gottlieb. From *The Orwell Conundrum: A Cry of Despair or Faith in the Spirit of Man?* 155–68. © 1992 by Carleton University Press. Reprinted by permission.

"Totalitarianism: A New Story? An Old Story?" by Laurence Lerner. From *Telling Stories: Studies in Honour of Ulrich Broich on the Occasion of His 60th Birthday*, edited by Elmar Lehmann and Bernd Lenz: 284–95. © 1992 by B.R. Grüner. Reprinted by permission.

"The Ghostly Bells of London" by Robert Plank. From *George Orwell's Guide Through Hell: A Psychological Study of 1984*: 23–31. © 1994 by the Borgo Press. Reprinted by permission.

"Newspeak and the Language of the Party" by Roger Fowler. From *The Language of George Orwell*: 211–40. © 1995 by Roger Fowler. Reprinted by permission.

"The Hell of *Nineteen Eighty-Four*" by Malcolm Pittock. From *Essays in Criticism* 47, no. 2 (April 1997): 143–64. © 1997 by Oxford University Press. Reprinted by permission.

"The Masks of Passion" by Steven Carter. From *A Do-It-Yourself Dystopia: The Americanization of Big Brother*: 83–91. © 2000 by University Press of America. Reprinted by permission.

"The Heresy of Common Sense: The Prohibition of Decency in *Nineteen Eighty-Four*" by Anthony Stewart. From *George Orwell, Doubleness, and the Value of Decency*: 123–52. © 2003 by Taylor & Francis Books. Reprinted by permission.

"Doublespeak and the Minority of One" by Homi K. Bhabha. From *On Nineteen Eighty-Four*, edited by Abbott Gleason, Jack Goldsmith, and Martha C. Nussbaum: 29–37. © 2005 by Princeton University Press. Reprinted by permission.

Every effort has been made to contact the owners of copyrighted material and secure copyright permission. Articles appearing in this volume generally appear much as they did in their original publication with few or no editorial changes. Those interested in locating the original source will find bibliographic information in the bibliography and acknowledgments sections of this volume.

Index

Characters in literary works are indexed by first name (if any), followed by the name of the work in parentheses